If you have a home computer with internet access you may:
  -request an item be placed on hold
  -renew an item that is overdue
  -view titles and due dates checked out on your card
  -view your own outstanding fines

To view your patron record from your home computer:
Click on the NSPL homepage:
http://nspl.suffolk.lib.ny.us

**North Shore Public Library**

# THE GOD STRATEGY

## How Religion Became
## a Political Weapon in America

DAVID DOMKE AND KEVIN COE

### OXFORD
UNIVERSITY PRESS

2008

# OXFORD
## UNIVERSITY PRESS

Oxford University Press, Inc., publishes works that further
Oxford University's objective of excellence
in research, scholarship, and education.

Oxford   New York
Auckland   Cape Town   Dar es Salaam   Hong Kong   Karachi
Kuala Lumpur   Madrid   Melbourne   Mexico City   Nairobi
New Delhi   Shanghai   Taipei   Toronto

With offices in
Argentina   Austria   Brazil   Chile   Czech Republic   France   Greece
Guatemala   Hungary   Italy   Japan   Poland   Portugal   Singapore
South Korea   Switzerland   Thailand   Turkey   Ukraine   Vietnam

Copyright © 2008 by Oxford University Press, Inc.

Published by Oxford University Press, Inc.
198 Madison Avenue, New York, New York 10016

www.oup.com

Oxford is a registered trademark of Oxford University Press

Library of Congress Cataloging-in-Publication Data
Domke, David Scott.
The God strategy : how religion became a political weapon in America /
David Domke & Kevin Coe.
p. cm.
Includes bibliographical references and index.
ISBN 978-0-19-532641-3
1. Religion and politics—United States.   2. United
States—Religion—1960–   I. Coe, Kevin M.   II. Title.
BL2525.D65 2007
324.973'092—dc22        2007014782

1 3 5 7 9 8 6 4 2

Printed in the United States of America
on acid-free paper

# CONTENTS

※

# THE GOD STRATEGY

# INTRODUCTION

※

# A New Religious Politics

On the evening of July 17, 1980, in Detroit's Joe Louis Arena, Ronald Reagan delivered his acceptance speech for the Republican Party's presidential nomination. Addressing a crowd of typically raucous delegates and a national television audience, Reagan was approaching the end of his speech when he departed from the prepared remarks he had supplied to the news media, a move certain to capture journalists' attention. Reagan abruptly said: "I have thought of something that is not part of my speech and I'm worried over whether I should do it." He paused, then continued:

> Can we doubt that only a Divine Providence placed this land,
> this island of freedom, here as a refuge for all those people in the
> world who yearn to breathe freely: Jews and Christians enduring
> persecution behind the Iron Curtain, the boat people of Southeast
> Asia, of Cuba and Haiti, the victims of drought and famine in Africa,
> the freedom fighters of Afghanistan and our own countrymen held
> in savage captivity.

He went on: "I'll confess that"—and here his voice faltered momentarily—"I've been a little afraid to suggest what I'm going to suggest." A long pause ensued, followed by this: "I'm more afraid not to. Can we begin our crusade joined together in a moment of silent prayer?" The entire hall went silent, and heads bowed. Reagan then concluded: "God bless America."[1]

It was grand political theater. It was a moment when religion and partisan politics were brought together through mass media as never before. It was a moment when religious conservatives became a political force in the United States. It was, simply put, a moment when a new religious politics was born.

It also was strategic to the hilt. Modern political communications are carefully scripted and rehearsed, with meticulous management of every detail—from the knowing smiles and poignant pauses to the clothes worn, backdrops used, and words chosen. The Reagan campaign and presidency did not create this dynamic, but they perfected it. The 1980 campaign was Reagan's third run for the White House, and his message was sharp this time out. His advisers had put his convention speech through five drafts over six weeks to make sure it appealed simultaneously to Christian conservatives—fundamentalists and evangelicals who had come together to form a crucial voting bloc—and to the broader American public.[2] When the moment arrived, the former Hollywood actor and two-term California governor offered a vision of America grounded in faith and morality, punctuated by his closing words and polished delivery. All of it came through.

Consider the reaction of *Newsweek* magazine: "In a rite as peaceful and as triumphal as a beatification, the Republican Party finally anointed Ronald Reagan as its Presidential nominee last week and sent him forth on what he called a 'crusade' to save America from its recent past." In a similar vein, *Washington Post* media critic Tom Shales said: "A more than faintly religious tone is being maintained by the Reagan candidacy. He has spoken repeatedly of leading a 'crusade,' and beginning a crusade with prayer is not exactly unheard of in the old history books. At times, the convention resembled the new breed of evangelical talk shows carried on TV stations throughout the country." Reagan's message found both of its intended audiences. In a poll of the general public taken in the days following the GOP convention, 67% expressed a favorable reaction to the event. Four months later, Reagan won the presidency with a coalition that included a significant number of evangelicals.[3] In succeeding years, conservative Catholics joined them, drawn by the same blending of morality, faith, and nation that Reagan offered. A new era of religious politics had arrived—to the delight of many, to the chagrin of others, and with enduring impact on all.

Twelve years later, it was the Democratic Party's turn. Having endured three terms of Republican rule in the White House, Democrats in 1992 saw an opportunity for revival in a sagging economy and an election season turned on its head by the on-again, off-again saga of Ross Perot's third-party candidacy. For three presidential elections, Democrats had done little to publicly appeal to religious Americans. In his party nomination acceptance address in 1980, the pious Jimmy Carter made no mention whatsoever of God. Walter Mondale in 1984 and Michael Dukakis in 1988 made between them only a handful of religious references. In 1992, however, Bill Clinton, the Arkansas governor upon whom Democrats had pinned their hopes, decided to travel a very different pathway in his challenge to Republican president George H. W. Bush. Clinton selected Al Gore as his running mate to produce the first all–Southern Baptist presidential ticket in the nation's history—a choice that captured the attention of this traditionally conservative religious community. Further, from the opening gavel, the Democratic Party's national convention at New York's Madison Square Garden struck a decidedly religious tone. Speakers from Jesse Jackson to Mario Cuomo wove faith into their addresses. The result, one commentator put it, was that the convention felt "like a cross between the Academy awards, a Las Vegas nightclub act and a religious revival meeting."[4]

On the convention's final night, July 16, 1992, Clinton brought it to a crescendo. He centered his acceptance speech on "the New Covenant"—a phrase rich in biblical grounding, most notably in the words of Jesus at the Last Supper. The new covenant, Clinton said, was to be "a solemn agreement between the people and their government" that would undergird his plans to address the nation's economic woes, balance the budget, improve education, and expand health care. Clinton also quoted Scripture, spoke of the importance of religious faith, and invoked God several times. The address reached its peak when Clinton expressed his desire for a more inclusive U.S. society, saying: "There is no them, there is only us." With the audience chanting "us," Clinton's pacing became more deliberate. "One nation," he began. Each word came slowly: "under God"—and here he let slip enough of his southern drawl to momentarily extend the word God—"indivisible." The audience took its cue, and joined Clinton for the exclamation point: "with liberty and justice for all!" As the crowd erupted, Clinton hammered home his vision for America: "That—That, is our Pledge of Allegiance, and that's what the New Covenant is all about."[5] Twelve years nearly to the day from Reagan's 1980 address, Clinton had delivered a speech with a similar combination of faith, morality, and nation.

Clinton's message was impossible to miss. The *New York Times* characterized the speech as "steeped in the values of faith and family," and a *Chicago Sun-Times* commentator quipped that Clinton "quoted Scripture almost as much as [evangelist] Robert Schuller on Sunday morning TV." Conservatives were immediately concerned. Vice president Dan Quayle accused Clinton of taking a page out of the Republicans' book, fundamentalist preacher Jerry Falwell charged Clinton with "misquoting and manipulating the Holy Scripture for political purposes," and televangelist and one-time GOP presidential candidate Pat Robertson said Clinton's use of the phrase new covenant was a sort of "pseudo-Christianity" that bordered on blasphemy. Clinton was not cowed. Within days, he was in a Presbyterian church in West Virginia fielding questions about his faith—a conversation broadcast over the Vision Interfaith Satellite Network to more than 15 million homes nationwide. All of this prompted the *Boston Globe* to declare, "After years of secular squeamishness, the Clinton-Gore ticket is bringing God and country back to the Democrats."[6] It is no coincidence that the only successful Democratic presidential candidate since 1976 was one willing and able to present himself to the public in religious terms. Clinton had well learned what has become perhaps the most important lesson in contemporary American politics: to compete successfully, politicians need not always walk the religious walk, but they had better be able to talk the religious talk.

For good or for ill, God has always been a part of American politics. Religion formally entered the U.S. presidency at its inception, when George Washington, in his 1789 Inaugural address, declared that "it would be peculiarly improper to omit in this first official act my fervent supplications to that Almighty Being who rules over the universe." In the years since, presidents have spoken of a higher power, prayed and been prayed for, sought divine favor for America, and expressed gratitude for providential outcomes. This confluence of faith and American politics has commonly been called "civil religion," a phrase coined in the 1960s by sociologist Robert Bellah. Building upon ideas of earlier philosophers and thinkers, Bellah defined civil religion as "a set of beliefs, symbols, and rituals" through which a society "interprets its historical experience in light of transcendent reality." In general, civil religion in America has been perceived—by many scholars, at least—to be a benignly symbolic practice, without distinctly partisan motivations or implications.[7] But something profound has changed in recent decades.

In 1960, John F. Kennedy became the only Catholic ever to be elected U.S. president. To do so, he had to overcome concerns that his administration would be a tool of the Vatican. In a pivotal address in September 1960, Kennedy declared: "I believe in an America where the separation of church and state is absolute; where no Catholic prelate would tell the President—should he be Catholic—how to act, and no Protestant minister would tell his parishioners for whom to vote." It was a welcome message then; it would be almost unimaginable today. Consider that during the 2004 presidential campaign Jerry Falwell proclaimed, "For conservative people of faith, voting for principle this year means voting for the re-election of George W. Bush. The alternative, in my mind, is simply unthinkable." Focus on the Family founder James Dobson, whose theologically conservative radio programs, magazines, videos, and books reach more than 200 million people worldwide, broke with his traditionally nonpartisan ways to endorse Bush. And the U.S. Conference of Catholic Bishops decreed that Communion could be withheld from Catholics in public office who dissent from church teachings, claiming that politicians "have an obligation in conscience to work toward correcting morally defective laws"—those which allow abortion, in particular—"lest they be guilty of cooperating in evil." This forced Democratic Party presidential candidate John Kerry to explain how his Catholic faith accorded with his prochoice position on abortion.[8] It was the reverse of 1960: whereas Kennedy had worked to show independence from the Vatican, Kerry had to fend off criticism for insufficient fealty to the Catholic church.

And it's not only conservatives who are mixing faith and politics. In October 2004, more than 200 U.S. seminary and religious leaders signed a statement condemning what they called a "theology of war" in the Bush administration's rhetoric about terrorism. In 2005, Rabbi Michael Lerner launched the Network of Spiritual Progressives with a founding conference in Berkeley, California, that drew more than 1,300 religious leaders, politicians, and activists. In the spring of 2006, the U.S. Conference of Catholic Bishops again waded into the political arena—this time with a Justice for Immigrants campaign that directly challenged proposals in Congress which would have made it a crime to provide food and shelter to undocumented immigrants. And in the autumn of 2006, the liberal religious magazine *Sojourners*—whose founder and editor, Jim Wallis, penned the bestselling book *God's Politics* in 2005—and the organization Catholics in Alliance for the Common Good produced voter guides that challenged conservatives' long-time dominance of these publications.[9] As will become apparent in this book, this liberal-leaning religious politics was capitalized upon by a number of Democratic Party candidates.

On issue after issue, U.S. public debate today includes—and often is dominated by—faith-based perspectives espoused by politically adept individuals and organizations. Religion has always been part of the political subtext in the United States, but it is now a defining fault line, with citizens' religious affinities, regularity of worship, and perceptions of "moral values" among the strongest predictors of presidential voting patterns. Political leaders have taken advantage of and contributed to these developments through calculated, deliberate, and partisan use of faith. We call this the *God strategy*, and we document how it has been implemented, who has used it and why, and what it means for democracy. Central to this approach is a series of carefully crafted public communications employed by politicians to connect with religiously inclined voters. Sometimes these religious signals are intended for the eyes and ears of all Americans, and other times they are implemented in targeted ways, as veritable "dog whistles" that only distinct segments of the population fully receive.[10] In combination, these approaches seek to entice both the many religious moderates who want leaders to be comfortable with faith, as well as devout Protestants and Catholics who desire a more intimate convergence of religion and politics. The God strategy moved to the fore in 1980 and, in the years since, politicians—especially those in the Republican Party, though Democrats are now responding in kind—have utilized and refined this model to accrue political capital and transform the role of religion in American politics.

Few have used this approach more adeptly than George W. Bush. During his father's presidential campaigns in 1988 and 1992, the younger Bush helped to coordinate outreach efforts to religious conservatives. He learned their concerns, their language, and how to turn both into political advantage. Bush's response to this experience, according to a close friend and campaign colleague, was "I could do this in Texas. I could make this work in Texas." Bush did just that. Despite never having held political office, he scored a surprising victory in the 1994 governor's race and then easily won reelection in 1998. In 1999, Bush met with leading pastors in Texas, asked for their prayers, and told them he had been "called" to seek the presidency. Throughout the 2000 presidential campaign, he and strategist Karl Rove worked assiduously to attract religious conservatives and, once in the White House, Bush immediately issued an executive order to implement "faith-based" initiatives that eased restrictions on government funding of religious organizations' social service programs.[11] In subsequent years, this intertwining of religion and politics— tailored to fit a distinctly conservative ideology—has been a centerpiece of Bush's presidency. It does not always work for Bush or other politicians, but it often does.

In early 2003, for example, Bush faced a critical juncture in his administration's push toward war with Iraq: public support was lukewarm as the president delivered his State of the Union address to Congress and a U.S. television audience of 62 million. Many have fixated on "16 words" in the president's speech, since disavowed by the administration, about Iraq's alleged attempts to purchase uranium from Africa.[12] However, every bit as crucial in building U.S. public support for the war were 17 words delivered in the final minute of the address: "The liberty we prize is not America's gift to the world, it is God's gift to humanity." It was a bold linkage of administration goals with divine wishes, but Bush had the benefit of a platform built by more than two decades of religious politics. So he drove his message home: "We Americans have faith in ourselves, but not in ourselves alone. We do not know—we do not claim to know all the ways of Providence, yet we can trust in them, placing our confidence in the loving God behind all of life and all of history. May He guide us now. And may God continue to bless the United States of America." Polls showed that 75% of U.S. adults "approved" of Bush's speech and 71% of registered voters said its content was "excellent" or "good." Three weeks later, U.S. adults were asked by pollsters, "Do you like the way George W. Bush talks in public about his religious beliefs, or does this bother you somewhat?" Fully 63% said they liked it.[13] The God strategy was operating at full force, and many, many Americans were on board.

This book is an attempt to understand how this came to be. We focus on political communications and tactics—particularly within the presidency—to understand the nexus of faith, politics, and public opinion in America. Specifically, we examine the historical and social forces that laid the foundation for the ascendance of today's religious politics, then systematically track Republican and Democratic leaders' use of a series of religious signals in recent decades. We consider the nature of this approach, its electoral strengths and limitations, and the implications of its now-dominant presence. The evidence will reveal that Republicans generally have been more inclined and better positioned to capitalize on a convergence of religion and politics. Still, Democrats have occasionally been successful and are making substantial inroads, especially since the 2004 elections. Throughout the ensuing pages, we will argue that the substantial presence of God and faith in American politics over the past few decades did not occur by chance. It was not by chance that Reagan and Clinton used the religious imagery they did, in the manner they did, while addressing their parties' convention delegates and the nation. Nor was it by chance that Bush staked much of his electoral hopes in 2000 and 2004 on religion. It was the God strategy.

# CHAPTER ONE

✳

## One Nation under God, Divisible

Almost 200 years ago, Alexis de Tocqueville toured the United States and took stock of the nation's fledgling experiment in democracy. He wrote that "the religious atmosphere of the country was the first thing that struck me on arrival in the United States." Visitors might say the same today. More than any other Western or industrialized nation, America is a place where one's beliefs about God are a significant component of daily life. A Pew Research Center study of 44 nations in 2002, for example, showed that religion is much more important to Americans than to people living in other affluent nations. Nearly six out of every ten U.S. adults told Pew researchers that religion plays a "very important" role in their lives. This roughly doubled what was found in Canada, in Western Europe, and in Japan and Korea. Even in heavily Catholic Italy, fewer than three in ten people said religion was very important. In-depth analysis by Pew found a steady decrease in citizens' religiosity as a nation's per-capita income rose, with one exception: the United States. The Pew report concluded that on matters of religious importance, "Americans' views are closer to people in developing nations than to the publics of developed nations." Every one of the nations in which citizens placed greater importance on religion was in Latin America, South Asia, Africa, or conflict-laden areas of the Middle East.[1]

Additional public opinion data among U.S. adults buttress these statistics. In survey after survey, more than 90% of Americans say they believe in God or a universal spirit. In the words of pollster George Gallup, Jr., "So many people in this country say they believe in the basic concept of God, that it almost seems unnecessary to conduct surveys on the question." Further, large majorities of American adults have integrated elements of faith into their daily experiences. On a consistent basis, roughly 70% say they pray several times a week or more, and about 60% claim that faith provides a "great deal" or "quite a bit" of guidance in their day-to-day lives. Similar results can be found in the confidence of U.S. adults about their religious beliefs: nearly 90% consistently say "I never doubt the existence of God," and slightly more than 80% consistently say that people will be called before God on a judgment day.[2] In short, faith runs wide and deep in America.

It is perhaps inevitable that religion and politics have converged now and again in U.S. history. Tocqueville followed his impression of American religiosity with these words: "The longer I stayed in the country, the more conscious I became of the important political consequences resulting from this novel situation." Theology and ideology have periodically formed a powerful nexus, including during the abolition movement, the post–Civil War recapture of power by southern whites, the Social Gospel activism of the late nineteenth and early twentieth centuries, the temperance movement that led to Prohibition, Cold War fears of "godless communism," and the civil rights movement.[3] Today, this religious heritage—deeply ingrained in the American imagination—is increasingly used for partisan purposes. This is occurring across a range of leaders and institutions, but in recent decades public debate on religion and politics has been driven by Christian conservatives—specifically, fundamentalists, conservative evangelical Protestants, and conservative Catholics, who since the late 1970s have been finding common political ground. These voices have been louder and more politically determined than their liberal counterparts, and we will show how the God strategy emerged as a direct response to the rising prominence of these voters.

Our inquiry begins with what scholars have identified as the origin of the modern presidency: the Inauguration of Franklin Roosevelt in 1933. Roosevelt is an appropriate place to start for a number of reasons. For one, during his administration the United States changed significantly, with presidential, federal governmental, and national power growing substantially. Beginning with FDR allows us to largely hold constant the cultural place of presidents. Second, radio and television gained prominence starting roughly at this time, giving presidents a greater capacity to speak to the public en masse and increasing the need for political leaders to carefully craft their messages. Both of these factors are particularly pronounced during the high-state occasions of Inaugural and State of the Union addresses. Third, U.S. demographics and citizenship participation expanded in this modern period, with greater racial, ethnic, and religious diversity. Presidents today must appeal to, respond to, and represent a much more diverse nation; in such an environment, the confluence of religion and politics takes on greater import for national inclusion and exclusion. Fourth, scholars have identified the late 1940s and the 1950s as a period of "unparalleled rhetorical escalating of the American civil religion." The Roosevelt administration was the lengthy predecessor to those that governed during this period.[4] Finally, the Scopes trial in 1925 was an important moment for religious conservatives, reverberating into Roosevelt's tenure as president and marking the start of today's religious politics.

## A POLITICAL AWAKENING

In the early years of the twentieth century, a group of Bible teachers and evangelists published a series of paperback volumes titled *The Fundamentals*. These writings offered a vigorous articulation of a theologically conservative version of Christianity in the face of perceived threats by communism, modern science, and historical criticism. Over time, these volumes became a point of reference for a broader movement. In particular, fundamentalists rallied around opposition to the teaching of evolution in public schools. With William Jennings Bryan as a public advocate, antievolution sentiment gained momentum, and laws against the teaching of evolution were put on the books in several states. Such laws were rarely enforced, but a showdown was inevitable. It came in 1925 in Dayton, Tennessee. In the now-famous trial that was a forerunner of today's culture wars, public school teacher John Scopes was convicted of teaching evolution. Despite this ostensible victory for religious conservatives, the national media depicted fundamentalists as backward buffoons outside the mainstream.[5] In the aftermath, many fundamentalists chose to retreat from civic life.

It was not a surrender, though. Scholar Nancy Ammerman suggests that "[w]hat may have appeared as the demise of a movement may better be seen as its transformation."[6] Fundamentalists began to build denominations, clergy networks, church-connected institutions such as schools and colleges, book and magazine publishing houses, and radio, television, and direct-mail operations, all of which yielded a "dense, sophisticated, multicentered national cultural infrastructure."[7] This subculture combined literalist biblical beliefs with the technological and institutional realities of modern life while avoiding discrete public domains, including the political arena. It was an approach that allowed Franklin Roosevelt to draw heavily upon liberal-leaning Protestants and Catholics to build the New Deal coalition in the 1930s. The Social Gospel orientation of Roosevelt and his successor, Harry Truman, did not go unnoticed, however, and during World War II a group of moderate fundamentalists began to reengage with the broader society. These individuals called themselves "evangelicals" to highlight their interest in public engagement, and they formed the National Association of Evangelicals in 1942, opened Fuller Seminary in 1947, and instituted National Prayer Breakfasts in the early 1950s to bring together political and religious leaders, a tradition that continues to this day.[8] As the Cold War dawned, these developments produced a convergence of religion and politics.

The United States was a nation anxious about communism in the early 1950s. Senator Joseph McCarthy was at the apex of his pursuit of communists in America, and the U.S. government's plan to stop communism and the Soviet Union in Korea ended in stalemate after the deaths of more than 33,000 U.S. soldiers. A poll by the National Opinion Research Center in January 1954 asked adult Americans, "Do you think the Communist Party in the United States is tied up with a world-wide organization aiming to overthrow our government by force?" Almost 75% said yes. So substantial was the perceived threat that in another poll the same month an identical percentage said no when asked whether "members of the Communist Party in this country should be allowed to speak on the radio?" And in May 1954, when asked by Gallup pollsters if "a man can believe in Communism and still be a loyal American," 87% said no. At the heart of many Americans' concerns was a belief that communism stood in direct opposition to Western values of religious liberty, freedom, and individualism. Talk of "godless communists" became commonplace, and some leading U.S. clergy—including Billy Graham, who rose to national prominence during this era—organized days-long "crusades" that merged patriotism and Christian teachings.[9]

In this environment, political leaders in Washington took steps to formally enshrine Judeo-Christian traditions in America. In June 1954, following years of lobbying by the Catholic organization Knights of Columbus, the U.S. Congress passed and President Dwight Eisenhower signed a bill that added the words "under God" to the nation's Pledge of Allegiance. The congressional vote was unanimous in support of this change, and the House of Representatives in an accompanying report said:

> At this moment of our history the principles underlying our American Government and the American way of life are under attack by a system whose philosophy is at direct odds with our own. Our American Government is founded on the concept of the individuality and the dignity of the human being. Underlying this concept is the belief that the human person is important because he was created by God and endowed by Him with certain inalienable rights which no civil authority may usurp. The inclusion of God in our pledge therefore would further acknowledge the dependence of our people

and our Government upon the moral directions of the Creator. At the same time it would serve to deny the atheistic and materialistic concepts of communism with its attendant subservience of the individual.

These sentiments were echoed by Eisenhower: "[I]n this way we are re-affirming the transcendence of religious faith in America's heritage and future; in this way we shall constantly strengthen those spiritual weapons which forever will be our country's most powerful resource in peace and war." In 1956, Congress and the president acted again, making "In God We Trust" the national motto. By the late 1960s, the motto had made its way onto all U.S. currency.[10]

Even in this setting, though, religious conservatives restrained their political engagement. Anthropologist Susan Friend Harding points out that "leaders refrained from overtly 'mixing' religion and politics in public venues or events, avoided partisan activities, and restricted themselves to private 'fellowshipping' activities and to lobbying along the lines already established by mainline church organizations." The result, she said, was that there was little challenge to "secular modernity's presumption that the public arena was off-limits to openly Bible-believing voices." The dramatic social changes of the 1960s and 1970s proved a turning point, however, prompting many Americans to seek the stability offered by fundamentalist beliefs and fostering among religious conservatives a sense of urgency about the state of America.[11] In particular, Ammerman suggests that Supreme Court decisions outlawing prayer in public schools in 1962 and 1963 and U.S. duplicity and failures in Vietnam

> raised fears that the nation might no longer enjoy its world supremacy. Fundamentalists cared deeply about that possibility, partly because they feared the growth of communism, but also because they saw American military and economic might as guarantors of their ability [to] evangelize the world. For fundamentalists the United States has always been the "city on a hill" ordained by God as the light to the nations. From the beginning they had been committed to foreign missions, and now they wondered if the light of the gospel might go out because it would have no great chosen nation to carry it.[12]

Just as important was the civil rights movement, which relied heavily on the religious infrastructure of the black community and became a fault line among whites. Some segregationists drew upon religious rhetoric and institutions in

15

their opposition to the movement, organizing formal church protests and allying with sympathetic religious leaders. At the same time, considerable segments of the white religious community, including the leadership of the Southern Baptist Convention, accepted desegregation after the Supreme Court's 1954 ruling in *Brown v. Board of Education*. As these cultural concerns coalesced and the Democratic Party behind Lyndon Johnson stepped forward to promote racial equality, many white evangelicals in the South—a part of the nation that since the Reconstruction era had been a Democratic bastion known as the "solid South"—began a long and marked migration to the GOP.[13]

Richard Nixon was the first Republican president to capitalize upon these trends. He emphasized his conservative thinking on the issue of abortion, appealed to a "silent majority" to support U.S. military actions in Vietnam, and spoke at a Billy Graham revival in Tennessee—the only time Graham ever allowed a president to join him onstage. It did not last, of course: national outrage over the Watergate scandal doomed Nixon and his successor, Gerald Ford, and in 1976 the White House was won by Democrat Jimmy Carter, a former governor of Georgia and a devout Southern Baptist. *Newsweek* magazine proclaimed it "the year of the evangelicals" and an analysis of presidential voting trends reveals a significant movement among evangelical Protestants toward Carter. It was a shift not lost on political conservatives, particularly when the trend held in the 1978 midterm elections.[14] Over time, however, Carter's rhetoric and policies—particularly his perceived weakness as a leader and his strict separation of church and state—disappointed conservative religious leaders. An important breaking point was a meeting between Carter and a group of evangelicals in January 1980, on the anniversary of the 1973 *Roe v. Wade* decision, which had legalized abortion. Religious leaders left unimpressed. As a result, a "relationship that already had been strained was irretrievably broken."[15] It was unclear, though, whether religious conservatives would find what they wanted in the Republican Party.

Jerry Falwell, the pastor of Thomas Road Baptist Church in Lynchburg, Virginia, and host of *Old Time Gospel Hour*, a television show that reached millions of viewers each Sunday, began a public push for evangelicals and fundamentalists to unite under the label "born again." In *America Can Be Saved*, a sermon series published in 1979, Falwell argued:

> For too long we have sat back and said politics are for the people
> in Washington, business is for those on Wall Street, and religion is our
> business. But the fact is, you cannot separate the sacred and the secu-
> lar. We need to train men of God in our schools who can go on to

Congress, can go on to be directors in the largest corporations, who can become the lawyers and the businessmen and those important people in tomorrow's United States. If we are going to turn this country around, we have to get God's people mobilized in the right direction and we must do it quickly. Did you know that the largest single minority block in the United States that has never been capitalized on by anybody is the fundamentalist movement? If all the fundamentalists knew who to vote for and did it together, we could elect anybody. If every one of these people could be intelligently taught and mobilized, brother, we could turn this nation upside down for God![16]

Falwell joined with a few political organizers to launch the Moral Majority, with an agenda focused on families, abortion, prayer in schools, and traditional notions of sexuality and gender. Upon discovering that only about half of religious conservatives were registered voters, Falwell adopted a mantra: "Get them saved, baptized, and registered." And then he offered those new votes to presidential hopeful Ronald Reagan, but with strings attached. Prior to the Republican Party convention in the summer of 1980, as Reagan prepared to name his running mate, Falwell said: "If evangelicals are excited about the platform, which they are, and about both candidates, I'd say three or four million votes will be available to Mr. Reagan that have never been available to anybody." However, he added, should the GOP or Reagan not pay sufficient heed to the wishes of newly politicized religious conservatives, "They'll just sit on their hands as they've been doing for the last 30 or 40 years."[17] This wasn't the Scopes trial redux; Falwell and his followers weren't interested in winning battles while losing wars. Politicians who wanted the support of this emerging constituency would need to provide something in return.

## SIGNALS FOR THE INFORMATION AGE

The political engagement of Christian conservatives presented a significant opportunity for the political party that could capitalize on it. Polls in the late 1970s showed that 35–40% of Americans self-identified as "born again."[18] Many of these citizens resided in the southeastern United States, and although this region's white evangelicals had been leaving the Democratic Party since the 1960s largely because of its support for civil rights, the election of Jimmy Carter in 1976 suggested a potential opening for Democrats. At the same time, the Republican platform—which opposed abortion and emphasized a strong national defense—was attractive to Falwell and many of his followers. The preacher's rhetoric may have been overstated, but it held an important kernel of truth: historic political capital was up for grabs. Support among newly engaged fundamentalists and evangelicals could go far in building electoral majorities. The challenge was not a simple one, however. A single candidate might be able to appeal directly to these voters, but a political party seeking a coherent national identity faced a significant hurdle: any attempt to entice religious conservatives would have to avoid alienating moderate Americans, who were less likely to be comfortable with overt religiosity or heavy-handed moralizing. Carefully calibrated rhetoric, relationship skills, and policy goals were needed to walk this tightrope.

The Republican Party responded with the God strategy: a mixture of voice and agenda that has been primarily secularized, while—in the words of Doug Wead, who in 1988 headed George H. W. Bush's campaign outreach to evangelicals—deliberately finding opportunities to "signal" sympathy for religious conservatives' views. This approach has two compelling strengths. First, it goes far toward building and then maintaining an electoral base for a political party. Second, it provides a sizable space within which a party's leaders can appeal to moderate voters. Ronald Reagan put this strategy in motion in 1980, and the GOP subsequently employed it to accrue political power rarely attained before.[19] Republicans won the White House in five of the past seven presidential elections, captured the Congress in the 1990s, and then added to their majorities in both congressional chambers in 2002 and 2004, the first time this had happened for a sitting president since Franklin Roosevelt in 1936. Democrats stemmed this tide at least temporarily by taking back Congress in 2006—but only by also adopting the God strategy, as we will see. The implications of the GOP's recent dominance of American politics are vast. To note just two examples, Congress and the White House worked so closely in the early 2000s that George W. Bush went five and a half years without vetoing a bill—the longest span for a president since Thomas Jefferson—and seven of the nine justices on today's U.S. Supreme Court were appointed by Republican presidents.[20]

The rise of religious politics was instrumental in these developments. Since the mid-1970s, Republicans have enticed religious conservatives with little challenge from Democrats, with only two significant exceptions: in the 1990s with Bill Clinton and in 2006, when several Democratic candidates infused their campaigns with faith. In general, though, the Democratic Party has been between a rock and a hard place with regard to religion, whereas Republicans have been more or less unfettered. At the heart of the God strategy have been four signals:

1. Acting as political priests by speaking the language of the faithful
2. Fusing God and country by linking America with divine will
3. Embracing important religious symbols, practices, and rituals
4. Engaging in morality politics by trumpeting bellwether issues

In combination, these signals have provided a compelling synthesis of faith and politics that appeals to many Americans—especially, but not only, Christian fundamentalists, conservative evangelicals, and conservative Catholics.

Of course, political leaders might use these words and engage in these behaviors for a variety of reasons, first and foremost because they are religious and believe in them. This is a reasonable possibility, so our position is not that the religious sentiments conveyed by political leaders are fabrications. Rather, we are agnostic about the authenticity of politicians' religious beliefs. It is impossible to know whether a politician truly shares or cares about the religious sentiments of the citizenry. One would need to be a mind reader to say with certainty. What we do know is what political leaders say and do—and both have far-reaching implications. Further, the words and actions of today's U.S. political leaders are commonly planned in advance, especially when they are religious in nature and particularly when they occur in the contexts that will be our focus. The position we adopt, then, is straightforward. Are these religious signals authentic? Perhaps. Are they strategic? Absolutely. Far from a contradiction, these are the realities of modern American politics.[21]

Together, these four signals define today's religious politics, with leaders of both major parties using them for advantage. Republicans, though, have been more successful in cultivating personas as faith-invoking leaders, nation-loving patriots, comrades-in-fellowship, and moral policymakers. Such messages are communicated behind the scenes, of course, but there is special significance in *public* signaling—which leads us to focus on public communications in the political arena. In the parlance of religious believers, public signals provide a "witness" for a particular set of values, and this witness accepts real political risk by choosing this path. Notably, the signals have to be perceived as congruent with one's personal life, a test Bill Clinton ultimately failed in the minds of many religious conservatives. At the same time, too much religiosity or overt morality can drive away moderate Americans. In the words of long-time GOP operative Doug Wead, speaking in 2004: "That is the great danger for a politician with the evangelical constituency. As a Republican, you can't win without them. But sometimes, you can lose with them, too, because of the backlash." As a result, he said, politicians "have to be careful how and [in] what way you appeal to them."[22] Hence, we see a God strategy that walks a fine line between religious conservatives and the broader public.

If done well, this approach offers a payoff uniquely suited to today's information age. Consider that from the 1930s through the 1970s, a handful of radio and television networks dominated the political attention of Americans. This ended in 1980 with the creation of the Cable News Network, the nation's first 24-hour television news channel. Today, there are three such channels: CNN, Fox News, and MSNBC, and four if one adds CNN Headline News. In 1982, USA Today was launched as a national newspaper; today, USA Today and the Wall Street Journal boast national readerships of more than 2 million each, and the New York Times is at nearly 1.1 million. And while newspaper circulation in general is declining, Americans have no shortage of daily papers from which to choose—nearly 1,500 at last count.[23] In the late 1980s, Rush Limbaugh took his radio program national, and he now is syndicated on more than 600 stations across the country and world, draws roughly 20 million listeners, and heads conservatives' dominance of the medium. The political Left responded by launching in 2004 Air America, a progressive talk radio network that has since struggled financially. In the early 1990s, the Internet entered the purview of the mass U.S. public, and by 2006 nearly one in three people were accessing online news at least three days a week. Further, online blogs and video sites such as YouTube are increasingly influencing the political process.[24] In short, today's media environment is a daunting new world.

It's an age for which religious signals are a perfect fit. Scholars have noted that one way in which U.S. citizens negotiate the extraordinary flow of information is by finding shortcuts in their decision making. This makes sense. There is no reasonable way for people to monitor, care about, or digest the endless array of issues, personalities, and competing agendas in today's political culture. As a result, individuals look for ways to simplify their intake and evaluation of information. One means of political decision making that has become increasingly commonplace is to rely upon cues—that is, credible people or information that can be confidently used to guide decisions.[25] Religious signals by political leaders provide exactly this: cues that Americans use to truncate their information exposure and consideration. Indeed, such signals are particularly potent because they connect with what are often core values and beliefs in people's lives. When such a connection is made, it shrinks the time and energy that people invest in politics because key concerns—perhaps the key concerns—have been addressed. Further, such cues tend to be concise, which allows them to be easily transmitted both through mainstream media, such as newspapers and television, and via the more narrowly targeted media of talk radio and online sites.[26]

Religious signals, therefore, have the ability to trump many other traditionally relevant considerations, and the God strategy is an attempt to capitalize on this dynamic. For politicians who practice this method, the ideal electoral outcome is one that was captured on a *CBS Evening News* broadcast in May 2004. As scholar Robert Ivie recounted it:

> [CBS news correspondent Jim] Axelrod's election-year report came that night from Allentown, Pennsylvania, a so-called "swingtown" that anchorman Dan Rather billed as "a microcosm of America in most every way—including how it votes in presidential elections." [Allentown resident Jodi] Crawford's husband was a National Guardsman with a year left on his tour of duty in Iraq. A soldier in his platoon had just been killed in combat. Crawford was understandably worried and wished that the war could suddenly end so that her husband could return home safely. Yet her faith in the president was unshaken. She would vote for George W. Bush "because he's a Christian."

A similar sentiment was offered in a June 2006 *New York Times* article that explored why Bush's public approval ratings remained high in Utah while bottoming out elsewhere. "When I watch him, I see a man with his heart in the right place," one Utah resident said. "I like George Bush because he is God fearing, and that's how a lot of people in this area feel." As a student at Brigham Young University told the *Times*, "I'm not sure of anything he's done, but I like that he's religious—that's really important."[27]

These anecdotes illustrate the political power of the God strategy: to encourage members of the electorate to use their religious concerns as the decisive factor in voting decisions. When this is successfully accomplished, today's never-ending news cycle is rendered increasingly superfluous. Good or bad developments for the economy? Plans in Congress to address health care or immigration? A new trade agreement? Overseas developments with global implications? All recede in importance for citizens who have received a signal that they trust to guide their political decisions. In recognition of this dynamic, political campaigns work relentlessly to provide cues about core values that voters immediately grasp and about which they care deeply. For many Americans, these values are grounded in faith. The result is that elections increasingly have become what scholars call "moral referendums."[28] One is hard-pressed to imagine another cue with such ability to dominate the contemporary American political arena. In short, religious signals not only capitalize upon the emergence of religious conservatives as a political force, but also provide an ideal antidote for the information overload so common today. It's a potent combination.

## POLITICAL TRANSFORMATIONS

The patterns described above and to be examined in detail in subsequent chapters have coincided with, capitalized upon, and contributed to a series of transformations in U.S. politics. Since the nation's founding, the large majority of voters have been mainline Protestants—that is, Lutherans, Methodists, Presbyterians, Episcopalians, American Baptists, Congregationalists, and members of the United Church of Christ—or, increasingly beginning in the nineteenth century, Catholics. In the late 1960s, though, Americans began a steady movement away from mainline Protestant churches, a development encouraged by the spirited "free market" of religion that characterizes the United States. Data collected each even year by the nonpartisan American National Election Studies (NES) show that the percentage of the U.S. adult population identifying as mainline Protestants declined from 44% in 1972 to 20% in 2004. These individuals migrated primarily to two places: evangelicalism, which grew from 17% to 22% of U.S. adults as it moved beyond its strength in the Southeast, and a "no affiliation" category made up of agnostics, atheists, and citizens uninterested in institutionalized religion, which grew from 4% to 16%. Catholics hovered around 25% of the population throughout. Together, these categories account for more than four-fifths of U.S. voters, and the trends align with a historic restructuring among American Protestants, which has been documented by scholars.[29] It is the confluence of faith and politics that is our primary interest, of course, and since the early 1970s the NES data show four patterns.

The first is the substantial movement among evangelical Protestants and Catholics toward a sense of identification with the Republican Party. The NES surveys allow us to track the religious and political orientations of U.S. citizens of voting age over time. Figures 1.1 and 1.2 show that evangelicals and Catholics, once bitterly at odds in America, have increasingly found common cause with the Republican Party. Consider that in 1972, according to NES data, more than 50% of U.S. evangelicals identified with the Democratic Party, compared to roughly 35% with the Republican Party. A pro-Democratic tilt among these citizens ensued through the Jimmy Carter years, but then a tectonic shift toward the Republican Party took place following Ronald Reagan's election in 1980—moving the party allegiances of evangelical Protestants into a dead heat. They remained there well into the 1990s before another decided migration toward the GOP, and by 2004 fully 56% of evangelicals identified with Republicans, compared to 35% with Democrats.[30] The trend is striking: in three decades there was a complete reversal in the partisan identification of evangelical Protestants.

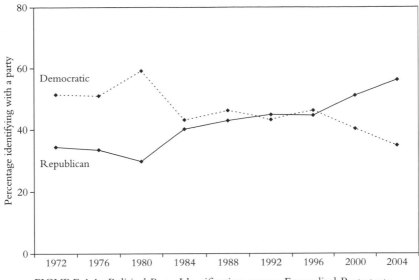

FIGURE 1.1. Political Party Identification among Evangelical Protestants

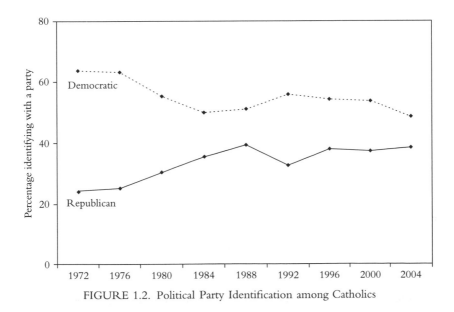

FIGURE 1.2. Political Party Identification among Catholics

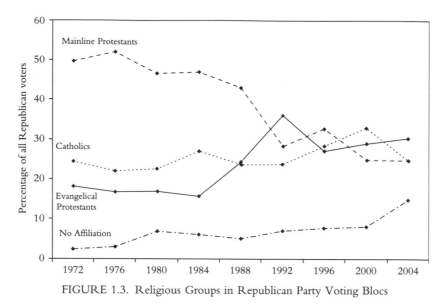

FIGURE 1.3. Religious Groups in Republican Party Voting Blocs

During the same time period, Protestants in mainline denominations leaned toward the Republican Party without dramatic change, but significant movement toward the GOP was also visible among Catholics. In 1972, Catholics were strongly Democratic: NES data show that in that year 64% identified with Democrats, 24% with Republicans. After 1976, however, the pro–Democratic Party preference began to decline steadily—such that it was cut in half by 1988, when 51% of Catholics identified with Democrats and 39% identified with the GOP. This trend slowed and reversed slightly in the 1990s during the Clinton presidency, but then resumed beginning in 2000. In 2004, for the first time, the number of U.S. Catholics identifying with the Democratic Party dipped below 50% while Republican identification was at 39%. These patterns suggest that the God strategy has resonated not only with evangelical Protestants, but with some Catholics as well. Indeed, Charles Colson, a former aide to Richard Nixon and director of the Prison Fellowship Ministries, declared in 2000 that evangelical and Catholic conservatives had forged an "ecumenism in the trenches" of cultural battles, so much so that they now "stand shoulder to shoulder as the most significant religious bloc in America."[31] When they have, they've increasingly stood with Republicans.

The growing identification with the Republican Party by evangelicals and Catholics has been accompanied by a rising centrality for each in the GOP's voting bloc. This is particularly so for evangelicals. Figure 1.3, still using the NES data, tracks the religious identification among those who voted for a

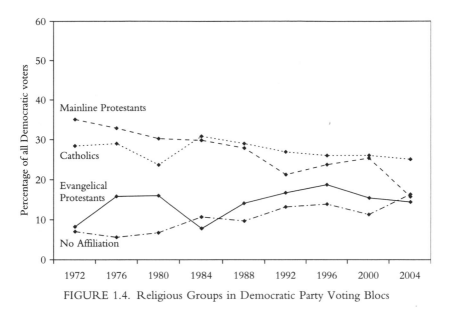

FIGURE 1.4. Religious Groups in Democratic Party Voting Blocs

Republican candidate in presidential elections 1972–2004. The four largest religious categories are shown. At the beginning of this time period, mainline Protestants accounted for fully half of all GOP voters, an electoral presence more than twice that of Catholics and roughly three times that of evangelical Protestants. Three decades later, these three groups were essentially equivalent in size in the GOP coalition, with evangelicals slightly ahead in 2004. Further, evangelicals can be distinguished in their ardor for Republicans. According to Scott Keeter, director of survey research for the nonpartisan Pew Research Center, white evangelical Protestants living in the South increasingly identified with the GOP in the 1990s, but since 2000 and especially after the terrorist attacks of September 11, 2001, evangelicals in other regions began to join the fold. The result, Keeter noted in 2006, is that "white evangelicals are approaching the same degree of political solidarity with the GOP that African-American voters accord the Democratic Party."[32] In other words, they have become the party's base.

Analysis of similar data for the Democratic Party over the same time period offers further insight. Figures 1.3 and 1.4 show the rising prominence of "no affiliation" voters for both parties and the dilemma faced by Democrats. This category of noninstitutionally religious citizens, agnostics, and atheists rose from 3% of GOP voters in 1972 to 15% in 2004, and from 7% to 16% of Democratic voters during the same period. These individuals are clearly larger on the electoral map these days.[33] At the same time, the data show the differing dynamics of religious politics for the two parties. These differences emerge when one compares within each party the relative importance of evangelical Protestants—the group most supportive of a convergence of faith and politics—to the unaffiliated bloc, the group that one might presume is most opposed to this approach. Among Republican voters in 2004, 30% were evangelicals and 15% were unaffiliated, for a ratio of 2:1. These numbers make it a no-brainer for the GOP to engage in religious politics. In contrast, among Democratic voters in 2004, 14% were evangelicals and 16% were unaffiliated. As a comparison, consider that in 1976, when Jimmy Carter was elected, evangelicals were 16% of the Democratic voting bloc and the unaffiliated were 6%—a ratio even more favorably disposed toward religious politics than Republicans enjoy now. In today's U.S. politics, therefore, it is far more difficult for the Democratic Party to successfully implement the God strategy.

That does not mean that some Democrats have not successfully done so. And indeed, the data suggest that the march toward the Republican Party by evangelical Protestants and to a lesser extent by Catholics in recent decades has not been inexorable. When the Democratic Party nominated Carter, evangelicals' presence in the party's voting bloc doubled. These voters departed just as precipitously, though, when Democrats turned in 1984 to northern liberal Walter Mondale. Eight years later, in 1992, Protestants of all stripes were divided in their opinions of George H. W. Bush. In this context, Bush faced a Republican primary challenge from conservative firebrand Pat Buchanan—who won 37% of the GOP vote in the year's first primary, in New Hampshire—and the Democrats nominated Bill Clinton and Al Gore, a pair of Southern Baptists. The combination of dismay over GOP leadership and the Democrats' own religious politics propelled evangelicals to their greatest levels of importance in the Democratic fold in 1992 and 1996. These starts and stops in evangelical Protestants' support for Democratic Party candidates point to how today's confluence of faith and politics might have been much different had either party made different choices along the way—or if they do so now.

Taken together, these transformations in the American electorate underscore the sizable opportunities and real challenges faced by politicians in recent decades who have attempted to negotiate the landscape of religious politics. Some leaders have had more success than others. But all who employed the God strategy and all who experienced it have been part of these shifts and developments. Just as politicians carefully calibrate their rhetoric and actions, so too do voters commonly have agendas. Many citizens—especially but not only those who are distinctly religious—desire leaders who can guide the nation in matters political *and* spiritual. Indeed, a large majority of Americans sees the two domains as inextricably linked: in both 2000 and 2004, 70% of registered U.S. voters told Pew researchers that it was important "that a president have strong religious beliefs."[34] Such an outlook means that when political leaders employ religious signals, an accumulation of political capital is not the only outcome. Such signals by America's highest national political leaders also validate or invalidate particular religious perspectives, invigorate or stall social movements, and demarcate for citizens the appropriate relationship between faith and nation. The outcomes, in short, are both political and religious. Let us turn, then, to see the God strategy in action.

# CHAPTER TWO

❋

## POLITICAL PRIESTS

For most of a mid-December evening in 1999, the Republican Party primary debate in Des Moines, Iowa, followed a predictable pattern. The six candidates on stage—Gary Bauer, George W. Bush, Steve Forbes, Alan Keyes, Orrin Hatch, and John McCain—fielded questions, argued, cracked jokes, and made their case for the party's presidential nomination. The live audience offered periodic applause when a candidate struck a resonant chord; many others watched on television. As the debate neared its conclusion, one of the moderators, local newsman John Bachman, posed a question sent in from an Iowan watching the debate: "I'd like to run the table quickly with one individual question. What political philosopher or thinker, Mr. Forbes, do you most identify with and why?"[1] Forbes said John Locke, because "[e]ven though there are some flaws, I think he set the stage for what became a revolution." Keyes followed, and he opted for the nation's founders, because they created "instruments of government that have preserved our liberty now for over 200 years." Bush was to answer next. He was known as a savvy politician—in Texas he had knocked off popular Democrat Ann Richards to become governor in 1994 and then coasted to reelection in 1998—and he seized the moment.

With all eyes on him, Bush answered, "Christ, because he changed my heart." There was a pause; a beat or two passed in the room as the answer settled. Bush gave a quick, confident nod, indicating he was content to leave it at that. But Bachman followed up: "I think the viewer would like to know more on how he's changed your heart." Bush smiled momentarily, then turned serious as he said, "Well, if they don't know, it's going to be hard to explain. When you turn your heart and your life over to Christ"—and here Bush had the perfect words to connect with religious conservatives—"when you accept Christ as the savior, it changes your heart. It changes your life. And

29

that's what happened to me." Bush's response drew loud applause from the audience. But it also did more: it established a norm. Hatch followed Bush by saying that Christ's influence upon him "goes without saying," adding, "I bear witness to Christ, too. I really know him to be the savior of the world. And that means more to me than almost anything else I know." McCain, ever the maverick in 2000, named Theodore Roosevelt. Last up was Bauer, a religious leader with a lineage in the Reagan administration. He offered a veritable sermon on the importance of Christ, concluding, "If America's in trouble in the next century, it will be because we forgot what he taught us." Bush's signal had been sent and received, and the dynamic of the debate was changed. That's the power of the God strategy.

The national news media immediately took up Bush's words for discussion, calling it his "Christ moment." The statement created such a stir that *Washington Post* columnist E. J. Dionne dubbed it "the pronouncement heard 'round the world." Among those critical of Bush's answer, some questioned its sincerity while others found it vague or exclusionary. For many, though, Bush's answer resonated. Polls showed that 40% of likely Republican caucus participants identified as evangelical or "born-again" Christians. As Dee Stewart, the executive director of the Republican Party of Iowa, put it, "The Republican debate has religion intertwined in its discourse. Our caucus attendee is not going to be offended by a discussion of God or moral values in politics."[2] And more broadly, for people of conservative faith nationwide—a group that by 2000 had become a crucial part of the GOP voting bloc—Bush's words hit home. Evangelist Billy Graham, for example, called Bush's response "a wonderful answer." The president of the Southern Baptist Convention's Ethics and Religious Liberty Commission, Richard Land, had this to say: "I was watching the debate with my wife and daughter in the room, neither of whom are political junkies. And when they heard that answer they both stopped what they were doing, looked at me and said 'Wow.' " Land explained the reaction: "[Bush] talks their language. Most evangelicals who heard that question probably thought 'That's exactly the way I would have answered that.' " Indeed, the *Post*'s Dionne quoted another debate observer—a declared Southern Baptist Democrat and not a Bush fan—who nonetheless said, "That's how we talk about our faith."[3] Exactly.

## THE FOUNDATIONAL SIGNAL

Politicians seeking to appeal to religiously inclined voters must be able to speak the language of the faithful. George W. Bush's talent for connecting with religious voters helped him to win the presidency in 2000—he received nearly

80% of white evangelicals' votes in that election—and, once he took office, this capacity became a hallmark of his public persona. But Bush is only the latest purveyor of this pattern of American religious politics. We begin our analysis of the God strategy with a focus in this chapter on presidential use of religious language since 1933. We examine how often presidents have employed such language and how much of it they have used. The evidence will show that beginning with Ronald Reagan, religious communications increased to levels never before seen in the modern presidency. They have yet to recede. We demonstrate this striking development by tracking religious language in every major national address given by presidents from Franklin Roosevelt's Inauguration on March 4, 1933, through the six-year mark of George W. Bush's presidency in early 2007—nearly 360 speeches in all.[4] These addresses were broadcast to the nation, were covered in the press, emphasized serious and wide-ranging matters, and went far in shaping U.S. public opinion.[5] One might reasonably conclude that these speeches represent the most significant public contributions to American political communications over the past eight decades.

Our focus is on two related yet distinct types of religious communication: invocations of God and invocations of faith. To invoke God is to make direct reference, often by name, to a supreme being. Examples include any mention of God, Christ, the Creator, Providence, the Almighty, or the like. Such language is the most explicit type of religious communication that any person, including a U.S. president, can use. Invocations of faith are more subtle, but not necessarily less important. To invoke faith is to use terms that over time have become laden with spiritual—especially Christian—meaning, such as Scripture, blessing, heaven, faith, mission, pray, and so on. Such language does not inevitably carry religious meaning for all listeners, but there is a vocabulary of faith embedded in American culture that conveys religious sentiment to anyone listening for such cues—and millions are doing so.[6] As a result, invocations of God and faith function as a crucial, foundational signal for political leaders trying to communicate their beliefs and convince religiously inclined Americans that they share their world view. In particular, an ability to speak the language of believers can be powerful for a president, who is frequently in the spotlight and is most commonly called upon to be America's "high priest" in times of crisis, national celebration, political turmoil, or tragedy.

Whether a president communicates in ways that connect with religious conservatives is something this constituency especially notices. Consider the perspective of Doug Wead, a political strategist who was George H. W. Bush's point person with evangelicals in 1988. Wead has advised political leaders to "signal early, signal often." Doing so, Wead told *Frontline* in 2004, is one means of making a "nod" to a key segment of the public—a way "to signal respect to the evangelical community, to say, 'We don't exclude you. If I'm president, I will love and respect you as much as any other American. I'm not going to judge, or deny you, just because of your religion.' Evangelicals feel that." This view is echoed by Richard Cizik, the vice president for governmental affairs for the National Association of Evangelicals, which represents more than 60 denominations and 30 million citizens nationwide. Asked about the religious allusions common in George W. Bush's public communications, Cizik said: "The president...used terminology designed, I think, to indicate [to] the evangelicals that 'Hey, I'm one of you,' so to speak....It accomplished his purposes. He sent a message, I think, to evangelicals, 'Hey, I understand.' "[7] In simple and pragmatic terms, a president who speaks the language of religious believers does much to suggest that he understands them and deserves their political support.

In part, the desire among religious conservatives to hear presidents speak their language stems from concerns about the secularization of modern society, a view that has encouraged these voters' increased political participation and fueled controversies about religious symbolism in government institutions.[8] In promoting language about God and faith, religious groups encourage—sometimes explicitly, sometimes implicitly—the vitality of their belief systems. Numerous anthropologists and sociologists have observed that religion is, at its core, a "system of symbols."[9] This means that people must learn their faith and then continually recreate their understandings of it; through this process, religious teachings are renewed and passed down through generations. Because the communications of political leaders circulate widely in U.S. society, the presence of religious themes can be an especially important factor in the public's ongoing religious socialization. Further, when these themes are made salient by politicians and news media, citizens become more likely to view faith and religious beliefs as important and to draw upon these criteria when evaluating politicians and political issues more generally.[10] Ultimately, what words become consistent and persistent matters deeply for society.

The patterns in religious language identified in this chapter should be viewed as both a cause and a consequence of the changing electoral dynamics in recent decades. Increases in presidential religious communication prompt citizens, journalists, and other politicians to take notice. Language never simply reflects society; rather, the words people choose always influence the way we—all of us—think, feel, and behave. Consequently, any significant shifts in presidential rhetoric over time encourage congruent changes in on-the-ground politics. At the same time, the shifts in religious language that we will observe reflect deliberate decisions by presidents to send distinct signals, particularly to fundamentalists, conservative evangelicals, and conservative Catholics, who began to form a coherent electoral bloc in recent decades. In the words of Richard Land of the Southern Baptist Convention in 2004: "We need to vote our values, our beliefs and our convictions. We shouldn't be endorsing candidates. We should be looking for candidates who endorse us."[11] For a president, there is no more important or politically expedient way to endorse religious voters than to speak their language.

## INVOKING GOD

The place to begin is by identifying how often presidents have invoked a divine entity in their public communications.[12] Figure 2.1 shows the percentage of White House addresses to the nation, separated by president, that included an explicit reference to a supreme being. Our reading of every word of these speeches revealed that presidents from Roosevelt in 1933 through Jimmy Carter, who exited office in 1981, invoked God in roughly half of their national addresses. There were some differences: most notably, John Kennedy, Richard Nixon, and Carter were half again lower in their invocations of God. Nonetheless, the fundamental trend is apparent: explicit invocations of a higher power have been a regular feature of the American presidency. Beginning in 1981, however, such appeals no longer were just common among

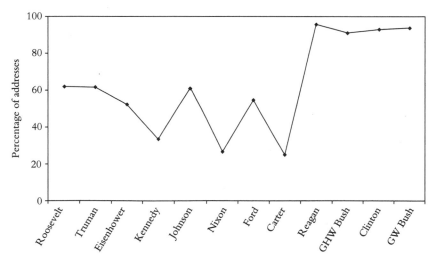

FIGURE 2.1. Presidential Addresses to the Nation with Invocations of God

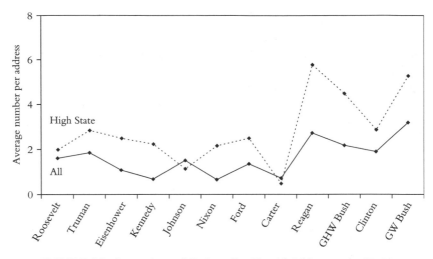

FIGURE 2.2. Invocations of God per Presidential Address to the Nation

presidents; they became omnipresent. In their presidential addresses to the nation, Ronald Reagan invoked God 96% of the time, George H. W. Bush did so at a 91% clip, Bill Clinton came in at 93%, and George W. Bush (through six years of his presidency) followed suit 94% of the time. Since the mid-1970s, invocations of God have become a fixture in American presidential addresses, every bit as de rigueur as the band striking up "Hail to the Chief" to announce the arrival of a president.

As a next step, we examined how often—that is, how many times in each address—God was invoked. It might be the case, for example, that the past four presidents referenced God in more speeches but still were congruent with previous presidents in total invocations. Figure 2.2 shows the average number of God references per address for each of the presidents since 1933, with two trend lines. One line shows the per-address average of God invocations for all speeches to the nation; the other shows the average for the subset of addresses that occurred in the high-state occasions of Inaugural and State of the Union addresses. These speeches are important to distinguish because they tend to draw larger public audiences and more news coverage. Comparison of these high-state addresses with the entire collection of speeches therefore allows us to gauge the perceived political capital of invoking God. If there have been consistently more invocations in Inaugurals and State of the Unions than in the broader compilation of addresses, we might surmise that U.S. presidents see religious language as politically valuable. Further, the ceremonial nature of Inaugurals and State of the Unions means that any invocation of a divine power in these contexts necessarily fuses a religious outlook with America as a nation; as a result, a higher visibility for God on these occasions would have significant meaning for the American public's sense of nationhood.[13]

The trend lines show a marked increase in the volume of explicit language about God in the presidency since 1981. Figure 2.2 shows that the four most recent presidents invoked God far more than previous modern presidents, regardless of the speaking context. Looking at the entire collection of addresses, the highest mean among the first eight presidents—by a sizable margin—was Harry Truman with 1.87 references to God per address. Beginning in 1981, the means were 2.7 for Ronald Reagan, 2.2 for George H. W. Bush, 1.89 for Bill Clinton, and 3.2 for George W. Bush. Inaugural and State of the Union addresses reveal a similar pattern, but with consistently more God invocations—an outcome suggestive of the political capital thought to accrue with such language. Again, in the first group of presidents, Truman was the high-water mark, averaging 2.86 references to God per address. Beginning in 1981, the means elevated to 5.8 for Reagan, 4.5 for the elder Bush, 2.89 for Clinton, and 5.3 for Bush the son. For both trend lines, presidential invocations of God in a typical address 1981–2007 were *more than double* the average for addresses delivered 1933–1980.[14] The data in Figures 2.1 and 2.2, then, show that the election of Ronald Reagan was a watershed moment. It's not that explicit language about God entered the presidency in 1981; it's that with Reagan explicit language about God became publicly embedded in the presidency—and, by extension, in U.S. politics.

Close examination of a small number of addresses is instructive of these trends. We begin by comparing two presidential prayers that commenced Inaugural addresses: one by Dwight Eisenhower in 1953 and one by George H. W. Bush in 1989. The symbolism of Inaugurals ensures that in these speeches a president's religious language—or lack thereof—is particularly noted. For example, William Pennell, the pastor of a Baptist megachurch in Georgia, expressed this reaction to Jimmy Carter's presidential beginning in 1977: "I was thrilled at the thought of a born-again in the White House," until Carter in his Inaugural address "mentioned the Lord's name less often than any other president"—a point borne out in Figure 2.2. Yet the prayers by Eisenhower and Bush were the only ones delivered in Inaugural addresses.[15] Eisenhower's prayer, in its entirety, went as follows:

> Almighty God, as we stand here at this moment my future associates in the executive branch of government join me in beseeching that Thou will make full and complete our dedication to the service of the people in this throng, and their fellow citizens everywhere. Give us,

we pray, the power to discern clearly right from wrong, and allow all our words and actions to be governed thereby, and by the laws of this land. Especially we pray that our concern shall be for all the people regardless of station, race or calling. May cooperation be permitted and be the mutual aim of those who, under the concepts of our Constitution, hold to differing political faiths; so that all may work for the good of our beloved country and Thy glory. Amen.

Eisenhower's focus was primarily on the motivations and actions that he, Congress, and the American public might exhibit. Indeed, he spoke of citizens and diversity, of laws and the Constitution. In contrast, George H. W. Bush focused a significant portion of his prayer on God's character and wishes, and he spoke in a distinctly personal manner. Bush's prayer, in its entirety, consisted of these words:

Heavenly Father, we bow our heads and thank You for Your love. Accept our thanks for the peace that yields this day and the shared faith that makes its continuance likely. Make us strong to do Your work, willing to heed and hear Your will, and write on our hearts these words: "Use power to help people." For we are given power not to advance our own purposes, nor to make a great show in the world, nor a name. There is but one just use of power, and it is to serve people. Help us remember, Lord. Amen.

For both presidents, the prayers expressed a desire to serve God and people. What differed was how this desire was communicated. Eisenhower invoked God three times and prioritized the American public and nation, an approach emblematic of the abstract "civil religion" common among presidents during America's first 200 years. In contrast, Bush invoked God six times, prioritized God and divine will, and spoke in the far more intimate manner commonly found in modern evangelicalism, using such words as Father, love, hearts, You and Your, and Lord. Bush's approach was a significant rhetorical elevation of God and a palpable shift in God's role vis-à-vis the nation's leaders and citizens. His words also recalled an era of religious understanding that pre-dates the scientific rationalism derided by many conservative Christians. As one observer put it: "[Bush's] text was pre-Enlightenment, words that could have been spoken with equal impact in the 17th century about the restorative powers of faith and prayer and good deeds and the balm of living in a community." Bush carried this theme throughout the Inauguration, concluding the weekend with a nationally televised prayer service at the National Cathedral, where he urged 200,000 churches nationwide to pray for his administration.[16] Bush's politics were exactly the type desired by the many Americans interested in a president who is not only a political leader but a spiritual one as well.

A second useful comparison can be made between Franklin Roosevelt's address to the nation two days after the Japanese attacks on Pearl Harbor in 1941 and George W. Bush's response to the terrorist attacks of September 11, 2001.[17] Pearl Harbor was bombed on December 7, 1941. Franklin Roosevelt requested a declaration of war against Japan from Congress on December 8,[18] and the following evening he spoke to the nation in one of his fabled fireside chats. Roosevelt began by detailing the state of relations between Japan and the United States and the record of Italian, German, and Japanese aggression over the previous decade. As a result of these developments, he said, "We are now in this war. We are all in it—all the way. Every single man, woman, and child is a partner in the most tremendous undertaking of our American history." He then spent most of the address on the plans of the federal government and responsibilities of U.S. citizens. It was not until the final word of the speech that Roosevelt explicitly invoked God. He closed with these words:

> We are going to win the war and we are going to win the peace that follows. And in the difficult hours of this day—through dark days that be yet to come—we will know that the vast majority of the members of the human race are on our side. Many of them are fighting with us. All of them are praying for us. For in representing our cause, we represent theirs as well—our hope and their hope for liberty under God.

The attack on Pearl Harbor was the worst by a foreign entity in America's history, and in comforting and rallying the nation Roosevelt overtly invoked God one time. FDR did not formally address the nation again until his annual State of the Union in early January 1942.

Sixty years later, when terrorists attacked the United States in 2001, George W. Bush formally addressed the nation via live television three times in the space of nine days: from the Oval Office on the evening of September 11, at the National Cathedral as part of a memorial service on September 14, and before a joint session of Congress on September 20. All three speeches invoked God a number of times. On September 11, Bush spoke for only five minutes, concluding with these words:

Tonight I ask for your prayers for all those who grieve, for the children whose worlds have been shattered, for all whose sense of safety and security has been threatened. And I pray they will be comforted by a power greater than any of us, spoken through the ages in Psalm 23: "Even though I walk through the valley of the shadow of death, I fear no evil, for You are with me."

This is a day when all Americans from every walk of life unite in our resolve for justice and peace. America has stood down enemies before, and we will do so this time. None of us will ever forget this day. Yet, we go forward to defend freedom and all that is good and just in our world.

Thank you. Good night, and God bless America.

Three days later at the National Cathedral, on a day that he had proclaimed to be a national day of prayer and mourning for the victims of the attacks, Bush overtly invoked God and quoted biblical texts several times. He concluded this way:

On this national day of prayer and remembrance, we ask almighty God to watch over our nation and grant us patience and resolve in all that is to come. We pray that He will comfort and console those who now walk in sorrow. We thank Him for each life we now must mourn and the promise of a life to come.

As we have been assured, neither death nor life, nor angels nor principalities nor powers, nor things present nor things to come, nor height nor depth, can separate us from God's love. May He bless the souls of the departed. May He comfort our own, and may He always guide our country.

God bless America.

Finally, Bush spoke before Congress and the nation on September 20 in an address watched by 82 million Americans, the largest audience for a political event in U.S. history.[19] The speech ran 3,013 words, two words fewer than Roosevelt's fireside chat 60 years earlier. Bush began by thanking U.S. allies, American families, and Congress for their support and perseverance in recent days—including, he noted, Congress's singing of "God Bless America" on the steps of the Capitol. The president then offered an explanation of who the terrorists were, why they had attacked the United States, and what steps the government and citizens would or should take. Along the way, he framed the conflict in distinctly religious terms by twice referencing "Allah," almost certainly the first time that the Muslim word for God had been invoked in a U.S. presidential address.[20] At the end, Bush declared: "The course of this conflict is not known, yet its outcome is certain. Freedom and fear, justice and cruelty have always been at war, and we know that God is not neutral between them." He then added, "Fellow citizens, we'll meet violence with patient justice, assured of the rightness of our cause and confident of the victories to come. In all that lies before us, may God grant us wisdom, and may He watch over the United States of America." Recall that after Pearl Harbor, FDR spoke to the nation once and invoked God one time. In the days following the 2001 terrorist attacks, Bush addressed the nation three times and invoked God more than 20 times in those speeches.

Bush put religious politics front and center in this defining moment for the nation, and the approach reaped rewards. Tony Carnes, the senior news editor for *Christianity Today*, a leading publication among evangelicals, responded this way: "President Bush, from the day of the attacks on the world trade center, has led the nation with a deft spiritual presence that radiates solidarity with people of all faiths." Peggy Noonan, who served as an adviser and speechwriter for Ronald Reagan and George H. W. Bush, had this to say: "In 1964, Time Magazine famously headlined 'God Is Dead.' I hope now, at the very highest reaches of that great magazine, they do a cover that says 'God Is Back.'" It's a headline, indeed, that could have been published on the day that Reagan entered the White House—or virtually any day since. In December 2001, Pat Robertson resigned as head of the Christian Coalition with little effect or public stir, a development that prompted the *Washington Post* to declare, "For the first time since religious conservatives became a modern political movement, the president of the United States has become the movement's de facto leader."[21] Behold the God strategy.

## INVOKING FAITH

As a next step, we examined the usage of more subtle forms of religious imagery and vocabulary in presidential communications. Specifically, we were interested in assessing how common in presidential speeches were terms that did not explicitly invoke God, but nonetheless were laden with spiritual, particularly Christian, significance. Such invocations of faith include angel, confession, evil, faith, miracle, mission, pray, proverb, sacred, sin, and worship, among others. Some of the included words can be used to address topics that are not distinctly religious, but even in such instances the religious connotations of the term still accompany its usage, so that the words inevitably suggest an element of faith.[22] This is particularly the case for devout religious believers, who commonly filter many, if not all, of the messages they encounter through a spiritual prism. Such individuals include large numbers of religious conservatives in the United States, but also millions of others who see their spiritual life as important. References to faith are part of everyday conversation for many Americans. Whether presidents have also used this manner of speaking was the guiding question of interest for this analysis.

Invocations of God and faith exist in a symbiotic relationship in American presidential communications. That is, each type of language reinforces and draws upon the other, working in tandem to express a religious outlook. At the same time, presidents may be more comfortable expressing one type of communication than the other, depending on the realities of the historical moment, their own political and religious perspectives, and the goals of their administration. It may be, therefore, that even though overt God references increased in the presidency after 1980, more subtle invocations of faith stayed constant or perhaps even declined. If, on the other hand, presidential references to faith have also risen in recent decades, this would further substantiate a shift in the public role of religion in American politics. With this in mind, Figure 2.3 shows the average number of faith invocations per address for each of the presidents since 1933. Two points became apparent in the data.

First, there is a notable increase in the volume of subtle religious language in the presidency since 1980. Whether one's focus is on all speeches to the nation or on those delivered during high-state occasions, Figure 2.3 shows that the three highest volumes of faith references in the modern presidency, and four of the top five, occurred among the four most recent presidents. Looking at the entire sample, the highest mean among the first eight presidents was Franklin Roosevelt with 9.9 faith terms per address. Beginning in 1981, the means were 10.4 for Ronald Reagan, 8.6 for George H. W. Bush, 11.8 for Bill Clinton, and 12.7 for George W. Bush. Second, in Inaugural and State of the Union addresses, a similar pattern is present, but with much more invoking of faith. Again in the first group of presidents, Roosevelt was tops with 13.7 faith terms per address. Beginning in 1981, the means elevated to 21.6 for Reagan, 13.3 for G. H. W. Bush, 20.2 for Clinton, and 16.7 for G. W. Bush. For both trend lines, the number of references to faith in a typical presidential address 1981–2007 was *more than 50% higher* than the average for addresses delivered 1933–1980.

Among the four most recent presidents, invocations of faith were highest for Reagan, Clinton, and George W. Bush. These findings merit elaboration. For one, these data bear out that Reagan was unmatched in the modern presidency in his expression of a religious world view, at least in his national

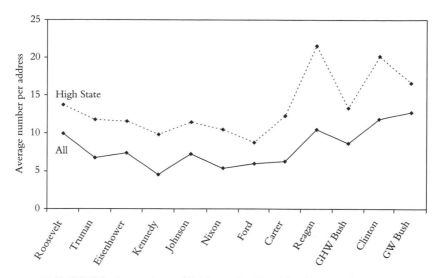

FIGURE 2.3. Invocations of Faith per Presidential Address to the Nation

addresses. He delivered the most addresses invoking God, was highest along with George W. Bush on the per-address averages for God invocations, and exhibited along with Clinton and Bush the most invocations of faith per address. Put simply, Reagan's presidency was unprecedented in its public religiosity—and George W. Bush and Clinton were not far behind. Indeed, the younger Bush was right with Reagan on all of these measures. As for Clinton, his high level of faith language was indicative of his apparent ease among religious communities, including both African American worshippers and southern white evangelicals, and begins to reveal how a Democratic Party politician can succeed with religious politics. In invoking God, Clinton was higher than pre-1981 presidents yet distinctly lower than Reagan and the Bushes. But Clinton more than held his own in invoking faith, a component of the God strategy likely to connect with religiously inclined citizens yet perhaps not overly trouble the large number of secular voters in the Democratic base.

One additional point emerged. Over time in the presidency, there has been a shift in faith-based terminology that is suggestive of how people might interpret the pressing issues faced by the nation. This shift was apparent in our reading of the addresses, so we looked more closely at two terms that can be used to describe tasks that must be undertaken: mission and crusade. Both terms have been used historically to refer to military combat, and both also have been employed over time in a decidedly religious manner. At all times, these words invoke dimensions of each of these lineages, making them uniquely potent

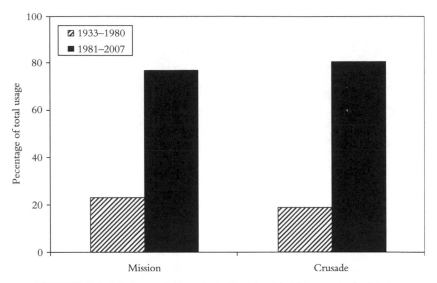

FIGURE 2.4. Mission and Crusade in Presidential Addresses to the Nation

political terminology. Given the trends observed thus far, it seemed plausible that mission and crusade have appeared more often in presidential communications in recent decades as part of the overall ascendance of religious politics. With this in mind, we identified when these terms were used in addresses to the nation during the modern presidency.[23]

Mission was the far more common of the two terms, appearing 200 times across the full collection of national addresses, while crusade appeared 21 times. What's most important here is not total usage, though, but when these terms have been employed. Figure 2.4 shows the proportional usage of these terms in two time periods: 1933 to 1980 and 1981 to early 2007. A full 77% of all usages of mission and 81% of all instances of crusade in major presidential addresses have occurred since Reagan took office. Stated another way, beginning in 1981, the use of mission in presidential addresses to the nation tripled and the use of crusade quadrupled. These patterns are even more notable when we consider that our sample included 100 more addresses by presidents prior to Reagan than since his Inauguration. The implications of the increased emphasis on mission and crusade, particularly in a post–September 11 world where global religious tensions have heightened, are profound. These words are used to identify American governmental actions at home and abroad and therefore function as a meaningful political and religious signal not only for Americans, but for citizens worldwide.

Finally, we looked closely at two addresses that are instructive of the trends in presidential invocations of faith and that highlight how such terminology might be deliberately employed. Specifically, we considered how presidents responded to major political misfortune in congressional midterm elections. In the eight decades encompassed by our analysis, there were three midterm elections in which the political party of a sitting president experienced an electoral wipeout, losing large numbers of seats and control of both chambers of Congress: 1946, 1994, and 2006.[24] Harry Truman was in office for the first, Bill Clinton for the second, and George W. Bush for the third. We selected the two presidents of the same party—Democrats Truman and Clinton—and examined whether they utilized religious rhetoric in their efforts to reconnect with the American public and to regain the political high ground. We closely read each of the State of the Union addresses that followed these shifts in congressional power, and focused on these two presidents' invocations of faith.

Truman became president in April 1945 upon the death of Franklin Roosevelt, and within a few months he presided over the close of World War II. An electoral shift away from Democratic Party dominance was perhaps inevitable, but Truman nonetheless had to answer for the Republican Party's pickup of 67 seats and both houses of Congress in the 1946 midterm elections. On January 6, 1947, Truman opened his State of the Union by noting the partisan distribution of seats in the Capitol: "It looks like a good many of you have moved over to the left since I was here last." He followed this line by noting that he was the 20th U.S. president to encounter a Congress controlled by an opposing party. Truman then delivered an address that was typical in its invocations of faith: across his high-state addresses Truman averaged 11.7 faith terms, and in this one he had 15. Further, he was in no hurry to invoke faith: only three terms appeared in the initial two-thirds of the address, while seven of them—spiritual, spirit (twice), solemn, devotion, and faith (twice)—came in one passage as he approached the closing. For Truman, the midterm electoral loss prompted a State of the Union speech that was ordinary in its emphasis on faith.

Clinton took a dramatically different approach after the Republican Party picked up 60 seats and control of both branches of Congress in the 1994 midterm elections. In his State of the Union address on January 24, 1995, the religious language—invocations of both faith and God—was present early and often. Clinton began with this sentence, "Again we are here in the sanctuary of democracy, and once again our democracy has spoken," and then went on:

So let me begin by congratulating all of you here in the 104th Congress and congratulating you, Mr. Speaker. If we agree on nothing else tonight, we must agree that the American people certainly voted for change in 1992 and in 1994. And as I look out at you, I know how some of you must have felt in 1992.

I must say that in both years we didn't hear America singing, we heard America shouting. And now all of us, Republicans and Democrats alike, must say, "We hear you. We will work together to earn the jobs you have given us. For we are the keepers of a sacred trust, and we must be faithful to it in this new and very demanding era."

Over 200 years ago, our Founders changed the entire course of human history by joining together to create a new country based on a single powerful idea: "We hold these truths to be self-evident, that all men are created equal, . . . endowed by their Creator with certain unalienable rights, and among these are life, liberty and the pursuit of happiness."

Three sentences later, Clinton said: "I came to this hallowed chamber two years ago on a mission, to restore the American dream for all our people and to make sure that we move into the 21st century still the strongest force for freedom and democracy in the entire world." Already knee-deep in religious language, he soon turned to the primary theme of his address—the same motif that had launched his presidential victory two years earlier:

So tonight we must forge a new social compact to meet the challenges of this time. As we enter a new era, we need a new set of understandings, not just with government but, even more important, with one another as Americans. That's what I want to talk with you about tonight. I call it the New Covenant. But it's grounded in a very, very old idea, that all Americans have not just a right but a solemn responsibility to rise as far as their God-given talents and determination can take them and to give something back to their communities and their country in return.

In these opening paragraphs of his address, Clinton twice invoked God and eight times used faith terms. People tuning in to see how the president was responding to the public's electoral rebuking received an immediate answer: Clinton had rediscovered religion. It turned out he was just getting started.

In the course of his speech, Clinton invoked faith in 49 separate instances. This amount was the highest of any presidential address in our analysis by a wide margin, and overall it was two and a half times as much as Clinton averaged across his high-state speeches (his mean was 20.2 on these occasions).

The centerpiece was the "new covenant," an idea that he referenced 13 times that evening. For Clinton, this idea was his religious ace in the hole, and he pulled it out when it was most needed. But there were other key faith words as well. The word church, for instance, had never before passed Clinton's lips in a national address; in this speech it was present six times. It was joined three times apiece by sacred, religious, and reverend, while congregations, sanctuary, and worship were each there twice.[25] Clinton's address could have just as easily been delivered from a church pulpit on Sunday morning as from the bully pulpit he had on Capitol Hill that evening. Time and again he hit religious themes, and he brought the address to a climactic close:

> We all gain when we give, and we reap what we sow. That's at the heart of this New Covenant. Responsibility, opportunity, and citizenship, more than stale chapters in some remote civic[s] book, they're still the virtue by which we can fulfill ourselves and reach our God-given potential and be like them and also to fulfill the eternal promise of this country, the enduring dream from that first and most sacred covenant. I believe every person in this country still believes that we are created equal and given by our Creator the right to life, liberty and the pursuit of happiness. This is a very, very great country. And our best days are still to come.
>
> Thank you, and God bless you all.

In a comparable moment of political hardship a half-century earlier, Truman had stuck to his script with a business-as-usual amount of faith language. Not so for Clinton. The 1994 midterm elections were a major setback for his presidency; in the aftermath and with the nation watching and listening, Clinton employed the God strategy with full force.

## TURNING POINTS

We have observed two patterns so far. First, since Franklin Roosevelt was elected in the early 1930s, presidents have with some regularity explicitly invoked a higher power and also spoken in more subtle religious terms. Religion has always been a public part of the American presidency, and this has continued to be the case in the modern era. That said, our second point is more compelling: the volume of religious language in the presidency increased sharply when Ronald Reagan took office in 1981 and has remained high since. Whether the focus is on God specifically or faith generally, whether the context is a standard national address or one delivered during a high-state occasion, a new breed of religious politics has been practiced by the four most recent presidents. In both common and unique ways, these presidents utilized the God strategy. A careful reader might still wonder, however, if increases in presidential religiosity are not only a recent phenomenon but one driven primarily by other factors. In particular, three alternative explanations merit examination: the potential impacts of a wartime context, a president's party affiliation, and a future stand for reelection.

The United States has been involved in several sustained military conflicts since the early 1930s: World War II, Korea, Vietnam, the Persian Gulf War, and more recently in Afghanistan and Iraq. In such environments, presidents may have employed more religious language. For example, invocations of God and faith could have done much to mobilize U.S. public opinion, justify the conflict, and buoy the nation in these periods. It is also possible that political ideology can explain the ascendance of religious politics. Three of the last four presidents have been Republican, after all, and it may be that being a member of the GOP—for a number of ideological, political, and practical reasons—is the crucial determinant in the volume of a president's religiosity. A third possibility is that the pressure of facing a future reelection campaign has compelled presidents to employ more religious language. With this political reality looming, perhaps presidents felt a greater need to communicate in religious terms so as to curry favor with voters of faith. With all of this in mind, we compared the increase in presidential invocations of God and faith that occurred beginning with the Reagan presidency to possible increases grounded in these three alternative explanations.[26]

Figure 2.5 shows the percentage increase of each of these potential turning points in presidential religiosity. Looking at the three alternative explanations, the data indicate that from 1933 to 2007, the presence of America being at war and the president being Republican were indeed significantly related to an increase in God references. Presidents were 22% more likely to invoke God if their address was delivered during wartime, and Republicans were 27% more likely to invoke God than were Democrats. The impact of these two factors upon faith language was negligible, though. Also apparent in Figure 2.5 is that whether a president's address came when a future election loomed had little relation to invoking either God or faith. When we turn to the final bars in the figure, however, we see that these three alternative explanations pale in comparison to the rise in presidential religious language that began with Ronald Reagan. Beginning in 1981 and through the six-year mark of George W. Bush's presidency, invocations of God in presidential addresses increased by an astounding 111% from what they had been, on average, over the previous five

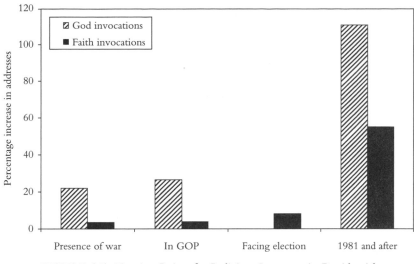

FIGURE 2.5. Turning Points for Religious Language in Presidential
Addresses to the Nation, 1933–2007

decades. In a similarly dramatic fashion, presidential invocations of faith were
55% higher among the four most recent presidents. Neither war, nor political
party, nor election context can adequately account for these increases in presidential religiosity. The past four presidents' religious language far exceeded
anything that came before in the modern presidency.[27] Whatever one's view
may be of the past four presidents, they are the founding fathers of today's
religious politics.

Like the original founders, these presidents have set a standard that those
who follow have sought to emulate. On that December evening in Iowa in
1999, George W. Bush changed the Republican Party primary debate when he
declared Jesus Christ to be his favorite philosopher. Bush's words established a
norm, and other candidates responded by voicing their own religious outlooks.
It follows that invocations of God and faith by America's four most recent
presidents have changed the nation's presidential politics. One example of the
shifting dynamic can be observed in the candidates' speeches delivered at the
Republican and Democratic presidential nominating conventions every four
years. These conventions became national spectacles beginning with live
television coverage in 1952,[28] and from that year through 1976, Democratic
and Republican presidential candidates averaged 2.4 invocations of God and
11.8 faith terms in nomination acceptance speeches.

In 1980, Ronald Reagan's victory established a new norm for the presidency. Ever since, U.S. presidential candidates who want to be taken seriously by religious voters, particularly conservatives, now face a come-to-Jesus moment in which they must display public religiosity in a manner that is inevitably calculated and yet cannot appear overtly so. The convention acceptance speech, in which candidates introduce themselves to much of the nation, is that moment for most presidential nominees.

Among Republicans, the response to the God strategy implemented by Reagan in 1980 was immediate. Beginning in 1984, and up through the election in 2004, the GOP presidential nominee in his convention acceptance speech invoked God an average of 5.2 times per address—more than doubling the previous level—and included 19.5 faith terms per speech, a 65% increase. In the Democratic Party, the evidence suggests that presidential candidates avoided religious politics until Bill Clinton arrived on the scene. Following Clinton's lead, though, Democratic presidential candidates bought into this approach as well. From 1992 through 2004, in their convention addresses, Democratic nominees averaged 4.3 God invocations and 16.5 faith terms—respective increases of 77% and 40% over the pre-1980 levels.

In the United States today, presidential candidates are afraid of being perceived as the apostate in the room. To signal that they're not, they become political priests by speaking the language of the faithful. In this respect, religious conservatives have successfully accomplished one of their primary goals: to reestablish God and religious faith at the center of American political life. In 1984, Richard John Neuhaus, editor of the Catholic journal *First Things*, decreed that the nation's public square was "naked" because, in his view, God and religious faith had been banished from the conversation.[29] No one could reach such a conclusion today.

# CHAPTER THREE

❈

## GOD AND COUNTRY

Jimmy Carter's "malaise" speech was the final straw. Over the course of two decades, Americans had endured assassinations, racial strife, duplicity and death in Vietnam, and the disgrace of Watergate. They had faced economic recession, rapid inflation, and spiraling energy costs. And now their president was floundering. In July 1979, Carter's pollster told him that for the first time "people no longer believed that the future of America was going to be as good as it was now." The president responded by inviting dozens of prominent Americans—members of Congress, governors, labor leaders, academics, and clergy—to his Camp David retreat to solicit their advice. Carter listened for a week, then emerged to deliver a national address in which he shared more than a dozen of the comments he had received: nearly all were critical of Carter or the nation. He declared that America faced a "crisis of confidence" that threatened "the very heart and soul and spirit of our national will," and he proceeded to ponder the causes, to share his concerns and hopes, and to suggest remedies. It was a speech unlike any in presidential history. The public reaction was initially favorable, but within a week criticism from pundits and cultural leaders began to rain down.[1] Seizing on a term that the president's pollster had used in a memo, critics dubbed this Carter's "malaise" speech and assailed him for expressing doubts about the nation and questioning its character—statements considered unacceptable when spoken by the president.

But this was about far more than Carter's words. Also at stake was a deeply held conviction that underlies the office of the presidency and is embedded in the American psyche: the United States is a "chosen nation," a country called by God to accomplish great things. In the words of historian Conrad Cherry, "Throughout their history Americans have been possessed by an acute sense of divine election. They have fancied themselves a New Israel, a people chosen for the awesome responsibility of serving as a light to the nations." This self-image, in turn, "has served as both a stimulus of creative American energy and a source of American self-righteousness. It has long been, in other words, the essence of America's motivating mythology." Such an outlook is particularly central for Christian conservatives, who have conceived of America as a special place from which to spread the teachings of their faith.[2] The deeper issue that Carter's speech brought to the fore, then, was this: if the United States was in decline, Christianity might go with it. When Islamic militants in Iran took more than 60 Americans hostage in early November 1979, the relationship between God and country became even more salient.

Ronald Reagan had just the words for the moment. Nine days after the hostage crisis began, he announced his candidacy for the presidency. In a nationally broadcast event that was the most expensive presidential campaign announcement in history, Reagan declared: "In recent months leaders in our government have told us that, we, the people, have lost confidence in ourselves; that we must regain our spirit and our will to achieve our national goals. Well, it is true there is a lack of confidence, an unease with things the way they are. But the confidence we have lost is confidence in our government's policies," not in the nation itself. Reagan then made his case for how he would lead, closing with these words:

> We who are privileged to be Americans have had a rendezvous with destiny since the moment in 1630 when John Winthrop, standing on the deck of the tiny *Arbella* off the coast of Massachusetts, told the little band of Pilgrims, "We shall be a city upon a hill. The eyes of all people are upon us so that if we shall deal falsely with our God in this work we have undertaken and so cause Him to withdraw His present help from us, we shall be made a story and a byword throughout the world."
>
> A troubled and afflicted mankind looks to us, pleading for us to keep our rendezvous with destiny; that we will uphold the principles of self-reliance, self-discipline, morality, and—above all—responsible liberty for every individual [so] that we will become that shining city on a hill.
>
> I believe that you and I together can keep this rendezvous with destiny.

Straight from Jesus's Sermon on the Mount, Winthrop's city-on-a-hill metaphor has wide resonance in the United States. To make sure of it, Reagan burnished the phrase with a special touch: as he told the *Washington Post*,

Winthrop "didn't say 'shining.' I added that." Just as important, Winthrop's words are *the* founding narrative among Christian conservatives, uttered more than a century before the first Great Awakening and the Declaration of Independence. Reagan had used the phrase before in front of smaller audiences, but invoking it at a moment of grave national doubt signaled that, in his view, the United States was still God's country, still the ordained leader of the free world. The response was immediate: within weeks, a coalition of some 50 Christian professionals organized and pledged to raise $450,000 in support of Reagan's campaign.[3] With his shining message, Reagan became the anti-Carter. To Carter's malaise, Reagan brought a convergence of God and country that was perfectly worded and timed. In short, Reagan brought the God strategy.

## MYTHIC AMERICA

A widely held sense of the United States as a divinely chosen place provides an especially fertile foundation for political leaders to employ religious rhetoric. With this in mind, we focus in this chapter on ways that modern presidents have talked about the nation, including whether claims about America have been closely connected with the invocations of God and faith identified in chapter 2. Scholar Benedict Anderson suggests that in today's world, in which nation-states often cover vast geographic spaces and encompass millions of people, the best we can do is to "imagine" a national community.[4] That is, because we don't all share the same experiences, we are forced to create images of a collective entity known as "the nation," through historical narratives, cultural symbols, language, customs, and personal experiences. Presidential addresses to the nation, which travel widely via news outlets and receive considerable attention among the citizenry, have great power to shape public impressions of what the United States is and what it means to be American. In turn, how citizens imagine the nation ripples through their everyday lives. In the words of Sheldon Hackney, who in the mid-1990s led a national conversation on American identity at the behest of President Bill Clinton, "[W]ho are we? That is the question, and it is a crucial question. Who we think we are shapes what we do."[5]

America's national self-image was threatened beginning in the 1960s by significant social and cultural forces. War, civil rights clashes, urban upheaval, sex and drugs, governmental lies, and economic recession all took a toll. These developments combined with U.S. Supreme Court decisions banning prayer in public schools and legalizing abortion to compel conservative religious leaders such as Jerry Falwell, Pat Robertson, and Tim LaHaye (who would go on to write the multimillion-bestselling *Left Behind* books) to enter the political fray. It was a marked change of course after decades of cultural retreat.[6] In their minds, the nation's troubles were first and foremost spiritual. Falwell declared that his reading of Old Testament prophets prompted him to see personal sin as tied to a nation's character, and in his view the United States had become "one of the most blatantly sinful nations of all time." As a result, he felt obliged to follow the prophets' model of publicly calling out the nation. He did so by embarking on national crusades aimed at birthing a mixture of "spiritual revival and political renewal" that would return the nation "to the greatness it once had as a leader among leaders in the world." He and others also established several organizations in the late 1970s to connect religious conservatives with mainstream U.S. politics, including the National Federation for Decency (1977), Moral Majority (1979), Religious Roundtable (1979), Christian Voice (1979), and National Affairs Briefing (1980). The network would continue to grow in subsequent years, eventually coalescing around the Christian Coalition in the 1990s.[7]

These leaders and organizations sought to spur a spiritual revival that would save America. Political scientist Michael Lienesch explains that, for religious conservatives, "revival is a public rite, a powerful ritual of renewal that can transform entire churches, move thousands to their feet in assembly halls or sports arenas, and even affect entire cities or countries. Thus they find it easy to think of nations, like people, repenting their sins, humbling themselves for God, and seeking salvation." A national renewal, it was thought, would return America to a mythic state of righteousness. For some who saw the United States as a distinctly "Christian nation" from its beginning, the desire was, in the words of Robertson, to "return to the moral integrity and original dreams of the founders of this nation."[8] Others pointed to the 1950s as a pinnacle of U.S. moral leadership. Ralph Reed, Jr., who headed the Christian Coalition when it was founded in 1989, said: "What religious conservatives really want is to reclaim some strengths of the America that most of us grew up in, the post–World War II America that was proud, militarily strong, morally sound, and looked up to by the rest of the world." Similarly, Focus on the Family founder James Dobson has highlighted the 1950s as a period of "cultural stability" shattered by societal upheaval in subsequent decades. The result of this outlook, according to Lienesch, is that Christian conservatives followed Old Testament prophets by adopting a "rhetoric of renewal" that has emphasized moral reform and the need for national revival.[9] As will become apparent, this prophetic approach to America was incorporated by savvy politicians.

In this chapter, we examine four distinct ways that presidents can highlight American identity, focusing on presidential addresses to the nation. Presidents have to first *invoke* the nation, that is, to name it by using words such as nation, country, United States, and America. To invoke the nation is symbolically powerful because it allows presidents, in a single phrase, to recall the myriad positive images of patriotism and sacrifice that many citizens associate with America. Once this is done, presidents then can *set apart* the nation by declaring it to be a special, distinctive place. This kind of language taps into the mythology of the United States as divinely chosen, an outlook held by many and at the core of religious conservatives' world view.[10] Third, presidents might seek to *renew* the nation by calling for national revival and rebirth. Such language is directly responsive to religious conservatives' concerns about national decline but also avoids—unlike Jimmy Carter in his malaise speech—direct criticism of the nation or its citizens. Finally, presidents can *sanctify* the nation by explicitly asking God's blessing upon it. Such language creates an overt pairing of America and Providence that goes far toward the fusion sought by religious conservatives. Together, these four techniques comprise a powerful part of the God strategy, one that recent presidents have taken to new heights.

## CONSECRATING THE NATION

Presidents are the nation's foremost political storytellers, spinning narratives about America's past, present, and future. Nowhere are presidential visions of and for the nation so expected, so commonplace, and so unabashedly laid bare as in Inaugural addresses. These speeches allow presidents to put their unique stamp on the presidency and, most crucially, to imagine the character of the nation—both for themselves and on behalf of citizens—as they desire it to be. Inaugural events also are the apex of U.S. high-state occasions, the American equivalent of royal coronations. Our analysis of God and country began, therefore, by focusing on the 20 Inaugural addresses delivered since 1933. We included all Inaugurations, because all were momentous occasions for American politics. We noted every time a president used the words nation, country, United States, or America, and then compared the presence of these terms in the speeches of the four most recent presidents to the usage by the previous eight.[11] Figure 3.1 shows that presidents beginning in 1981 employed much more of this language: the average use of three of the four terms— nation, country, and America—increased noticeably beginning with Ronald Reagan. Taken together, presidential invocations of the nation for the period

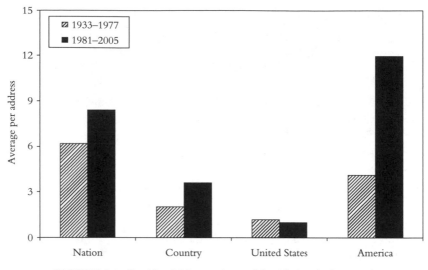

FIGURE 3.1. Presidential Invocations of the Nation in Inaugurals

1981 through 2005 were *nearly double* what they were among presidents from FDR to Jimmy Carter, increasing on average from 13.5 invocations of all terms combined per Inaugural address prior to 1981 to 25 in the years since. The nation has become a far more prominent part of Inaugural addresses in recent decades, corresponding to the political emergence of religious conservatives.

But this is not the whole story. Figure 3.1 reveals two important additional patterns. First, the largest increase in national invocations, by a considerable margin, occurs with America: since 1981 this term increased *nearly threefold*, elevating from 4.1 references per Inaugural address to 12. Second, the term America has been so popular among the past four presidents that it is now the preferred way of invoking the nation, being used nearly 50% more than the second most popular term, nation. This marks a distinct reversal from the period 1933–1977, when presidents placed greatest emphasis on the term nation and used it roughly 50% more often than America. These shifts point to the nation's rising prominence on the world stage and the deliberate choices made by presidents in their words. America, for example, brings with it a broader set of cultural mythologies than do any of the other ways of invoking the nation. Consider the manner in which America, the word, is embedded in the nation's culture: it is ascribed to symbols (the American flag), success stories (the American Dream), cultural slogans (America: Love It or Leave It), industrial pride (Made in America), even songs ("God Bless America," "America the Beautiful").[12] The term connotes a set of historical, social, and political images that nation, country, and United States do not. The evidence from these Inaugural addresses suggests that it is precisely such mythic ideas that the four most recent presidents have attempted to evoke.

Presidents John F. Kennedy and George W. Bush offer an interesting comparison. Democratic senator Kennedy in 1960 won the presidency over Republican Richard Nixon, who was a sitting two-term vice president in the popular Eisenhower administration. The popular vote almost perfectly split between the two candidates: 49.7% for Kennedy and 49.5% for Nixon. On the heels of this narrow victory, Kennedy delivered one of the more memorable Inaugural addresses in history, which included this famous passage:

> And so, my fellow Americans: ask not what your country can
> do for you—ask what you can do for your country.
> My fellow citizens of the world: ask not what America will do for
> you, but what together we can do for the freedom of man.
> Finally, whether you are citizens of America or citizens of the
> world, ask of us here the same high standards of strength and sacrifice
> which we ask of you.

In these sentences, Kennedy invoked the nation four times, twice referring to the country and twice to America. These references were exactly half of his national invocations in this address. Two other times he used the term country, and two times he used the term nation. He made no other references to America, nor did he once use the words United States. All told, Kennedy invoked the nation a grand total of eight times in this famous Inaugural.

Forty years later, Texas Republican governor Bush gave his first Inaugural address. Like Kennedy, Bush was a Harvard-educated politician from a powerful family. Like Kennedy, Bush entered the presidency facing a divided nation after barely defeating a two-term sitting vice president in a popular administration (Al Gore, in this case). Unlike Kennedy, however, Bush invoked the nation early and often in his Inaugural address—31 times, nearly four times that of Kennedy. Bush referred 11 times to the nation and nine times to the country, and like the three presidents who preceded him, he gave America a prominent position. Bush invoked America 11 times— more than all of Kennedy's national invocations—and made overt its mythic nature by rhythmically focusing the speech on a series of passages that described "America, at its best." Four times, Bush used this phrase, and each time he completed it with a claim about virtuous national traits. Four years later, in his second Inaugural, Bush took it up another notch: he invoked the nation 42 times, including 19 references to America, and again utilized an

America-centric phrase to pace the address. This time it was "America's ideal of freedom," which Bush used three times. And for good measure Bush invoked the United States five times, the most of any president in any Inaugural from 1933 to today.[13]

Such prominent and unabashed invocations of the nation were precisely what many religious conservatives wanted to hear in a presidential Inaugural. Albert Mohler, president of the Southern Baptist Theological Seminary and a prominent conservative radio commentator, had this to say in the *Baptist Press* on the day of Bush's second Inaugural:

> The nation and the world will be listening to hear what President George W. Bush will signal in what may be one of the most remembered speeches of his presidency. America is no longer a young nation seeking to be recognized by the world as one among equals. Now, America stands preeminent in the world, and America's president is the most significant leader on the world stage.

In making America the centerpiece of his address, Bush delivered. Richard Land, president of the Southern Baptist Convention's Ethics and Religious Liberty Commission, called the second Inaugural "a great speech that reaffirmed the timeless verities of the American people—that freedom is the God-given right of every human being and that America is the hope for freedom-loving people all over the world."[14] Any way you look at Bush's address, the nation was exalted. This has been increasingly so since Reagan took office.

Of course, presidents do more in Inaugural addresses than just invoke the nation; they also make claims about its values, its heritage, its people, its current challenges, and its future. As a second step, we wondered if there have been shifts in presidential characterizations of the nation that correspond with the political emergence of religious conservatives beginning in the 1970s. In particular, two claims about American identity have special appeal for religious conservatives while also resonating among the broader citizenry: the idea that the United States is a chosen nation set apart from others and the idea that a national renewal or revival will lead the nation toward its full, divinely decreed potential. With this in mind, we examined how presidents have invoked these two themes in their Inaugurals. We carefully reread the 20 Inaugural addresses from Roosevelt's in 1933 through Bush's in 2005 and took note of two patterns. First, we identified whenever a president used words suggesting that America was a nation set apart: this included terms such as unique, special, chosen, unmatched, best, beacon, and greatest. Second, we noted whenever a president used words suggesting that America needed, or would benefit from, a

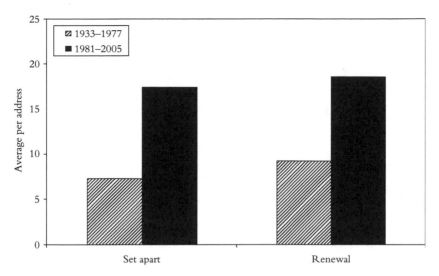

FIGURE 3.2. Presidential Claims about American Identity in Inaugurals

period of renewal: this included terms such as beginning, rebirth, reawaken, rededicate, revive, and renew.[15]

Figure 3.2 compares how often presidents emphasized these two themes in Inaugural addresses before and since 1981. The picture is striking: the four most recent presidents have been significantly more likely to characterize the nation as set apart and to talk about national renewal. In their emphases on these themes, Presidents Ronald Reagan, George H. W. Bush, Bill Clinton, and George W. Bush roughly doubled the presidents who preceded them. Specifically, talk of America as set apart rose from an average of 7.3 references per address prior to 1981 to 17.4 per address afterward, and renewal language rose from an average of 9.2 instances prior to 1981 to 18.6 per address thereafter. Put another way, the typical Inaugural from Roosevelt's first in 1933 through Jimmy Carter's in 1977 contained about 17 separate instances in which presidents characterized the nation as set apart or in need of national renewal. These themes, then, have been staples of presidential rhetoric. In recent decades, however, presidents elevated these ideas to defining features of Inaugurals. From the moment Reagan took the oath of office in 1981, presidents have averaged 36 separate instances in which they characterized the nation as set apart or spoke of national renewal. For Americans and especially religious conservatives convinced of the nation's chosen status and committed to renewing its moral leadership as a city on a hill, these shifts in presidential claims about the nation could not be more appealing.

Further insight into presidential emphasis on American identity can be gained by looking at the relative usage of these two themes—a nation set apart and renewal of the nation—by each of the last four presidents. The two Bushes were the least likely of the pack to highlight these ideas, although their invocations were still high compared to the pre-Reagan average. Bush Sr.'s Inaugural in 1989 contained 28 instances of the themes, while Bush Jr. averaged 30.5 claims of America being set apart and national renewal in his two Inaugurals. Reagan's number was higher: he averaged 35 instances of the themes and, following Carter into office, declared that his presidency would be a "new beginning" for the nation. Reagan, in 1981, said:

> It is time for us to realize that we are too great a nation to limit ourselves to small dreams. We are not, as some would have us believe, doomed to an inevitable decline. I do not believe in a fate that will fall on us no matter what we do. I do believe in a fate that will fall on us if we do nothing. So, with all the creative energy at our command, let us begin an era of national renewal. Let us renew our determination, our courage, and our strength. And let us renew our faith and our hope.

Reagan's vision of a national rebirth was carried on by George H. W. Bush in his single Inaugural, coming at the Cold War's end: "The new breeze blows, a page turns, the story unfolds. And so today a chapter begins, a small and stately story of unity, diversity, and generosity—shared, and written, together." Twelve years later, Bush's son picked the same metaphor in his emphasis on the unique character of America: "We have a place, all of us, in a long story—a story we continue, but whose end we will not see. It is the story of a new world that became a friend and liberator of the old, a story of a slave-holding society that became a servant of freedom, the story of a power that went into the world to protect but not possess, to defend but not to conquer." Bush carried this motif of a set-apart nation throughout the address, and then as he approached his finish, connected it to national renewal: "We are not this story's Author, who fills time and eternity with His purpose. Yet His purpose is achieved in our duty, and our duty is fulfilled in service to one another. Never tiring, never yielding, never finishing, we renew that purpose today, to make our country more just and generous, to affirm the dignity of our lives and every life." He added, "This work continues. This story goes on. And an angel still rides in the whirlwind and directs this storm."

It was Bill Clinton, though, who set the standard for language about American identity. In his Inaugural addresses, Clinton emphasized America as set apart and in need of national renewal an average of 46.5 times—30% more than anyone else. Clinton began his first Inaugural, in 1993, with this sentence: "My fellow citizens, today we celebrate the mystery of American renewal." He then proceeded to hammer the point home by making national rebirth the central theme of both of his Inaugurals. Clinton spoke of "a new season of American renewal," a "new era," a "new generation," and a "new world" of "new responsibilities," "new promise," "new miracles," "new government," "new spirit," "new vision," and "new ties that bind." Clinton also trumpeted the United States' unique status in the world, calling America the country that "must continue to lead the world," "the world's greatest democracy," "the envy of the world," and a "blessed land of new promise." And, to conclude his first Inaugural, he brought these two themes together in dramatic fashion, adding a heavy dose of religious language for good measure:

> Today we do more than celebrate America. We rededicate ourselves to the very idea of America, an idea born in revolution and renewed through two centuries of challenge; an idea tempered by the knowledge that, but for fate, we, the fortunate, and the unfortunate might have been each other; an idea ennobled by the faith that our nation can summon from its myriad diversity the deepest measure of unity; an idea infused with the conviction that America's long, heroic journey must go forever upward.
>
> And so, my fellow Americans, as we stand at the edge of the 21st century, let us begin anew with energy and hope, with faith and discipline. And let us work until our work is done. The Scripture says, "And let us not be weary in well doing: for in due season we shall reap, if we faint not." From this joyful mountaintop of celebration, we hear a call to service in the valley. We have heard the trumpets. We have changed the guard. And now, each in our own way and with God's help, we must answer the call.

There was no mistaking Clinton's dominant theme, and those on both sides of the partisan aisle applauded the message. Conservative columnist William Safire, for instance, declared Clinton's emphasis on renewal to be "[s]imple, direct and fitting," concluding: "[Clinton] wanted to get the point across of a nation born again, subtly evoking Abraham Lincoln at Gettysburg, and the new man drove it home." And a commentator in the *St. Louis Post-Dispatch* had this to say:

> Faith and change, of course, were the central themes of Bill Clinton's Inaugural speech. The word itself, change, echoed like a

refrain, four times in the first three paragraphs alone, and its melody was reprised again and again: the mystery of American renewal; a spring reborn; courage to reinvent America.

The use of these words and figures of speech were no casual rhetorical device, intended to briefly set a mood. The speech lasted 14 minutes and the words change, renew and renewal appeared no fewer than 11 times, from beginning to end. While they were offstage, their work was carried on by revitalize, reborn, reinvent, reform, rebuild, reconnection, rededicate. . . .

Renewal. Reform. Rededicate. Reconnecting. These are the summoning words to search our past for something that will justify us. This is the message of faith in Bill Clinton's speech. Somewhere behind us, in a purer moment of the nation's spirit, lies the source of strength for tomorrow, if we can only find it again and use it.[16]

The patterns in Clinton's Inaugurals, in combination with earlier insights into his religious communications, are illustrative of religious politics in practice. As we have seen, Clinton was lowest among the past four presidents on invocations of God, yet was neck and neck with Ronald Reagan and George W. Bush for the most invocations of faith among modern presidents. We now see that Clinton outpaced Reagan and both Bushes in presenting America as a set-apart nation ripe for renewal. In all cases, Clinton chose a public religiosity that spoke to many of the nation's religious faithful while minimizing the risk of pushing away those hesitant to hear the president talk too explicitly about God. For the first Democratic president since Franklin Roosevelt to be elected twice, implementation of the God strategy was as much about emphasizing faith and nation as it was about explicit invocations of God. None of this was by chance. Thirteen years before he entered the White House, Clinton was governor of Arkansas—and he was one of the people Jimmy Carter invited to Camp David in 1979 to discuss the state of the nation. It was Clinton to whom Carter was referring when he shared this comment in his malaise speech: "This from a southern governor: 'Mr. President, you are not leading this nation—you're just managing the government.' " Clinton did not make the same mistake. When religious conservatives came out of the political wilderness in the 1970s, he—as well as Reagan and the Bushes— watched and listened. For good or for ill, what they learned was how to use religious politics to lead the nation.

## GOD BLESS AMERICA

In the minds of many Americans, God and country have been side-by-side railroad tracks running across centuries, converging at the horizon. In the 1970s, though, religious conservative leaders made it clear that they wanted more. Their desired image of God and country was perhaps closer to a DNA helix: a spiral with tightly interwoven strands. It may be, therefore, that recent presidents have sought to more closely align the United States with a divine being. One pragmatic way to do this is by using public addresses to overtly connect the nation with a higher power. With this in mind, we looked for presidential communications that sanctified the nation by asking God to bestow favor upon America. In this analysis, we moved beyond Inaugurations to all presidential addresses to the nation from Roosevelt in 1933 through the six-year mark of George W. Bush's presidency in early 2007—a total of 358 speeches. We did so because overt linkages of America with a higher power are much more notable if present in a broader collection of presidential addresses than if they occur only in Inaugurals, a context in which presidents are given considerable license in their religious rhetoric.

We began with a focus on the phrase "God bless America" in presidential addresses. This statement succinctly combines an explicit reference to a supreme being with the term America, the most symbolically charged invocation of the nation. God bless America is today such a familiar political slogan that some might be surprised to learn of its relative youth: the phrase did not gain ubiquity in presidential speeches until the 1980s. Prior to Ronald Reagan taking office, the phrase had been used in a major national address exactly once: by Richard Nixon on April 30, 1973, as he concluded a speech about the Watergate scandal. That's one use of the phrase in 48 years and 229 presidential addresses to the nation. In contrast, from 1981, when Reagan took office, through six years of George W. Bush, the phrase God bless America was used 34 times. When the phrase "God bless the United States of America" is included as well, Nixon's single use remains its only instance prior to 1981 while the count jumps to 49 in the years thereafter.[17] Put simply, God bless America and its similar counterparts—which together constitute perhaps the most explicit statements a president can make to connect God and country—were *almost entirely absent* from the modern presidency until Reagan took office. Since then, they have become a political staple.

It is possible, however, that even though the phrase God bless America is new, the idea itself is quite old. Presidents may have long been saying essentially the same thing but with different phrasing. To account for this possibility, we read the concluding paragraphs of all the addresses to identify if presidents perhaps utilized other, albeit similar language to request divine favor. We took care to note any instance when a president used words even remotely parallel to today's phrase of "God bless," or to its inherent idea that a divine being might bless, watch over, guide, or protect the nation or its inhabitants.[18] There were a number of these instances across the presidencies, such as "May God protect each and every one of us" and "May God's grace be with you in all the days ahead"—which was Richard Nixon's parting line in his resignation speech in 1974. Of these parallel phrases, the two most common were "May God give us wisdom" (or a close variant) and "With God's help."

Figure 3.3 shows that such statements were present in a minority of addresses from 1933 to 1980, whereas they since have become nearly a constant. Through 1980, the president who most commonly closed his addresses with a request for divine favor upon America or Americans was Gerald Ford, who did so 46% of the time. Five of the eight presidents from Roosevelt to Carter did so less than 30% of the time. Beginning in 1981, the relationship between God and country became much more intimate. Reagan and George H. W. Bush each closed their national addresses with a request for divine favor more than 90% of the time, and Bill Clinton and George W. Bush followed suit 89% and 84% of the time, respectively.

Further, among the past four presidents, there have been some intriguing variants of the God and country phrasing. For example, 14 of Reagan's first

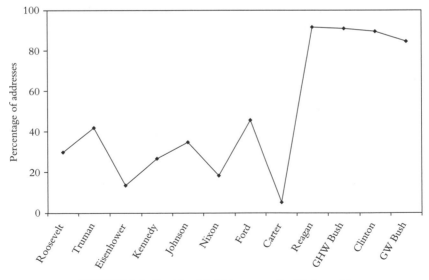

FIGURE 3.3. Presidential Addresses to the Nation with
Closing Request for Divine Favor

15 such statements were "God bless you," with the sole exception being a "God bless us, every one" (quoting the familiar phrase from Charles Dickens's *A Christmas Carol*). Then, in an October 1983 speech about the deaths of 241 U.S. soldiers in Beirut, Reagan introduced "God bless you, and God bless America." For the remainder of his presidency, Reagan alternated these shorter or longer phrasings, with very few exceptions. Only once after 1981 did Reagan not ask for divine blessing in the concluding portion of an address: his speech to the nation in January 1986 after the explosion of the space shuttle *Challenger*. Reagan ended his final presidential address, his farewell in January 1989, with an extra flourish: "God bless all of you, and may God bless this great nation, the United States of America."

George H. W. Bush's Inaugural closed with "God bless you. And God bless the United States of America." Then, in his first State of the Union address in 1990, he mimicked word for word Reagan's farewell line: "God bless all of you, and may God bless this great nation, the United States of America." During the Gulf War, Bush several times concluded speeches by asking for divine blessing on the troops, and made an especially interesting shift in his January 1991 address marking the opening of U.S. air strikes against Iraq, saying: "May He continue to bless our nation, the United States of America." With these words, Bush explicitly made it taken for granted that the nation had long experienced divine favor, a view sure to resonate with many Americans. Bush used this phrasing one other time, and in his 1992 State of the Union he offered, "God bless you, and God bless our beloved country."

Clinton's preferred phrasing was a stand-alone "God bless America," which he used 10 times in 28 speeches. He concluded three addresses with "May God bless you all," and concluded a September 1994 speech about possible military action in Haiti with "May God bless the people of the United States and the cause of freedom." Clinton again extended his standard conclusion in his second Inaugural in January 1997, when he ended with these words: "May God strengthen our hands for the good work ahead, and always, always bless our America." Two years later, in June 1999, when speaking about peacekeeping developments in Kosovo, Clinton ended with "May God bless our wonderful United States of America." Finally, in January 2001, he concluded his farewell address with the by-then-familiar combination of "God bless you, and God bless America."

George W. Bush utilized a range of phrasings during his first six years in office, including "In all that lies before us, may God grant us wisdom, and may He watch over the United States of America," which is how he concluded his address to a joint session of Congress following the attacks of September 11, 2001. Bush's signature form was that which his father had introduced: "May

God continue to bless America," which the younger Bush used with minor variations seven times between the September 11 attacks and his Republican Party presidential nomination acceptance speech in the summer of 2004. Not to be missed, though—and assuredly not missed by many religiously inclined Americans, whose faith often informs their foreign policy preferences—was Bush's wording in December 2003 after announcing the capture of Saddam Hussein: "May God bless the people of Iraq, and may God bless America." All of these phrases, now standard fare at all levels of U.S. politics, grew out of the Reagan era. This language has been fueled by a convergence of politics and faith, but in this case the simplicity of God bless America helped it to become embedded in political rhetoric. This phrase has become the signature tagline of today's religious politics, a branding every bit as memorable as Nike's "Just do it" or Coca-Cola's "The real thing." In this case, the words originated not on Madison Avenue but on Pennsylvania Avenue.

## PETITIONERS AND PROPHETS

Finally, we undertook an examination of how presidents have highlighted American identity by emphasizing "freedom" and "liberty" in national addresses. These two ideas are often used interchangeably by U.S. political leaders, and they have long been central to American mythology. This remains the case today: in a 2004 public opinion poll in key electoral states, adults were asked for one word that best conveyed their sense of what it means to be American. Almost half said "freedom." These values are so ingrained in the nation's mindset that they are enshrined in more than 400 literal symbols, such as the Liberty Bell, Statue of Liberty, Freedom Trail in Boston, and Freedom Tower, which is being built on the site of the former World Trade Center towers in New York.[19] These ideas are more than just nationally resonant; in the minds of many Americans, freedom and liberty occupy a vital point of intersection for the political and religious heritages that have defined the nation. Consider the words of French observer Alexis de Tocqueville, who wrote in the 1830s that, at its core, America's success in democracy "is the product (and one should continually bear in mind this point of departure) of two perfectly distinct elements which elsewhere have often been at war with one another but which in America it was somehow possible to incorporate into each other, forming a marvelous combination. I mean the spirit of religion and the spirit of freedom." Indeed, a nexus of freedom and liberty with the Christian faith is so central to the world view of religious conservatives that Jerry Falwell in 1976 changed the name of his theologically conservative

Christian college from Lynchburg (Virginia) Baptist to Liberty Baptist, and then in 1985 he changed it again to Liberty University.[20]

Freedom and liberty occupy this sacrosanct position because they are perceived to be the foundation of America's status as a chosen nation. That is, those who believe the United States has a divinely decided role in the world tend to point to the creation, defense, and global spread of freedom and liberty as the reason for the nation's unique position. Consider the words of Richard Land of the Southern Baptist Convention, speaking in 2005 at Wheaton College, a flagship evangelical university:

> I do believe that God has blessed our nation in providential ways and that the Bible tells us that to whom much is given, much is required and that America has a special purpose in the world. And that purpose is to be the defender of freedom, the propagator of freedom, not in attempting to impose American ideals on the world, but our belief that these are universal ideals. Freedom is a universal ideal.

Further, this task is simultaneously spiritual and national. Christian fundamentalists and conservative evangelicals are forever mindful of the "great commission" biblical mandate in the Book of Matthew, which instructs believers to "go therefore and make disciples of all the nations." This command can best be lived out in places where political and religious freedoms are present. As a result, for many Christians in America, making sure that freedom and liberty flourish locally and globally is akin to doing God's will.[21] We wondered, therefore, whether the four most recent presidents, in addition to emphasizing American identity in ways already identified in this chapter, have been more likely than previous presidents to connect freedom and liberty with claims about God in national addresses.

To fully understand the significance of such linkages in the God strategy, it is also important to ascertain whether recent presidents have adopted the style of speaking about the nation commonly used by religious conservatives. According to political scientist Michael Lienesch, leaders such as Jerry Falwell and Pat Robertson have practiced "a prophetic brand of politics" that emphasizes moral revival and how the nation might accomplish such redemption.[22] With this in mind, we considered whether there has been a shift in how presidents have connected a higher power with the principles of freedom and liberty. One way to link these two is for a president to speak as a *petitioner* of God, an approach distinguished by requests and gratitude for divine guidance in the nation's pursuits. May God bless America is an instance of petitioner language. Another way for a president to link God and country is to speak as if he is a *prophet* of God, an approach distinguished by declarative statements of God's will and wishes for the nation. A prophetic style of speaking is likely to have great appeal for religious conservatives, and thus great value for politicians seeking to connect with these voters.

We explored these matters in two steps. First, we noted whenever presidents in national addresses connected explicit invocations of God with claims about freedom and liberty. It turns out that presidents have made such a linkage in nearly one-fifth of their addresses, 18% to be precise. This is not a widespread presence, but neither is it a rarity. We then examined whether, in making these linkages, presidents positioned themselves as a petitioner or as a prophet.[23] These are very different ways of speaking, with the prophetic style much closer to the view of God and country sought by many religious conservatives. Figure 3.4 shows that recent presidents have traveled far down this road. From 1933 to 1980, presidents used a petitioner speaking style 86% of the time when connecting God with freedom and liberty in national addresses. For example, in Franklin Roosevelt's famous "Four Freedoms" speech in 1941, he spoke as a petitioner: "This nation has placed its destiny in the hands and heads and hearts of its millions of free men and women; and its faith in freedom under the guidance of God." A striking reversal occurred beginning with the Reagan presidency: from 1981 through early 2007, presidents used a prophetic

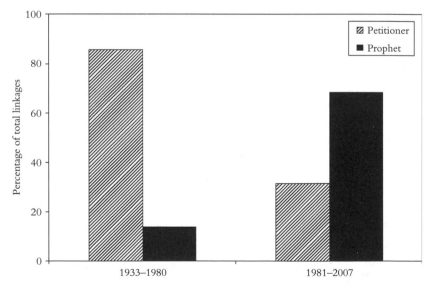

FIGURE 3.4. Presidential Speaking Style When Linking
God with Freedom and Liberty

speaking style 68% of the time when linking freedom and liberty with God. For example, George W. Bush said this in his 2004 State of the Union address: "I believe that God has planted in every human heart the desire to live in freedom." It is hard to imagine a more meaningful shift in presidential pairings of God and country.

Additional examples from presidential addresses help to make this transformation more concrete. Presidential statements from a petitioner posture were often simple, like Truman's statement in a July 1950 speech discussing the developments in Korea: "Our country stands before the world as an example of how free men, under God, can build a community of neighbors, working together for the good of all." Eisenhower in his 1954 State of the Union went further in linking God with freedom from the petitioner posture:

> Happily, our people, though blessed with more material goods than any people in history, have always reserved their first allegiance to the kingdom of the spirit, which is the true source of that freedom we value above all material things. . . .
> So long as action and aspiration humbly and earnestly seek favor in the sight of the Almighty, there is no end to America's forward road; there is no obstacle on it she will not surmount in her march toward a lasting peace in a free and prosperous world.

Kennedy ended his 1962 State of the Union with similar remarks: "[N]o nation has ever been so ready to seize the burden and the glory of freedom. And in this high endeavor, may God watch over the United States of America." Johnson, in a July 1967 address, used the petitioner posture by invoking a familiar refrain from the Pledge of Allegiance: "Let us then act in the Congress, in the city halls, and in every community, so that this great land of ours may truly be 'one nation under God—with liberty and justice for all.'" Nixon, in his 1970 State of the Union, sought divine guidance in this fashion: "May God give us the wisdom, the strength and, above all, the idealism to be worthy of that challenge, so that America can fulfill its destiny of being the world's best hope for liberty, for opportunity, for progress and peace for all peoples." Then Ford, in his 1977 State of the Union, struck a nearly identical tone: "May God guide this wonderful country, its people, and those they have chosen to lead them. May our third century be illuminated by liberty and blessed with brotherhood, so that we and all who come after us may be the humble servants of thy peace."

In contrast to these voices, presidents since 1981 have commonly spoken as if they were prophets, issuing claims about God's desires for the values of freedom and liberty. This shift was most pronounced among Reagan and the younger Bush, both of whom made prophetic linkages between God and freedom a regular feature of their speeches: nearly a quarter of their addresses (and fully half of their Inaugurals and States of the Union) contained such a linkage. Reagan set a prophetic tone right from the start, saying in his Inaugural: "We are a nation under God, and I believe God intended for us to be free." In his second Inaugural address four years later, Reagan offered a similar sentiment:

We raise our voices to the God who is the Author of this most tender music. And may He continue to hold us close as we fill the world with our sound—in unity, affection, and love—one people under God, dedicated to the dream of freedom that He has placed in the human heart, called upon now to pass that dream on to a waiting and hopeful world.

Then, in a September 1986 speech about drug abuse, Reagan recalled phrasing from the address which began this book—his presidential nomination acceptance speech in 1980: "Think for a moment how special it is to be an American. Can we doubt that only a Divine Providence placed this land, this island of freedom, here as a refuge for all those people on the world who yearn to breathe free?" And in his final State of the Union address, in 1988, Reagan declared:

[T]hese ideas were part of a larger notion—a vision, if you will, of America herself—an America . . . whose divergent but harmonizing communities were a reflection of a deeper community of values—the value of work, of family, of religion—and of the love of freedom that God places in each of us and whose defense He has entrusted in a special way to this nation.

George W. Bush struck a similar prophetic tone frequently during his first six years in office. He began in the aftermath of September 11, when he spoke to a joint session of Congress and a television audience of more than 80 million, saying: "Freedom and fear, justice and cruelty have always been at war, and we know that God is not neutral between them." A year later, on the anniversary of the attacks, Bush once again used the prophetic posture: "Our deepest national conviction is that every life is precious, because every life is the gift of a Creator who intended us to live in liberty and equality." Then, in his 2003 State of the Union, as he built his case for the invasion of Iraq, Bush ratcheted up the language: "Americans are a free people, who know that freedom is the right of every person and the future of every nation. The liberty we prize is not America's gift to the world, it is God's gift to humanity." Bush went on to offer a similar sentiment in his 2004 State of the Union, and in his 2005 State of the Union he put it this way: "The road of Providence is uneven and unpredictable—yet we know where it leads: It leads to freedom." For Bush, like Reagan, the prophetic posture—and its attendant certitude about God's desires—was the dominant mode of linking God and freedom.

Bush the father and Clinton fit this story too, but with some twists that provide further insight into the God strategy. Overall, these presidents linked freedom and liberty with God far less than did Reagan or Bush the son. George H. W. Bush made only one such linkage, and Clinton only five—with Bush's single linkage and two of Clinton's five coming from the prophetic posture. It is revealing, though, that these presidents employed the prophetic approach at key political moments. Bush did so in his 1990 State of the Union, the same year he later famously broke his "no new taxes" campaign promise.[24] Clinton's two uses of the prophetic style came in his 1995 State of the Union, just after Republicans had gained control of both houses of Congress in the 1994 midterm elections. As detailed in chapter 2, Clinton's speech in January 1995 was a key moment in which the Democratic president sought to regain his footing and to begin work with an oppositional Congress. In this context, Clinton made the only two prophetic claims in all of his national addresses as president. At a time when Americans, particularly conservatives, were sure to be listening to see how he responded, Clinton spoke in a language that gave him the best chance of connecting with them.

He made sure of that, in fact. Clinton did so by invoking the most famous pairing of God and country in the nation's history: the passage from the Declaration of Independence which decrees that citizens are "endowed by their Creator with certain unalienable rights," one of which is liberty. It is a phrase and idea embedded deep in the nation's self-image. Clinton used these words twice in his 1995 address, positioning them as bookends near the opening and closing of his speech. Such repetition and placement were indicative of the value of the message and his decision to sound this note loudly. Just five years earlier, George H. W. Bush had made a remarkably similar decision. In his sole linkage of freedom and God during his presidency, Bush in his 1990 State of the Union address cited exactly the same passage from the Declaration of Independence. It was the case, then, that these presidents—rivals in 1992 who nonetheless shared an understanding of the importance of religious politics—employed the prophetic voice in moments of political need and, when they did, pulled out the rhetorical big guns: the words of the nation's founders. George H. W. Bush and Clinton played the prophet card less frequently than did Reagan and George W. Bush, but they played it no less adroitly. In drawing upon the Declaration of Independence, they invoked the gold standard of American identity.

So mythic among religious conservatives are the ideas and words from 1776 that they are considered to be synonymous with the nation itself. It is not uncommon, for example, for some fundamentalists and conservative evangelicals to conflate the Declaration of Independence with the U.S. Constitution, which formally codified the law of the land in 1789. Jerry Falwell, in his 1980 manifesto for religious politics, *Listen, America*, wrote:

> We must not forget that it is God Almighty who has made and preserved us [as] a nation. Let us never forget that as our Constitution declares, we are endowed by our Creator with certain inalienable rights. It is only as we abide by those laws established by our Creator that He will continue to bless us with these rights. We are endowed our rights to freedom and liberty and the pursuit of happiness by the God who created man to be free and equal.... I am positive in my belief regarding the Constitution that God led in the development of that document, and as a result, we here in America have enjoyed 204 years of unparalleled freedom.[25]

The intertwining of these two founding documents—Falwell ascribed the Declaration of Independence's famous phrasing and birthdate to the U.S. Constitution—symbolizes the convergence of God and country sought by many religious conservatives when they reentered American politics in the 1970s. Beginning in the 1980 presidential campaign, U.S. political leaders incorporated this outlook into the political mainstream. From Reagan to George W. Bush, the four most recent presidents have imprinted on the national psyche a presidential vision of the nation that has been more religious than at any time since 1933. God and country have always been present in presidential rhetoric, but in the past few decades presidents have fused the two. The result is that, more than ever, America is now portrayed as God's country.

# CHAPTER FOUR

❋

## ACTS OF COMMUNION

Bill Clinton had heard the same story for weeks: he and the Democratic Party were out of step with religious Americans. It was late in the summer of 1992 and election day was drawing near. Clinton was leading Republican president George H. W. Bush in the polls, but the GOP was running hard. At the Republican National Convention, Pat Buchanan said, "There is a religious war going on in this country for the soul of America," and charged Clinton with being "on the other side." The Democratic nominee was fighting fire with fire, though: Clinton emphasized the new covenant in his convention speech, and he wanted to make faith the focus of another prominent address. But when and where? The campaign picked September 11 because Bush was to speak that day to the Christian Coalition, the most prominent organization of the religious Right. By speaking on the same day, Clinton would draw attention to his own religious politics. For the location, the campaign selected the nation's most renowned Catholic university: Notre Dame. There was only one problem. On September 12, Notre Dame was to host the University of Michigan in an important football game. Because of this, virtually no large rooms were available on campus. Finally, one was found, but it was booked for a concert the night before. Setup would require dozens of volunteers working all night.[1] For any other speech, the campaign would have simply sought another venue. But not in this case.

Clinton's address at Notre Dame was important for several reasons. For one, it came right after the traditional Labor Day kickoff of the final leg of the presidential campaign, meaning that many Americans would be tuning in for the first time. Second, going to Notre Dame was, in the words of Clinton's speechwriter, a "mirror image" of what John Kennedy had famously done in 1960: then, it was a Catholic speaking about faith before Southern Baptists;

now, it was a Southern Baptist speaking about faith before Catholics. Aligning himself with the mythic Kennedy could only help Clinton.[2] Third, as one conservative columnist put it, Notre Dame "wasn't friendly turf for Clinton" because its students historically leaned Republican. Indeed, Clinton was met by protests and his speech was interrupted by hecklers. Finally and most important, Notre Dame is a site of pride for American Catholics, of which there are many in the Midwest. "We need to carry them," a Clinton aide told the *Washington Post* in early September, adding that Southern Baptist Jimmy Carter "almost lost the [1976] election because of northern Catholics." With this in mind, Clinton was joined onstage by Catholic public officials, and he pointedly connected himself with their faith. He recalled his Catholic education, in primary school and then at Georgetown University, and said he was "deeply drawn to the Catholic social mission, to the idea that, as President Kennedy said, 'Here on earth, God's work must truly be our own.' "[3] In its aim, setting, and tone, Clinton's speech was a God-strategy signal that said to Catholics and other religious believers, "I'm one of you."

On all fronts, Clinton's visit to Notre Dame was a success. National media highlighted both presidential candidates' speeches that day, with CNN devoting a full hour on *Larry King Live* to the religious dynamics of the campaign. Further, news outlets said that the audience at Notre Dame, with few exceptions, embraced Clinton. A sampling of news reports described the crowd as "wildly enthusiastic" and "boisterous" and said Clinton received "rapturous" and "thunderous" applause, "thunderous cheers," and a "standing ovation." Boston mayor Raymond Flynn, who was with Clinton during the speech, said: "To go into the most Catholic college in America and get this kind of reception is a very encouraging sign." Most crucially, the event went far in legitimating Clinton among religious Americans of all stripes. In early November, conservative pundit Fred Barnes, then a writer for the *New Republic*, said that in going to Notre Dame, Clinton "aimed to dissolve doubts about his character and seriousness." There, he "was heckled by anti-abortion protestors sprinkled strategically through the audience and by Bush backers. He persevered." The result, Barnes said, was that "[a]ttitudes, even among conservative Catholics, toward Clinton have changed. George Weigel, a Catholic intellectual who supports Bush, says Clinton 'does not give off that aura of cold, rational secularism that [Michael] Dukakis did. He's not religiously tone deaf.' " Similarly, Harris Wofford—a Democratic senator in Pennsylvania, former Notre Dame law professor, and convert to Catholicism—later declared that Clinton's visit to Notre Dame had a positive "ripple effect" among people of faith.[4] Public acts of communion with religious believers can do that.

## RELATIONSHIP SIGNALS

Recent presidents have taken steps to speak the language of faith and to fuse God and country. These words and ideas resonate in American culture and, as a result, can be "broadcast" by political leaders.[5] That is, speakers can use these themes with most audiences and in most contexts with little risk of offending moderate voters. At the same time, an elevated emphasis on these communications is a political siren call for religious conservatives. More is needed, though, for a constituency to feel a deep connection with a politician or a political party. All groups want to be special, to sense that they are more than cogs in an electoral machine. One way politicians can deliver this feeling is to engage in "narrowcasting." When political leaders do this, they target a particular constituency with words and actions that are public but that fly below the radar of most Americans.[6] Such targeted signals convey a sense of *relationship* between sender and receiver—an especially meaningful feeling for religious conservatives, who often speak of a "personal relationship" with God and who make "fellowship" activities with other people of faith a central part of their lives. To engender a connection with religious conservatives, savvy politicians do more than talk about God, faith, and country: they also demonstrate an understanding and appreciation of these voters' concerns and values, practicing what scholars have called "the social embodiment of religious beliefs."[7] By doing so, political leaders engage in targeted acts of communion.

One such act is for political leaders to undertake symbolic pilgrimages to places of religious significance. The idea of a "pilgrimage" conjures an image of the faithful trekking across the globe to a sacred location. However, one might draw upon what scholar Juan Eduardo Campo has called "American pilgrimages" to gain insight into the political capital accrued by travels within the United States. Particularly valuable for the God strategy are public appearances at places overtly "connected with the values, symbols, and practices of American civil religion."[8] Bill Clinton's speech at Notre Dame is a perfect example; for religious symbolism in America, especially for Catholics, it is hard to top this location. A speech delivered there is simply different from the same speech delivered anywhere else. Of course, short of national addresses, the average American likely has no idea of, or interest in, where a politician is speaking. But when a political leader comes to their neighborhood, people hear about it and take notice.[9] That's what a political pilgrimage is: a visit to someone's neighborhood. In this case, it is a religious neighborhood. In this chapter, we identify presidential remarks delivered at religious institutions or before distinctly religious audiences.

Another narrowcast signal is for political leaders to exhibit a commitment to foundational religious practices. This might include, for instance, an emphasis on prayer, which is a central component of a religious world view. Consider that Focus on the Family, one of the most prominent conservative organizations of faith, devotes an entire section of its Web site to prayer, saying, "Whatever the Lord accomplishes through us, wherever success is found, prayer is always a factor. We appreciate your prayers as we seek God's will and direction for this ministry."[10] Perhaps even more powerful is for political leaders to celebrate religion or religious beliefs generally, such as the importance of the Bible, freedom of worship, and a view of God as the Creator. In demonstrably embracing elements of faith, political leaders suggest that they genuinely appreciate a religious community. Notably, presidents have a unique mechanism to engage in such acts of communion: presidential proclamations. These come in several forms, with the primary one being hortatory in nature; that is, they are symbolic and are issued to recognize, honor, and commemorate something. Such proclamations fly low on the radar, perhaps even off it, for most Americans, but they are prized by the targeted constituency.[11] As a second piece in this chapter, we examine presidential proclamations that emphasize key religious practices and beliefs.

A final act of communion considered here is the celebration of important religious rituals. Anthropologists and sociologists have noted the importance of rituals for religious faiths, observing that it is primarily through these practices "that religious conviction emerges on the human plane."[12] In other words, it is via consistent, habitual words and actions—such as the observation of holy days, worship attendance, and immersion in sacred texts—that abstract beliefs become concrete experiences. For Christian conservatives in America, one of the most important holy days is Christmas, which marks the birth of Jesus Christ. So culturally embedded is this ritual, of course, that it is the centerpiece of a substantial secular industry. For people of faith, though, Christmas has tremendous spiritual importance—a fact highlighted in recent years by attempts to "reclaim" a religious meaning for the holiday. In 2005, for example, the Alliance Defense Fund sponsored the Christmas Project, with the slogan "Merry Christmas: It's okay to say it." The religious significance of Christmas ensures that many politically attuned Christians note how presidents mark these occasions, even if the mass public does not.[13] We conclude this chapter, therefore, by examining presidential messages about Christmas.

The ways that political leaders have worked to create a sense of relationship with religious voters, rather than a feeling of political transaction, is our focus in this chapter. These fellowship activities were enacted in the public arena, but presidents performed them with confidence that they would receive little recognition among the general public. In this way, such acts of communion complement national addresses, which are directed to the masses and from which the religious faithful might extract particularized signals. The messages examined in this chapter are exactly the opposite: they are targeted to a key constituency with the expectation that the mass public will either not encounter them or not fully recognize their potency as religious signals. The dynamics of these differing types of communications are crucial to the God strategy: this is a calculus that is first, last, and always about walking a line between the general public and religious citizens, particularly conservatives. Both Republicans and Democrats have engaged in narrowly cast religious politics, but the GOP has been uniquely effective at delivering the something special sought by religious conservatives. It is Republicans' ability, desire, and success in doing so that has cemented their alliance with these voters in recent years.

## PRESIDENTIAL PILGRIMAGES

The idea of a pilgrimage is deeply rooted in the American experience. Families take vacations to national treasures such as the Grand Canyon, amusement parks such as Disneyland, and military battlefields such as Gettysburg. Sports fans visit mythic stadiums, from Boston's Fenway Park to the Indianapolis Motor Speedway to Lambeau Field in Green Bay, Wisconsin. Others visit sites of tragedy, such as Pearl Harbor in Honolulu, the Murrah Federal Building in Oklahoma City, and Ground Zero in Manhattan. Yet others travel to see famous birthplaces or homes, such as Mount Vernon and Graceland. In all instances, the symbolism of the site transcends the location. By traveling to these iconic places, Americans insert themselves into larger "national narratives" that are our cultural connective tissue.[14] In turn, officeholders or candidates can convey a sense of fellowship with a key constituency by visiting people or places that have elevated significance to the group. In so doing, political leaders insert themselves into religious narratives in subtle yet understood ways, and targeted groups appreciate this show of solidarity. In an age of the God strategy, therefore, one might expect to find U.S. political leaders undertaking more religious political pilgrimages.

We examined all public remarks made by presidents over the past eight decades, from the 1933 Inauguration of Franklin Roosevelt through the halfway point of George W. Bush's second term. This amounted to more than 15,000 speeches, and we noted every instance in which a president left the White House and spoke publicly at a religious location or with a religious population. Our focus was Christian-themed pilgrimages because of the political importance of Christian conservatives in recent decades. Four types of pilgrimages became apparent. First, presidents during foreign trips occasionally met with religious leaders or stopped at religious sites. Second, on U.S. soil, presidents delivered addresses at religiously symbolic universities and colleges, often at commencement or convocation ceremonies. Third, presidents spoke in churches in a range of contexts, including stump speeches, sermons, and funeral services. Fourth, presidents met in formal settings with religious leaders and groups to discuss policy ideas and goals. Each of these was a pilgrimage: a president paid homage to faith by going to a religious audience or location. We first identified how often these pilgrimages occurred during each four-year presidential term, an approach which revealed the differences within multiple-term presidents.[15] For this analysis, we calculated a projection for the final two years of George W. Bush's second term.

Figure 4.1 shows that religious pilgrimages by U.S. presidents have become more common over time, with distinct moments of elevation. Harry Truman in his one full term, 1949–1953, and Dwight Eisenhower right afterward in his first term undertook a dozen or so pilgrimages with religious meaning. Eisenhower's numbers dropped in his second term, 1957–1961, but presidential religious trips then rebounded to the same level through Richard Nixon's first term, 1969–1973. Thereafter, presidents significantly increased their religious pilgrimages, with leaps upward in the mid-1970s and then even more so since Ronald Reagan took office in 1981. This trend line suggests that U.S.

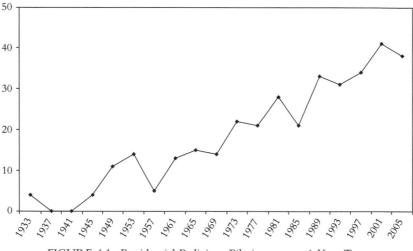

FIGURE 4.1. Presidential Religious Pilgrimages per 4-Year Term

presidents elevated their religious pilgrimages at the same time that Christian conservatives emerged from the political wilderness. Consider that by the close of Nixon's first term, presidents averaged just under 15 pilgrimages per four-year term. From Nixon's second Inauguration in January 1973 through Jimmy Carter's presidency in 1981—a span of eight years in which U.S. religious conservatives began to mobilize politically—presidential pilgrimages jumped to roughly 20 per term, an increase of one-third. Then, beginning with Reagan in 1981 through the halfway mark of George W. Bush's second term, presidents averaged more than 32 religious pilgrimages per four-year term—an increase of another 50%. These data show that the past four presidents did not invent the religious pilgrimage as a political signal, but they did take it to new heights. Nothing affirms a constituency's importance like a visit from the president.

A close look at these public remarks shows significant recent increases—and notable differences among presidents—in all four types of religious pilgrimage. Figure 4.2 shows these increases, and each pattern merits elaboration. First, foreign religious pilgrimages were nearly nonexistent from Roosevelt through Carter: there were three in 48 years. All were visits, by Nixon and Carter, to meet with the pope in Rome. Since Reagan took office, presidents have spoken publicly at overseas religious venues on 17 occasions. These include six visits to the Vatican, three church visits in Beijing, China, and three stops at religious sites in the former Soviet Union. In short, presidents have stepped up their "missionary" work: highlighting faith overseas is a sign to fundamentalists and evangelicals, who place great weight on the biblical mandate to bring the gospel to all nations.[16] George W. Bush has done this the most, averaging just over one such pilgrimage per year in his first six years. Bush's pilgrimages included a visit to Beijing's Gangwashi Protestant Church in 2005, which netted him a photograph with renowned evangelist Luis Palau on the front page of the *New York Times* and other leading newspapers, and prompted Southern Baptist Convention leader Richard Land to commend Bush in the pages of the *Baptist Press*. It was an ideal narrowcast signal: disseminated widely but meant for the faithful. Further, the importance of the pope in recent decades is indicative of the growing alliance between conservative Protestants and Catholics. A visit with Pope John Paul II, whose popularity extended beyond Catholic circles, was a can't-miss draw for recent U.S. presidents.[17]

Second, presidential visits to religious educational settings more than doubled in recent decades, from an average of 2.7 per four-year term from Roosevelt through Carter to 5.5 per term among chief executives thereafter.[18] In looking closely at the past four presidents, Reagan and George H. W. Bush most commonly utilized this signal: about one-fourth of their religious

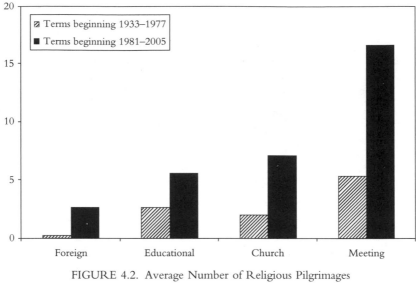

FIGURE 4.2. Average Number of Religious Pilgrimages
per Presidential 4-Year Term

pilgrimages were to educational sites, roughly double the numbers for Bill
Clinton and George W. Bush. Overall, the most popular venue was Georgetown University, where presidents spoke 15 times over the past eight decades. Next up was Notre Dame, where presidents spoke nine times: the first
was Roosevelt in 1935; the most recent was Bush in 2005. Baylor University, a
flagship Baptist-affiliated institution, was next in line with four stops. Visits to
universities dominated this type of presidential pilgrimage, but beginning with
Reagan they were joined by a small number of visits to religious primary and
secondary schools. In 1982, Reagan visited a Catholic elementary school in
Illinois, and he subsequently made two more similar stops during his presidency. George H. W. Bush followed with two visits of this kind, including a
stop at a Christian school in Georgia in May 1992—smack in the middle of his
reelection campaign—and Clinton spoke at two religious schools during his
presidency. The younger Bush did not make any such school visits through his
first six years in the White House.

Third, public remarks in church settings increased significantly with recent
presidents. From Roosevelt through Carter, presidents delivered public remarks in churches an average of twice during a four-year term. From Reagan's
Inauguration through the halfway mark of George W. Bush's second term,
that average tripled to more than seven per term—with Clinton truly in a
league of his own. He spoke in church settings 28 times, close to half of all his

public religious pilgrimages while in the White House. These remarks were wide in scope. Many were to primarily African American congregations; they came both on Sunday mornings (including a day in 2000 when he delivered lengthy addresses at two churches just hours apart) and at funeral services, and they included an extemporaneous talk in 1993 delivered in the Memphis pulpit from which Martin Luther King, Jr., had delivered his final sermon. The next closest among the past four presidents in this type of religious pilgrimage was George W. Bush, who delivered roughly one-fourth of his religious-pilgrimage speeches in church settings.[19] A final point about these communications is that Reagan represented the yin to Clinton's yang: not once during Reagan's presidency did he deliver formal public remarks in a church setting. These patterns thus reveal crucial partisan differences in how this facet of religious politics has been enacted. In this case, a Democrat dominated presidential visits to the church pulpit.

Presidents also met with religious leaders and communities in formalized conference settings, public meetings, and other gatherings. In the modern presidency this was the most common pilgrimage of a religious nature, embarked on more often than all of the others combined. To cite just one example, presidents since John Kennedy in 1961 have spoken annually at an ecumenical prayer breakfast in Washington, DC.[20] Even so, there was a significant increase in these pilgrimages beginning in the 1980s. From Roosevelt through Carter, presidents averaged 5.3 public meetings per term with religious groups. From Reagan through the halfway mark of Bush's second term, this average more than tripled to 16.6 per term.[21] These are now standard fare in the presidency. Further, there are notable partisan differences among recent presidents. Two-thirds of Reagan's pilgrimages were public meetings with religious groups, and the Bush family was not far behind: both father and son devoted more than half of their religious pilgrimages to meetings of this sort. In contrast, just over one-third of Clinton's religious pilgrimages were this type. Among recent presidents, then, Republicans engaged in this narrowcast far more often than a Democrat who also knew his way around religious politics.

But it's not just how often they met that's important, but also with whom. The National Religious Broadcasters Association and the National Association of Evangelicals are umbrella organizations that represent millions of religious Americans who lean conservative.[22] Since 1981, presidents have spoken 13 times to the annual conventions of these organizations; in every one of these instances it was a Republican president. Almost half of these visits came in presidential election years. The National Religious Broadcasters Association was so pleased with Bush's pilgrimage to its annual convention in 2003 that it issued a resolution honoring him. As a tax-exempt organization, the NRB had to stop short of explicitly endorsing Bush's reelection—but only barely. The resolution concluded this way: "We recognize in all of the above that God has appointed President George W. Bush to leadership at this critical period in our nation's history, and give Him thanks."[23] It was a bread-breaking moment.

Further, Reagan, Bush, and Bush spoke a total of four times to annual meetings of the Knights of Columbus, a conservative Catholic association; not once did Clinton do so. Another four times, one of the Presidents Bush spoke to the annual Southern Baptist Convention; Clinton never did so, even though he was Southern Baptist and the others were not. Reagan spoke to the Baptist Fundamentalism convention in 1984, the religiously conservative Concerned Women for America in 1987, and the Student Congress on Evangelism in 1988. Bush Sr. spoke to the Christian Coalition in 1992. George W. Bush spoke at several prayer breakfasts and events with Hispanic religious leaders, and also at conferences on faith-based initiatives convened by his administration.[24] Clinton spoke in none of these settings. In all instances, what drew together the recent Republican presidents and these organizations was a shared agenda distinctly conservative in its politics. The God strategy had gained a partisan edge.

## PROCLAMATIONS FROM ON HIGH

American presidents have a built-in means to create messages geared to a constituency: they can issue proclamations to honor or celebrate groups, causes, events, ideas, and people. Such symbolic statements have few downsides. Scholar Phillip Cooper notes that proclamations are entirely under the president's control and are rarely noticed by news media or the general public, yet their political payoff is high: "[It is] a matter of considerable distinction to be publicly recognized in a proclamation. If one's group or cause is so lauded, there is clearly a measure of legitimacy conveyed in the process—legitimacy that can translate into contributions or other forms of support. Such groups or individuals will never forget the president's support."[25] Further, as an act of communion, a proclamation has the extra benefit of being a concept imbued with spiritual meaning. People of religious faith, particularly conservatives, take seriously the biblical mandate to "proclaim" their beliefs about God.[26] All of these factors make presidential proclamations a potent tool to send a narrowcast message to religious believers.

In line with what we observed with religious pilgrimages, we wondered if beginning with Ronald Reagan's presidency there was an increase in presidential proclamations containing distinct religious dimensions. We combed through a total of more than 6,000 proclamations, identified all that were overtly religious in nature, and grouped these into three types.[27] The first cluster contained annual days of prayer, which began in the late 1940s and were soon formalized by Congress. The second grouping consisted of special days of prayer and reflection that presidents initiated to celebrate national developments or as responses to tragedy. Both of these types of proclamations—and particularly the latter, because of their special invocation—suggest that a president values a central religious practice, in this case prayer. Finally, there were proclamations that recognized religion or religious beliefs more generally. This latter category was an especially direct way for presidents to signal a relationship with the faithful—and particularly with religious conservatives, as we will see.

Figure 4.3 shows the presence of these kinds of presidential proclamations before and since Reagan took office. For each type, we compared the number of proclamations issued on average in four-year terms beginning 1933 through 1977 to the parallel average in terms beginning 1981 through 2005 (using just the first two years of George W. Bush's second term). Significant increases were apparent in all three categories, with the latter two especially instructive about today's religious politics.[28] The first category contains annual days of prayer, which since the early 1950s have consisted of two proclamations a year. One commemorates Memorial Day as a day of prayer for peace, and the other proclaims a national day of prayer, which now occurs in early May. These statements are fixtures of the modern presidency, to the delight of religious conservatives. Consider that there is a National Day of Prayer Task Force committed to "organizing and promoting prayer observances conforming to a Judeo-Christian system of values." The organization was first headed by Vonette Bright, wife of Campus Crusade for Christ founder Bill Bright, and has been chaired since 1991 by Shirley Dobson, wife of Focus on the Family founder James Dobson. The task force coordinates events for the day of prayer, connects with other conservative religious organizations, and highlights presidential communications about prayer.[29] With these annual prayer days in place, presidents interested in using proclamations to narrowcast a connection with religious believers had to find other proclamation targets. So they did.

One approach was to create special days of prayer or reflection tied to events of the moment. The middle bars in Figure 4.3 show that for presidents Roosevelt through Carter these kinds of proclamations were few and far between: an average of 1.1 per term. Beginning with Reagan, presidents nearly tripled such proclamations to an average of 2.8 per term. Reagan issued two of these, including a Day of Prayer for Poland and Solidarity with the Polish People in 1982, but this practice really took off after him. In fact, each of the

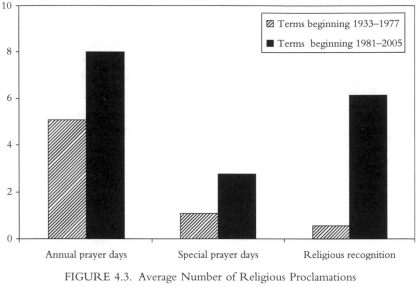

FIGURE 4.3. Average Number of Religious Proclamations
per Presidential 4-Year Term

last three presidents opened their tenures in office by issuing one of these special proclamations. George H. W. Bush proclaimed a National Day of Prayer and Thanksgiving in 1989, Bill Clinton declared a National Day of Fellowship and Hope in 1993, and George W. Bush offered his own National Day of Prayer and Thanksgiving in 2001. It turns out they were only getting started—especially the Bush family.

George H. W. Bush issued four special proclamations emphasizing prayer in 1990 and 1991, connecting the first three to the Gulf War. The last of these three came after the conclusion of U.S.–led military combat in Kuwait and proclaimed April 5, 6, and 7—a full three days, the final one being a Sunday— to be National Days of Thanksgiving. The proclamation opened with these words:

> As the Psalmist wrote, "O give thanks to the Lord for He is gracious, for His mercy endures for ever." Almighty God has answered the prayers of millions of people with the liberation of Kuwait and the end of offensive operations in the Persian Gulf region. As we prepare to welcome home our courageous service men and women and join in the joyful celebrations of the Kuwaiti people, it is fitting that we give thanks to our Heavenly Father, our help and shield, for His mercy and protection.[30]

It continued in this fashion, culminating with what Bush called a "timeless prayer found in scripture." That prayer, presented here exactly as issued, said:

> Thine, O Lord, is the greatness, and the power and the glory . . . for all
> that is in the heaven and in the earth is Thine . . . and Thou reignest
> over all. . . . in Thine hand is power and might; and in Thine hand it
> is to make great, and to give strength unto all. Now therefore, our
> God, we thank Thee and praise Thy glorious Name. As the Psalmist
> wrote, "Come behold the works of the Lord. . . . He makes wars to
> cease to the end of the earth."

Later, in December 1991, Bush proclaimed a Year of Thanksgiving for the Blessings of Liberty, in which he celebrated both the 200-year anniversary of the passage of the Bill of Rights and overseas expansion of freedom and liberty. This proclamation ended with an exhortation that included both the petitioner and prophetic styles we saw earlier: "Let us show through word and deed— including public and private prayer—that we are grateful for our God-given freedom and for the many other blessings that He has bestowed on us as individuals and as a Nation."

Clinton followed by opening his presidency with one of these special proclamations and then adding two more in his eight years. Then came George W. Bush, who was his father's son in using this signal, with one key difference: Bush the son proclaimed special days of prayer to commemorate national tragedies. The first was a National Day of Prayer and Remembrance in the aftermath of the terrorist attacks of September 2001, and he thereafter made this an annual proclamation. Further, each year, Bush designated three days of reflection upon the attacks, with the last one always a Sunday. His 2002 proclamation opened with these words:

> As we remember the tragic events of September 11, 2001, and the
> thousands of innocent lives lost on that day, we recall as well the
> outpouring of compassion and faith that swept our Nation in the face
> of the evil done that day. In designating September 6–8 as National
> Days of Prayer and Remembrance, I ask all Americans to join to-
> gether in cities, communities, neighborhoods, and places of worship
> to honor those who were lost, to pray for those who grieve, and
> to give thanks for God's enduring blessings on our land. And let
> us, through prayer, seek the wisdom, patience, and strength to bring
> those responsible for the attacks to justice and to press for a world
> at peace.

In 2005, following Hurricane Katrina, Bush announced another National Day of Prayer and Remembrance, giving him two special prayer proclamations that September. The proclamation began this way:

> Hurricane Katrina was one of the worst natural disasters in our Nation's history and has caused unimaginable devastation and heartbreak throughout the Gulf Coast Region. A vast coastline of towns and communities has been decimated. Many lives have been lost, and hundreds of thousands of our fellow Americans are suffering great hardship. To honor the memory of those who lost their lives, to provide comfort and strength to the families of the victims, and to help ease the burden of the survivors, I call upon all Americans to pray to Almighty God and to perform acts of service.

These proclamations, all emphasizing the importance of prayer, signaled to religious believers that these presidents understood and shared a key faith practice.

In the scope of the God strategy, though, it is hard to top the final cluster of proclamations, which highlight religion and religious beliefs generally. First and foremost, there was a tenfold increase in these proclamations after Reagan entered the White House. From 1933 through 1981, presidents issued an average of 0.58 such proclamations per four-year term; that average soared to 6.15 per term from the moment Reagan took office through the halfway mark of Bush's second term. It was as if a faucet that had for decades only dripped was suddenly turned on full blast. But there's more to this story: this increase was joined by a clear shift in the nature of these statements. Consider that there were seven proclamations of religious recognition in the 48 years from Roosevelt through Carter. The first was Dwight Eisenhower's declaration of National Salvation Army Week in 1954, the second was Lyndon Johnson's Commemoration of Poland's National and Christian Millennium in 1966, and the final five were proclamations of International Clergy Week in the 1970s. Each of these highlighted religious faith—with a preference toward Christianity—in a manner that did not target distinct segments among the faithful. Once Reagan took office, however, there were 40 proclamations of religious recognition in 26 years and virtually every one had distinct appeal for religious conservatives. Further, important differences emerged between the three Republicans and the lone Democrat among the past four presidents.

In January 1984, Ronald Reagan proclaimed a National Sanctity of Human Life Day to coincide with the anniversary of the *Roe v. Wade* Supreme

Court decision on abortion—which fell on Sunday that year. This proclamation opened with these words:

> The values and freedoms we cherish as Americans rest on our fundamental commitment to the sanctity of human life. The first of the "unalienable rights" affirmed by our Declaration of Independence is the right to life itself, a right the Declaration states has been endowed by our Creator on all human beings—whether young or old, weak or strong, healthy or handicapped. Since 1973, however, more than 15 million unborn children have died in legalized abortions—a tragedy of stunning dimensions that stands in sad contrast to our belief that each life is sacred.

On the appointed day, celebrated as Sanctity of Life Sunday by a wide range of Protestant churches, Reagan met with 30 antiabortion leaders prior to their demonstrations in the nation's capital. Afterward, heads of the National Right to Life Committee at a press conference declared that Reagan "is the only President we've had to support the unborn child," and consequently he had their full backing for a second term.[31]

With this as a send-off, one week later Reagan opened his reelection campaign with a speech in which he emphasized his concern about social issues, particularly his opposition to abortion. The audience for this speech? The National Religious Broadcasters Association, as Reagan sealed the act of communion with a pilgrimage. Reagan had found a powerful signal, and he turned this proclamation into an annual affair. He issued five more like it, the last coming in his final days in office. Tellingly, in all instances, these proclamations designated National Sanctity of Human Life Day to occur on the Sunday prior to the anniversary of *Roe v. Wade*, rather than on the date of the court decision. It was the perfect move when crafting a message for the faithful: Reagan was keeping the Sabbath holy—and wholly political.

George H. W. Bush followed with four Sanctity of Human Life proclamations during his presidency, emphasizing the Declaration of Independence and filling each with religious language. But then this well ran dry for religious conservatives: for the eight years of Bill Clinton's presidency, these proclamations disappeared. Here again is an instance in which Clinton, a Democrat, deviated from the script of his GOP counterparts. When the Republicans regained the White House, the proclamation returned. In January 2002, George W. Bush proclaimed National Sanctity of Human Life Day, and in so doing made an adept move: he connected the traditional emphasis on the

Declaration of Independence and general concern for human life with the defining moment of his presidency. The proclamation included these words:

> On September 11, we saw clearly that evil exists in this world, and that it does not value life. The terrible events of that fateful day have given us, as a Nation, a greater understanding about the value and wonder of life. Every innocent life taken that day was the most important person on earth to somebody; and every death extinguished a world. Now we are engaged in a fight against evil and tyranny to preserve and protect life. In so doing, we are standing again for those core principles upon which our Nation was founded.

Six years into his presidency, Bush had issued six proclamations about the sanctity of life. This well was flowing again for religious conservatives, and they were eager to drink from it. Bush's proclamations were regularly reported, and sometimes printed in full, in both the *Baptist Press* and the Christian Coalition's *Washington Weekly Review*.[32]

Reagan also was the trigger man for another series of proclamations connected to religious faith, this time beginning in 1986. In July of that year, he declared Let Freedom Ring Day, a proclamation timed to the 210th anniversary of the signing of the Declaration of Independence and the 100th anniversary of the newly restored Statue of Liberty. The proclamation began this way:

> For centuries, great occasions have been marked by the ringing of bells. When America's Independence was proclaimed in Philadelphia more than two centuries ago, the Liberty Bell announced the glad news—those joyful and triumphant words of Leviticus graven on the bell itself: "Proclaim liberty throughout the land, unto all the inhabitants thereof."

The proclamation then turned to the benefits of freedom and liberty, building to this:

> As the golden glow of the Statue of Liberty's rekindled torch calls forth the pealing of thousands of bells in every city, village, and hamlet throughout our land, let every American take it as a summons to rededication, recalling those words we sang as children:

"Our father's God, to Thee, Author of
Liberty, To Thee we sing,
Long may our land be bright with Freedom's Holy Light,
Protect us by Thy might, Great God, Our King."

Two years later, in September 1988, Congress passed a resolution designating a Religious Freedom Week. To coincide with it, Reagan issued a proclamation that echoed that of 1986:

America's creed of liberty has never been expressed better than in the words of the Book of Leviticus emblazoned on the Liberty Bell, "Proclaim liberty throughout all the land unto all the inhabitants thereof." The American people have long recognized that the liberty we cherish must include the freedom to worship God as each of us pleases.

Thereafter, a proclamation on religious liberty was issued off and on through the mid-1990s, when Clinton initiated an unbroken line of annual Religious Freedom Day proclamations. He did so, though, in a way that worked for him: all of these trumpeted freedom of worship, but they were not overtly religious and were not stated in distinctly Christian terms. Consider the tone of the opening words in Clinton's 1996 proclamation, the first of this series:

On this day over 200 years ago, Virginia's General Assembly passed a law that created the first legal protection for religious freedom in this country. Introducing his bill to the Virginia Assembly, Thomas Jefferson stated that he was not creating a new right confined simply to the State of Virginia or to the United States, but rather declared religious liberty to be one of the "natural rights of mankind" that should be shared by all people. Jefferson's language was shepherded through the legislature by James Madison, who later used it as a model for the First Amendment to the United States Constitution.

Today, more than 250,000 churches, synagogues, mosques, meeting houses, and other places of worship serve to bring citizens together, strengthening families and helping communities to keep their faith traditions alive. We must continue to ensure full protection for religious liberty and help people of different faiths to find common ground.

This tenor has remained in these proclamations, although Clinton's successor, George W. Bush, put his stamp on them. Clinton had designated a January date for this proclamation, which provided Bush with an opportunity when he came to Washington, DC. In reintroducing National Sanctity of Human Life Day, Bush had two religious recognition proclamations scheduled for the first month of the year. How, then, to handle this? In 2002, Bush issued them three days apart, on January 15 and 18, and then from 2003 through 2007, he issued these proclamations in consecutive order, three times doing so on back-to-back or the same days. The result was the creation of an under-the-radar set of "holy days" for religious conservatives. As presidential acts of communion go, this was close to perfect.

## PUTTING CHRIST IN CHRISTMAS

War is a common metaphor in American culture, used in familiar phrases such as "war on drugs" and "war on poverty." Religious politics, for example, is often linked to the notion of a "culture war." Thus Fox News Channel anchor John Gibson made a familiar move when he published in 2005 *The War on Christmas: How the Liberal Plot to Ban the Sacred Christian Holiday Is Worse than You Thought*. Religious conservatives were on board with Gibson's sentiment. The Family Research Council, in its own words, collected stories of the " 'grinches' out there determined to steal not only the spirit of Christmas but its meaning as well," which it compiled in a publication sardonically titled *Best of Christmas 2005*. Jerry Falwell and the conservative legal outfit Liberty Counsel organized a Friend or Foe Christmas Campaign that brought legal action against those perceived to be stifling Christmas expression, while other groups, including the American Family Association, organized boycotts of major retailers thought to be hostile to Christmas.[33] It was more of the same in 2006.[34] At a fundamental level, the notion of a war on Christmas resonated with conservative Christians: for years, there had been concern that the holiday was becoming too commercial and secular and that people no longer saw the birth of Jesus as "the reason for the season." Religious conservatives believe strongly in the importance of public rites, and in the case of Christmas many conservative Christians have tried to emphasize the religious significance of the holiday by looking for ways to "put Christ back into Christmas."[35] It turns out that American presidents since Ronald Reagan have been doing exactly this.

Calvin Coolidge in 1923 began a presidential tradition of marking the holiday season by lighting the national Christmas tree at a public ceremony. This event grew in scope over time, becoming in 1954 a Christmas Pageant of

Peace with smaller trees representing states and territories in the Union. By 2006, the event had reached impressive proportions, with activities, musical performances, clowns, and, of course, Santa Claus. Most important for the God strategy, presidents since Franklin Roosevelt have made formal remarks to accompany the tree lighting, with only a few exceptions. We read these speeches closely to see if presidents have put, or put back, Christ in Christmas. Presidents often have invoked Christ in these addresses and used a variety of terms to do so, including Christ, Jesus, Prince of Peace, Messiah, Savior, and Son of God.[36] The bars on the left side of Figure 4.4 compare the average number of Christ references in modern presidents' annual tree-lighting addresses. Prior to 1981, presidents averaged just under two references to Christ in these remarks. The average more than doubled thereafter, with Reagan through George W. Bush averaging closer to five references to Christ in these remarks. They made much more apparent a Christian reason for the season.

There are other presidential Christmas communications as well. Most notably, since the 1970s, presidents have often marked the occasion by issuing a formal Christmas message. These communications have the celebration of Christmas as their sole purpose, without the trappings of the tree-lighting festivities. As a result, they are out of sight for most Americans. Richard Nixon was the first to issue such a message, doing so twice during his five Decembers in office. By the end of Jimmy Carter's administration in 1981, these were a staple of presidents' Christmas communications. We identified references to Jesus in every formal presidential Christmas message since 1970.[37] The bars on the right side of Figure 4.4 reveal a trend similar to that seen in the tree-lighting addresses, but the difference here is sharper, perhaps encouraged by the even-narrower narrowcast position of these messages. In the eight formal presidential Christmas messages issued prior to 1980, presidents averaged only 0.38 references to Christ—not even half a reference per address. Since 1981, however, presidents have averaged more than six references in these messages—more than a *15-fold increase*. In both of these types of Christmas messages, then, recent presidents have done exactly what Christian conservatives desired: put Christ in Christmas.

Roosevelt's tree-lighting remarks often felt like a story that might be told to a child at bedtime—short allegories with a touch of whimsy and a clear moral. More than once, he referenced or read from Charles Dickens's *A Christmas Carol*. As was true of nearly all of the presidents' tree-lighting remarks, Roosevelt's were fairly religious in tone. Still, he made few references to Christ: five of Roosevelt's 12 messages had no such references, and three of them mentioned Christ just once. For example, in his first tree-lighting address, in 1933, Roosevelt began: "We in the nation's capital are gathered

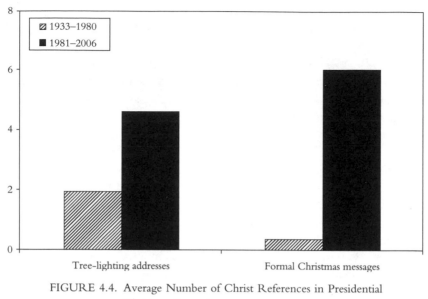

FIGURE 4.4. Average Number of Christ References in Presidential
Christmas Remarks

around this symbolic tree celebrating the coming of Christmas; in spirit we join
with millions of others, men and women and children, throughout our own
land and in other countries and continents, in happy and reverent observance
of the spirit of Christmas."[38] Roosevelt then thanked those citizens who had
sent him Christmas greetings, before concluding with a single reference to
Christ and a quote from *A Christmas Carol*:

> Even more greatly, my happiness springs from the deep conviction
> that this year marks a greater national understanding of the signifi-
> cance in our modern lives of the teachings of Him whose birth we
> celebrate. To more and more of us the words "Thou shalt love
> thy neighbor as thyself" have taken on a meaning that is showing
> itself and proving itself in our purposes and daily lives.
>
> May the practice of that high ideal grow in us all in the year to
> come.
>
> I give you and send you one and all, old and young, a Merry
> Christmas and a truly Happy New Year.
>
> And so, for now and for always "God Bless Us Every One."

Many of the tree-lighting remarks prior to 1981 had much the same feel as
Roosevelt's.

A particularly useful comparison can be made between Dwight Eisenhower and Ronald Reagan. Eisenhower was in the White House when the
lighting of the Christmas tree blossomed into the Pageant of Peace, and he
delivered an address on this occasion each year. Even though he presided when
Cold War fears of "godless communism" were commonplace, Eisenhower
invoked Christ only a handful of times in these Christmas addresses. In his first
seven speeches, Eisenhower four times made no reference to Christ and three
times made just one. Then in 1960, his final year in office, he made three
references. He began with these sentiments: "We commemorate the birth of
the Christ Child by the giving of gifts, by joining in carols of celebration, by
giving expression to our gratitude for the great things that His coming has
brought about in the world. Such words as faith and hope and charity and
compassion come naturally and gladly to our lips at this wondrous time of the
year." Eisenhower then spent the rest of his address developing a theme of
personal and national self-reflection, focusing on the nation's role in the world
and the changing nature of American society. Only in conclusion did he again
mention Christ:

> Each succeeding Christmas will, we pray, see ever greater striving
> by each of us to rekindle in our hearts and minds zeal for America's
> progress in fulfilling her own high purposes. In doing so, our ven-
> eration of Christmas and its meaning will be better understood
> throughout the world and we shall be true to ourselves, to our Na-
> tion, and to the Man whose birth, 2,000 years ago, we now celebrate.

Eisenhower's address struck a tone typical of tree-lighting addresses: he
delivered a speech that was primarily about the nation and referred to Christ
only to bookend those remarks. When Reagan entered the White House, he
reversed the pattern: his tree-lighting addresses commonly made Christ their
central theme, with references to the nation serving as the bookends. In seven
of eight addresses, Reagan mentioned Christ at least six times, including a 1983
speech that was a veritable homily on Christ. Reagan began by welcoming
the audience and expressing his sympathy for others around the world who
were "forbidden the freedom to worship a God who so loved the world that
He gave us the birth of the Christ Child so that we might learn to love each
other." Reagan continued:

> Many stories have been written about Christmas. Charles Dickens'
> "Carol" is probably the most famous. Well, I'd like to read some lines
> from a favorite of mine called, "One Solitary Life," which describes

for me the meaning of Christmas. It's the story of a man born of Jewish parents who grew up in an obscure village working in a carpenter shop until he was 30 and then for 3 years as a preacher. And, as the story says, he never wrote a book, he never held an office, he never had a family, he never went to college, he never traveled 200 miles from the place where he was born. He never did one of the things that usually accompany greatness.

While still a young man, the tide of popular opinion turned against him. His friends ran away. One of them denied him. He was turned over to his enemies. He went through the mockery of a trial. He was nailed upon a cross between two thieves. While he was dying, his executioners gambled for the only piece of property that he had on Earth. When he was dead he was taken down and laid in a borrowed grave.

And then Reagan brought home his message with a sentiment that he would return to more than once in his Christmas statements:

Nineteen wide centuries have come and gone. And today he is the centerpiece of much of the human race. All the armies that ever marched, all the navies that were ever built, and all the parliaments that ever sat, and all the kings that ever reigned, put together, have not affected the life of man upon Earth as powerfully as this one solitary life.

Religious voters wondering about Reagan's reason for the season received an unequivocal signal: it could be found in one solitary life. Since 1981, presidents have offered this same answer far more often than those who came before.

A similar shift over time is present in the formal Christmas messages. Nixon introduced these in 1970, just as religious conservatives in America began to stir politically. For Nixon, though, these were communications far removed from a religious signal: his two formal messages were short and businesslike affairs—three or four brief paragraphs with no mention of Christ whatsoever. His 1970 message, in full, read as follows:

Christmas is a family time. Let us make it, at Christmas 1970, a time when we have a very special sense of Americans as a national family. Let us put aside what divides us and rediscover what unites us— concern for one another, love of liberty and justice, pride in our own diversity. Let us resolve to work together to right old wrongs and heal old wounds, to do what needs to be done to make this a better country and a better world for all of our children.

Our greatest hope at Christmas 1970—and at every Christmastime of course—is for peace in the world. This Christmas we can be thankful that we are making progress toward peace.

Peace is a fragile thing, and there are dangers that threaten it in many parts of the world. But I firmly believe that, in this Christmas season, we can look forward with greater confidence than at any time since World War II to the prospect that our children can have, at last, what we all devoutly hope for: a generation of peace.

Nixon's successor, Gerald Ford, took much the same approach: he issued two Christmas messages over three years, and only once mentioned Christ. When self-professed evangelical Christian Jimmy Carter held the office, he issued a formal message about Christmas in every year of his term. But the same tenor held: in only one of the four did Carter mention Christ. Carter's entire Christmas message that year, 1978, was:

Rosalynn and I send our warmest wishes to our fellow citizens who celebrate the birth of Christ and who rejoice with us in the coming of the peace He symbolizes.

We welcome this opportunity to offer our thanks to those who have given us their encouragement and prayers.

We also join in this season's traditional expression of appreciation to God for His blessings in the past year. And we ask for His continuing guidance and protection as we face the challenges of 1979.

We hope that the months ahead will be good to each of you and to our country.

Relative to Nixon's and Ford's, Carter's Christmas message was sermonlike. But compared to what followed, it was little more than a "Merry Christmas."

Beginning with Reagan, these communications became unmistakable religious signals. Consider, for example, the act of communion proffered by George H. W. Bush in his formal Christmas statement in 1990. He began this way:

At Christmas, people of every age and every walk of life celebrate with a profound sense of wonder, joy, and gratitude for our Savior's birth in Bethlehem. Like the shepherds called from nearby fields and the Magi who journeyed from distant lands to welcome the Christ Child, we are drawn to this miraculous event in history.

Born in a stable and greeted by a handful of faithful and obedient men, Christ came to assume the role of a shepherd, thus fulfilling the words of the prophet Isaiah: "He shall feed His flock like a shepherd: He shall gather the lambs with His arm and carry them in His bosom."

Christ's brief time on Earth was devoted to tending the physical and spiritual needs of His flock: healing the sick, feeding the hungry, and illuminating the path to eternal salvation. His Incarnation radically altered the course of human history by challenging men and women to live according to the will of our just and merciful Father in Heaven. Today, Christ's message of hope and redemption—first delivered on that holy night in the City of David—continues to bring peace and joy to millions of people around the world.

But the elder Bush was only halfway home in his message. Having celebrated the religious roots of Christmas, he turned these faith principles into contemporary applications:

As we give and receive the goodwill of Christ during this holy season, let us be mindful of the true meaning of His life on earth and especially of His greatest commandment: to love God with all our heart and to love our neighbor as ourself. Events during the past year have given us a renewed sense of hope, yet in some parts of the world, peace remains an elusive blessing this Christmas. Even in some of our own cities, poverty, despair, and drug-related violence prevent families and individuals from sharing in the promise of this season. Therefore, let us strive, by following Christ's example in word and deed, to make peace on Earth a reality for all of God's children.

Barbara joins me in wishing all of our fellow Americans a Merry Christmas. May this festive and holy season be filled with the warmth of family and friends and with the deep joy of knowing God's love for mankind through the gift of His Son. God bless you.

Clinton and Bush the younger followed suit in their Christmas messages. In 1995, for example, Clinton included these words:

The Christmas story is dear and familiar to us all—shepherds and angels, Wise Men and King Herod, Mary and Joseph, and, at the heart of it all, a Child. This Child was born into poverty in a city too crowded to offer Him shelter. He was sent to a region whose people had endured suffering, tyranny, and exile. And yet this Child

94

brought with Him riches so great that they continue to sustain the human spirit two thousand years later: the assurance of God's love and presence in our lives and the promise of salvation.

Each year at Christmas, we celebrate these gifts with family and friends. We place candles in the window as a sign that there is always room for Christ in our homes. We put angels and stars and twinkling lights on the Christmas tree to remind us of the glory and mystery of Christ's birth. We sing the old and beloved Christmas carols to express the joy filling our hearts, and we share special gifts with those we love, just as God shared His Son with us. And, in contemplating the nativity scene under the tree or in a neighbor's yard, we realize that children hold a special place in God's heart, since He sent His only Son to us as a little Child.

Clinton was not going to be left out on this signal, but he was again distinct from his Republican counterparts. Among the past four presidents, Clinton was the only one to create a short holiday greeting that was made available for nationwide broadcast. In six of his eight years in office, Clinton and his wife, Hillary, developed such an address. Notably, these greetings were largely secular treatments of Christmas. They never mentioned Christ and mentioned God only when closing with "God bless you." Clinton, then, had it both ways. He took steps to appeal to devout Christians with his Christ-laden tree-lighting remarks and formal Christmas messages, but also served up a secularized greeting for those less interested in overt religiosity. The diversity of his constituencies compelled Clinton to offer multiple narrowcast signals.

Tellingly, George W. Bush issued only one of these Clintonian holiday greetings—and infused it with a mention of the "Prince of Peace" when he did so. For Bush, a separate and largely secular Christmas greeting was extraneous: he knew who was attending to his Christmas behavior, and he acted accordingly. So Bush dropped this greeting after 2001. In contrast, right from the start, his formal Christmas messages were chock-full of references to Christ. In 2001, his first year in office, Bush's formal message included these words:

According to the Gospel of Luke, two thousand years ago, the Savior of mankind came into the world. Christians believe that Jesus' birth was the incarnation of God on earth, opening the door to new hope and eternal life. At Christmastime, Christians celebrate God's love revealed to the world through Christ. And the message of Jesus is one that all Americans can embrace this holiday season—to love one another.

This Christmas we remember those who are without their loved ones. They continue to be in our hearts and prayers. May they experience peace, and may they find hope. And as we again celebrate Christ's birth, may the glorious light of God's goodness and love shine forth from our land.

In 2005, Bush began his message by quoting from the Book of Matthew: " 'Behold, a virgin shall conceive and bear a son, and his name shall be called Emmanuel'—which means, God with us." Bush then continued:

More than 2,000 years ago, a virgin gave birth to a Son, and the God of heaven came to Earth. Mankind had received its Savior, and to those who had dwelled in darkness, the light of hope had come. Each Christmas, we celebrate that first coming anew, and we rejoice in the knowledge that the God who came to Earth that night in Bethlehem is with us still and will remain with us forever.

Christmas is a season of hope and joy, a time to give thanks for the blessing of Christ's birth and for the blessings that surround us every day of the year. We have much to be thankful for in this country, and we have a responsibility to help those in need. Jesus calls us to help others, and acts of kindness toward the less fortunate fulfill the spirit of the Christmas season.

Just as Reagan had done before, Bush, Clinton, and Bush put Christ at the very heart of the Christmas season. For Christians looking for a sign that the president was with them, these signals shone like the Bethlehem star.

One final point clinches these trends. The Christian world view conceives of God as a Trinity, a three-part deity that consists of God the Creator, Christ the Redeemer, and a Holy Spirit. In most situations, an individual can reference these entities in an interchangeable manner, because all three are part of the orthodox Christian outlook. There are some instances, however, when one member of the Trinity is distinguished because of perceived functions or roles. The birth of Jesus is one of these moments. Those wanting to put Christ in Christmas, therefore, may not only emphasize Jesus more often, they also might seek to make Christ the primary form of address for God. That is, in speaking to and about a divine being, they might make mentions of Jesus especially prominent relative to other mentions of God. As a final step, then, we examined all references to a supreme being in presidential tree-lighting remarks and formal Christmas messages, with an interest in whether a reference was to Christ specifically or to God more generally. Figure 4.5 shows that from

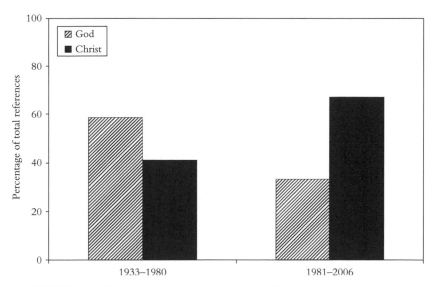

FIGURE 4.5. Divine References in Presidential Christmas Communications

1933 through 1980, presidents emphasized God in 59% of their references to a divine being, compared to 41% for Jesus. From 1981 through 2006, we see a reversal: in these years, presidents made Jesus their form of divine address 67% of the time, twice as often as they invoked God in some other form. For most moderates and nonbelievers, this is a superfluous distinction—which is exactly the point: it's a signal lost on them. For the Christian faithful, it's the ultimate narrowcast message.

These dynamics underscore the value of the acts of communion identified in this chapter. Among the general public, few pay much attention to where the president is speaking on a given day, what proclamations he issues, or how he celebrates holiday—or holy day—rituals. But for religious citizens, these communications and activities can be crucial signals that do much to establish the religious bona fides of the political leaders behind them. That's the power of narrowcasting. Targeted, under-the-radar messages denote who is part of the club. It's like a secret handshake, writ large and electoral: politicians who narrowcast religious cues are assigned considerable credibility by voters in the targeted constituency.

The political capital of such acts of communion cannot be overstated. Consider that during the 2006 midterm campaigns, National Public Radio's *Weekend Edition* news program spent time with a conservative evangelical megachurch in Columbus, Ohio, and with political activists working to connect politicians with religious voters. Almost to a person, the religious and political faithful interviewed by NPR said that religious words by politicians had to be accompanied by "authentic engagement" in faith practices.[39] Acts of communion go far to foster this sense of authenticity for political leaders. By buttressing words with deeds, they turn a political transaction into a relationship.

# CHAPTER FIVE

※

## MORALITY POLITICS

The ceremony was staged with the precision that defines modern American politics. President George H. W. Bush was framed by flags, standing tall before a gathering of U.S. political leaders and war heroes. Behind him, in perfect view of the television cameras, was the Marine Corps Memorial to the World War II battle of Iwo Jima, which lies adjacent to Arlington National Cemetery. When he spoke, Bush described America as "the freest, most generous nation on God's earth" and declared that they had come together to address a matter that "represents and reflects the fabric of our nation—our dreams, our destiny, our very fiber as a people." What had stirred the president so? Not war nor peace, not civil rights nor social disorder, not triumph nor tragedy. It was an act that most Americans never do nor see, one that across the entire United States occurs only a handful of times a year: Bush had come to talk about flag burning. He was responding to a Supreme Court ruling that laws prohibiting flag desecration were unconstitutional.[1] For Bush, this decision in June 1989 was a political godsend: more than 70% of Americans wanted legal protections for the flag, and 60% felt strongly about it. But an even bigger jackpot was at hand. To that point, religious conservatives had been lukewarm toward Bush, but polls showed that born-again evangelicals were more interested in the Court's decision than any other religious group and were the most likely to talk about it with family and friends.[2] For Bush, this ruling offered a chance for a religious signal.

The president wasted no time. The day after the Court's ruling on June 21, the usually stoic Bush expressed a "personal, emotional response" to the decision: "Flag-burning is wrong—dead wrong—and the flag of the United States is very, very special." These words showed up in news reports across the nation. Bush soon went further: on June 27, he held a press conference to announce that he would seek an amendment to the U.S. Constitution.[3] A desire to highlight this proposed legislation—to send the message in the clearest of terms—brought Bush to the Marine Corps Memorial in Arlington three days later. At a site commemorating one of the most famous flag raisings in the nation's history, he emphasized the moral gravity of his cause:

> As you view this memorial, think of its flag and of these men and of how they honor the living and the dead. Remember their heroism and their sacrifice, giving of themselves and others of their lives, fighting bravely, daring greatly, so that freedom could survive.... These Marines wrote a profile in courage, enduring a torrent of shells, pushing their way up that extinct volcano. And they stormed Mount Suribachi. And when they reached the top, the five men behind me raised a piece of pipe upright, and from one end flew a flag. And in the most famous image of World War II, a photograph was taken of these men and that flag.

He then closed by making certain that the religious faithful heard him. Bush said, "And what that flag embodies is too sacred to be abused," and he tailored his traditional final phrase to fit the moment: "For the sake of the fallen, for the men behind the guns, for every American, we will defend the flag of the United States of America. God bless this flag, and God bless the United States of America."

Ultimately, Congress stopped short of passing Bush's constitutional amendment, but he had made his point. Following Bush's visit to Arlington Cemetery, a former Boston University professor told the *Boston Globe*: "I think we have created something unique in the world: the flag as a religion, a civil religion."[4] Even more important, Bush had taken a stand on a symbolic, morally charged issue, and did so in response to a controversial Court ruling. We will see in this chapter that it is precisely this dynamic—judges coming down on the other side of a morally laden law—which angers religious conservatives to no end. Flag burning was not number one on their list of issues, but it mattered. As this issue periodically resurfaced in years to come, religious conservatives were often its strongest proponents. The Catholic organization Knights of Columbus, for instance, regularly passed resolutions affirming its "longstanding commitment" to a flag-burning amendment. In 2006, when such an amendment came within one Senate vote of passing the Congress, white evangelicals were the citizens most likely to say the issue was "very important." That same year, the Christian Coalition voiced its support for the amendment, as did Jerry Falwell's *National Liberty Journal* and Family Research

Council president Tony Perkins. In his organization's newsletter, Perkins even invoked the same image as Bush had in 1989: "I'd invite all of you who come to Washington to visit the Marine War Memorial right across the river. There, you will see the flag over Iwo Jima being raised by five Marines and a Navy corpsman."[5] Flag burning was an issue with strong moral symbolism for many Americans, especially religious conservatives—which made it ideal for the final piece of the God strategy.

## A MORAL REVOLUTION

Religious conservatives in the 1970s crystallized their push for spiritual and political renewal in the United States. They wanted to put God and faith back in the public arena, to reinvigorate the idea that America was a chosen nation, and to have U.S. political leaders recognize them. Check, check, check—each accomplished in spades in subsequent years. But all would be for naught unless the nation's moral compass was reset. In their minds, morality in America had begun a precipitous decline with Supreme Court rulings in the early 1960s that held mandated prayer in public schools to be unconstitutional. These rulings were "a seismic shock" to fundamentalists and evangelicals, and in their view things had gone downhill since.[6] In 1984, Jerry Falwell told PBS's *MacNeil/Lehrer NewsHour*:

> [U]ntil 21 years ago, 22 years ago, prayers were allowed. Since that
> time, in the last 22 years, the drug epidemic, the moral permissiveness,
> the terrible discipline and crime problems we have, the deteriorating
> SAT scores—I would put up the children, the graduates of the first
> 170 years of our schools' [history] against the last 22 years any day. And
> all I'm saying is that while you can't say the expulsion of prayer from
> schools caused all of that, God is light, and when you do not allow even
> the acknowledgement—though it's symbolism, not evangelism—of
> God in our schools, you invite every kind of social and moral and
> spiritual disease, which in fact we do have today.

Religious conservatives believed that a moral revolution was needed. In the words of Paul Weyrich, who helped to found the Moral Majority in 1979, "We are radicals working to overturn the present power structures in this country."[7]

Such an outcome has been sought on a number of matters, and in this chapter we consider five: school prayer, abortion, research on stem cells, the

Equal Rights Amendment, and gay and lesbian relationships. These issues highlight church-state relations, origins of life, and sexual and gender norms, all of which have been central concerns of Christian conservatives since they politically mobilized. We examine how the Republican Party—and not the Democratic Party—signaled that it offered the agenda sought by Weyrich and his allies. The evidence will show that the GOP engaged in what political scientists and sociologists call *morality politics*, a form of public debate characterized by claims about what is right, good, and normal.[8] Through their public communications, Republicans turned these issues into national, religious, and moral symbols. Their goals in doing so were to entice religious conservative voters and to bury the Democratic Party. They were successful on both counts for years. George H. W. Bush used this approach to perfection with flag burning, and ultimately it was used with matters of even greater concern to religious conservatives. The key has been the implementation of a two-step political maneuver.

As a first step, the Republican Party incorporated the core concerns of religious conservatives into the party's platform. In most cases, these voters sought the passage of new laws and the installation of new judges to uphold them. The former without the latter was viewed as inadequate: after all, it was the justices of the U.S. Supreme Court who banned school prayer, legalized abortion, and legitimized same-sex relationships.[9] Consequently, the contempt felt by many religious conservatives for the judiciary is raw. Consider the words of Falwell in 1980: "Nine men, by majority vote, said it was okay to kill unborn children." The following year, conservative organizations joined forces to create *A Blueprint for Judicial Reform*, a manual spurred by perceptions of a federal judiciary too activist and liberal, especially on social issues.[10] This anger at the courts has not dissipated, and it often peaks when a seat on the Supreme Court becomes available. In 2005, for example, religious conservatives concerned about Court decisions and judicial nominees held rallies—titled Justice Sundays—that were broadcast over the Internet, made available to Christian broadcast networks, and reached millions of U.S. homes. In promoting these events, Family Research Council president Tony Perkins said:

> Whether it was the legalization of abortion, the banning of school prayer, the expulsion of the 10 Commandments from public spaces, or the starvation of Terri Schiavo, decisions by the courts have not only changed our nation's course, but even led to the taking of human lives. . . . For years activist courts, aided by liberal interest groups like the ACLU, have been quietly working under the veil of the judiciary,

like thieves in the night, to rob us of our Christian heritage and our religious freedoms. Federal judges have systematically grabbed power, usurping the constitutional authority that resides in the other two branches of government and, ultimately, in the American people.[11]

As we will see, Republican Party leaders participated in these events—and, when doing so, employed a no-holds-barred brand of morality politics.

But the GOP did more than incorporate the goals of religious conservatives. Republicans also worked hard to show that they were motivated by principles, not partisan gain. The party did this in two related ways. First, the GOP elevated the gravity of issues such as abortion and same-sex relationships by calling for constitutional amendments and a reformed judiciary. Second, Republicans employed religious and moral language, a move that suggested that transcendent, "deeply held values" were at stake.[12] Both steps were valuable because these issues are, simultaneously, central concerns for religious conservatives and subjects on which Americans are deeply divided. Elevating them into symbols of national morality provided the GOP with a persuasive rationale for controversial agenda items: we are pursuing these matters, they could say, because of our beliefs about what is right and good for America and Americans. Framing their positions as acts of patriotism and principle did much to engender respect among voters, even those who disagreed. Further, this approach provided Republicans with capital among religious conservatives when the party failed to deliver desired policy changes, which sometimes occurred.[13] Morality politics, therefore, enabled the GOP to signal support for a key constituency's pet policies while providing a compelling justification that headed off criticisms of partisan pandering. It was not done easily, but it was done effectively.

## PLATFORM SIGNALS

Every four years, the Democratic and Republican parties, in conjunction with their presidential nominating conventions, produce platforms that declare their values, lay out visions for the future, and distinguish themselves from their opponents. Like the acts of communion identified in the previous chapter, platforms are opportunities to narrowcast messages to targeted segments of the electorate. Indeed, these communications are the ultimate signaling mechanism for policy goals: parties create platforms knowing that engaged groups will look for distinct "planks"—identifiable sub-areas in the platform—that discuss their pet concerns. Any single plank may be a relatively small part of the platforms, which are massive documents. From 1932 through 2004, for example, the average length of Democratic and Republican platforms was well over 16,000 words—more than five times longer than a typical presidential address to the nation, and enough to put the average person to sleep.[14] That's not a problem, though, because these documents are primarily written by and for the activists of each party, who pay close attention to what their leaders publicly stand for, as well as the key constituencies from which each party hopes to gain votes. Each of these groups scours the platforms to find the planks about which they care and to see how their concerns are treated. As a result, parties reserve some of their most measured language for these texts.

With this in mind, we examined Democratic and Republican platforms to gain insight into the utilization of morality politics. We focused on discussions of five issues central to the politics of religious conservatives: school prayer, abortion, research on stem cells, the Equal Rights Amendment, and gay and lesbian relationships. We read each party platform and noted all language directly tied to these issues.[15] We were interested first in when the topics entered the platforms, with an expectation that this occurred in the late 1970s in the aftermath of Supreme Court decisions and as a result of the political emergence of the Moral Majority and other religious conservative organizations. Figure 5.1 shows that this is precisely what occurred. The lines in the figure show the total number of words in each party's platform devoted to these five topics. From 1932 through 1968, there was almost no discussion of these matters. In 1972 and 1976, there was a small amount of discussion, a foreshadowing of what was to come. Then, in 1980, morality politics entered through the front door: there was an exponential spike in emphases on these issues by both parties. Thereafter, both Republicans and Democrats continued to accent these five issues.

A few points about the data merit elaboration. First, the small amount of pre–1970s language addressing these issues focused on the Equal Rights Amendment. Republicans introduced it first, in 1940, with a platform plank of "equal rights," which contained one sentence: "We favor submission by Congress to the States of an amendment to the Constitution providing for equal rights for men and women." Four years later, the Democratic platform said roughly the same, and the platforms of both parties contained such language through 1956, with Republicans carrying it through 1960. The ERA then disappeared from both platforms until 1972, when the parties reaffirmed their support for the amendment, which passed Congress that year and was sent to the states for ratification. A second point is that when morality politics emerged in earnest, the Democratic Party led the way. From 1972 through 1984, the Democratic platforms contained almost twice as much language on

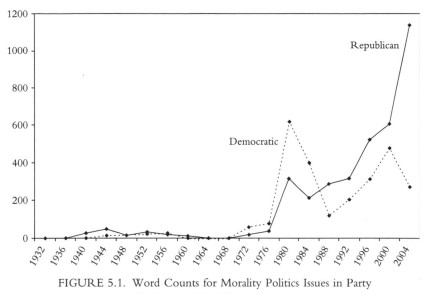

FIGURE 5.1. Word Counts for Morality Politics Issues in Party
Platforms, 1932–2004

these topics as did the Republican platforms. Democrats today may be split over morality and religion, but their party waded headlong into these matters not long ago. Third, since 1988, the GOP platform has consistently contained more on these issues, with a shift into overdrive in 1996. That year, Republicans increased their emphases on these key issues by two-thirds, the largest increase since 1980. The timing of this elevation was not happenstance. In the 1994 elections, Republicans gained control of both houses of Congress largely because of support among religious voters.[16] Having found a message that worked, the GOP ramped it up the next time it had the chance. The party has not looked back since.

One final observation can be drawn from Figure 5.1. These patterns again point to the 1980 election as the moment in which the God strategy moved to the center of American politics. *Newsweek* called 1976 "the year of the evangelicals," but our evidence indicates that 1980 was the year that morality politics were born, or perhaps born again.[17] Further, that year, the Republican Party switched its position from staunch support of the Equal Rights Amendment to explicit neutrality. This shift sent a strong message to religious conservatives that the GOP wanted their business. In 1976, the platform said, "The Republican Party reaffirms its support for ratification of the Equal Rights Amendment. Our Party was the first national party to endorse the E.R.A. in 1940. We continue to believe its ratification is essential to insure [*sic*] equal rights for all Americans." By the late 1970s, however, religious conservatives had widely mobilized in opposition to the ERA. They were concerned, in particular, that women would be forced to serve in military combat and that traditional family structures would be undermined. For example, Beverly LaHaye founded Concerned Women for America in 1979 in response to what she called "feminists' anti-God, anti-family rhetoric," and Phyllis Schlafly's Eagle Forum initiated a Stop ERA campaign.[18]

The GOP responded to these political tremors with a striking policy shift. After four decades of unequivocal support of the ERA, in their 1980 platform Republicans said this: "We acknowledge the legitimate efforts of those who support or oppose ratification of the Equal Rights Amendment." They then added:

> We reaffirm our Party's historic commitment to equal rights and equality for women. We support equal rights and equal opportunities for women, without taking away traditional rights of women such as exemption from the military draft. We support the enforcement of all equal opportunity laws and urge the elimination of discrimination against women. We oppose any move which would give the federal government more power over families. Ratification of the Equal Rights Amendment is now in the hands of state legislatures, and the issues of the time extension and rescission are in the courts. The states have a constitutional right to accept or reject a constitutional amendment without federal interference or pressure. At the direction of the White House, federal departments launched pressure against states which refused to ratify ERA. Regardless of one's position on ERA, we demand that this practice cease.

Support for families, opposition to military combat for women, criticism of federal pressure on the states—all were exactly what religious conservatives wanted to hear. And with those words, the ERA disappeared from the GOP platform, never to be mentioned again. In 1982, the amendment failed, three states shy of the 38 needed for ratification. In marked contrast, the Democratic Party upped its emphasis on the ERA, even mentioning it in its 1984 platform preamble—the opening words in which the party lays out its most treasured values. These platform developments were signals: bright, blinking signals. By 1984, the nation's two major political parties were on divergent tracks when it came to morality politics. One would increasingly advocate the agenda of religious conservatives. The other would not.

Figure 5.2 shows these differing pathways for the parties. The bars in this figure are derived from two pieces of information in the platforms. First, we noted the average amount that each party said about the five issues of focus, which allowed us to compare the relative emphasis that each side gave to these matters. Second, we noted whether a party's stated position on an issue was congruent with the policy wishes of religious conservatives. Since the mid-1970s, the Moral Majority and its successors have sought the installation of voluntary prayer in public schools, ending of legal abortion, restrictions on stem cell research, rejection of the ERA, and little to no legal recognition of same-sex relationships—especially of same-sex marriage. If a party's position was in line with these wishes, we assigned a positive value to the platform language about the issue; if a party's position was in opposition to this constituency's wishes, we assigned a negative value to the platform language about the issue. The resulting bars in Figure 5.2 show both the average number of words devoted to a topic and whether the party's position matched the agenda of religious conservatives. The platforms included in this analysis are from 1980, when religious politics emerged in a substantive manner, through 2004.

The data in Figure 5.2 reveal the yin and yang of American moral politics: Republicans have advocated the key policy goals of religious conservatives, while Democrats decidedly have not. Notably, each party was consistent in its

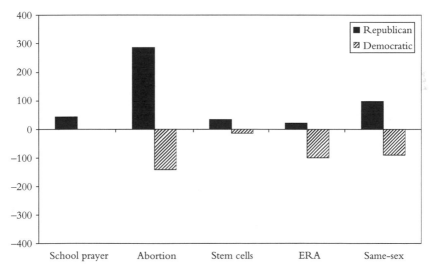

FIGURE 5.2. Average Word Counts and Congruence with Religious Conservatives on Morality Politics Issues in Party Platforms, 1980–2004

policy positions from 1980 through 2004, and in all of these instances the GOP offered an agenda congruent with the wishes of many Christian fundamentalists, conservative evangelicals, and conservative Catholics. Further, Republicans drove home their embrace of religious conservatives by placing greater emphasis on these topics. For example, the GOP devoted an average of 44 words in each platform to school prayer, whereas Democrats did not directly address it once. The GOP more than doubled the Democratic Party in its emphasis on abortion and nearly tripled it on stem cells. On same-sex relationships, Republicans' platform language was just slightly higher than Democrats' over the entire period, but from 1996 through 2004, it was more than double. Only on the ERA did Democrats devote more emphasis to one of these issues—in this case, at a fourfold clip. But even this was an adroit move by Republicans. In choosing to become silent on the ERA in its platform, the GOP appealed to religious conservatives while providing space for individual Republican politicians to appeal to moderate voters. It was the God strategy's big-tent philosophy.

We turn now to the second step in the morality politics approach. Incorporation of the key agenda items of religious conservatives propelled Republicans into risky political territory because these issues are accompanied by strong feelings. This required some careful maneuvering. For example, because of the perceived magnitude of these matters, it was possible that religious conservatives would not be satisfied by Republicans' embrace of their positions; more might be needed to convince these voters that the GOP genuinely was with them. Enactment of new policies would do it, but this was difficult given the divided state of Congress and the nation. Further, it is not unreasonable to suspect that some Republicans did not want to pass new policies, or at least sought to do so slowly—an approach likely to keep religious conservatives reaching for the policy carrots offered by the party.[19] However, if these constituents concluded that they were forever reaching for the unattainable, the GOP's morality politics—and perhaps even the entire God strategy—would fail. Finally, the Republican Party had to offer a rationale for its pursuit of these policies that would mollify politically and religiously moderate citizens. Without a compelling rationale, the GOP might be seen as pandering to religious conservatives. Republicans needed to perform a delicate dance. The solution was to elevate the party rhetoric, in two related ways.

One move was to issue calls for constitutional amendments and an overhauled judiciary, thereby suggesting that the party was motivated by fundamental concerns about the state of the nation. In Figure 5.3, the left two sets of bars show that from 1932 through 1976 Republicans and Democrats referenced the U.S. Constitution and the judiciary in almost identical amounts in their platforms, with slightly more language generally devoted to the Constitution.[20] Over these decades, the Constitution and the courts were treated as key components of the U.S. political system, central to what parties sought to accomplish. With the rise of religious politics in 1980, however, the Constitution and the judiciary became symbols of national morality, with the GOP issuing platform calls for amendments to institute voluntary prayer in public schools, to end legal abortion, and to prohibit same-sex marriage.[21] The result is that from 1980 through 2004 the GOP roughly tripled the Democrats in platform references to both the Constitution and the judiciary. Further, additional analysis shows that the parties diverged in even greater degree in the past few elections. In platforms 1996–2004, Republicans more than quadrupled Democrats in emphases on the Constitution and the courts. There is such synchronicity in the platform language because the GOP has consistently paired calls for constitutional amendments with criticisms of Court decisions and judicial ideologies. Symbolic acts such as these went far to convince religious conservatives to enter and then stay in the Republican fold, even when policy goals were not realized or were slow in coming.

The GOP was still on risky political terrain, however. In calling for amendments to the U.S. Constitution and judicial reform, Republicans declared that their positions were genuine concerns about the nation rather than

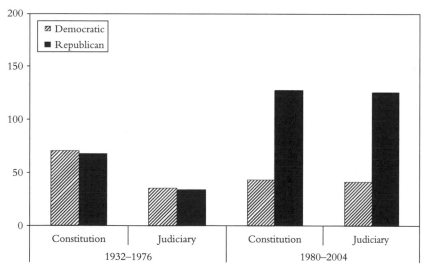

FIGURE 5.3. Total Word Counts for Constitution and Judiciary
in Party Platforms, 1932–2004

purely political. However, the party still needed to convince devout religious voters that they shared not only policy concerns, but their moral and religious values as well. Further, the GOP had to make sure its rationale was acceptable in the eyes of moderates. Republicans devised a plan: they grounded their policy positions in the language of faith and family. Earlier, we saw how religious terminology can send a signal to religious citizens while still operating within the parameters of mainstream debate. The language of family functions similarly. Family is a moral pillar among religious conservatives, and "family values" is the umbrella phrase under which many of their policy aims are grouped. But the idea of family also resonates among the broader public. With this in mind, we looked at invocations of faith and family in party platforms.[22] Faith language in this case included both explicit references to a supreme being and implicit religious terms such as pray, blessing, and so forth. Family language included all references to terms such as family, parents, marriage, wife, husband, and others of this kind.[23]

Figure 5.4 indicates that the themes of faith and family have long been common in party platforms. The left side of the figure shows that from 1932 through 1976, the parties were virtually identical in their emphasis on faith while Democrats were modestly higher on family. These ideas have been staples of American political debate. On the right side of the figure, we see a dramatic shift beginning in 1980. Once religious conservatives emerged as

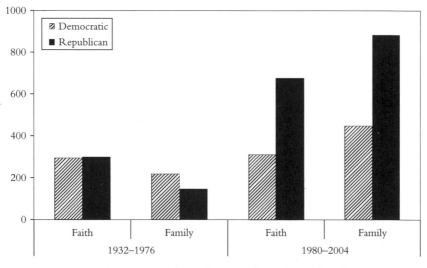

FIGURE 5.4. Total Word Counts for Faith and Family
in Party Platforms, 1932–2004

a sizable political presence, faith and family were elevated in both parties' platforms—and particularly by Republicans. In platforms from 1980 through 2004, Republicans emphasized faith twice as much as did Democrats (with the GOP devoting 350-plus more words to faith across the seven platforms) and did almost the same with family (with the GOP devoting 400-plus more words to family). In short, beginning in 1980, Republicans worked hard to signal that their agenda was driven by concerns about the nation as well as grounded in two traditional moral bulwarks—and if the party happened to benefit, so much the better.

Comparison of the 2004 party platforms illustrates these differences. Democrats devoted 140 words to faith and family, an increase of more than one-third on their per-platform average since 1980. They devoted an entire section to "Strong, Healthy Families," which included these words:

> Family is the center of everyday American life. Our parents are our first protectors, first teachers, first role models, and first friends. Parents know that America's great reward is the quiet but incomparable satisfaction that comes from building their families a better life. Strong families, blessed with opportunity, guided by faith, and filled with dreams are the heart of a strong America.

Yet Republicans went much further. Their platform had 256 words on faith and family—an increase of 17% on their already high average—and it emphasized these matters in multiple sections. When talking about education, there was a section titled "Options for Parents" that discussed "faith-based" schools. When talking about strong communities, there was a section on "Faith-Based and Community Initiatives" that described the leaders of such programs as "moral individuals created in the image of God." And there was a lengthy section on "Protecting Our Families," which included subsections on "Promoting Healthy Marriages and Responsible Fatherhood," "Protecting Family Privacy," and "Protecting Marriage." All of which was prefaced by this quote from George W. Bush:

> We are living in a time of great change—in our world, in our economy, in science and medicine. Yet some things endure—courage and compassion, reverence and integrity, respect for differences of faith and race. The values we try to live by never change. And they are instilled in us by fundamental institutions, such as families and schools and religious congregations. These institutions, these unseen pillars of civilization, must remain strong in America, and we will defend them.

We must stand with our families to help them raise healthy, responsible children.

In the 2004 platforms, then, the GOP more substantially undergirded its policies with a moral and religious outlook attractive to both a key constituency and broader America. It was a pattern that began in 1980, and in the years since Republicans closely aligned their positions with religious conservatives' key wishes and signaled a commitment to these issues.

This was precisely what religious conservatives hoped for—and worked hard to make happen. After the Republican Party platform in 2004 was completed, the Traditional Values Coalition issued a press release, in which it said:

> The Traditional Values Coalition praised the Republican platform's section on marriage today and encouraged its 43,000 member churches and their congregations to "keep your eye on the ball." . . . We met with the leadership of the Platform Committee and we are pleased to see that our recommendation to support a position which "fully protects marriage" was included.

Meanwhile, Janice Crouse, head of the Legislative Action Committee of Concerned Women for America, expressed satisfaction that "the platform was right down the line on our issues." And the Christian Coalition issued this statement:

> Christian Coalition of America applauds the Republican Party National Convention platform for being a pro-family conservative document and protecting the strong right-to-life position which has been in the Republican Party platform since President Ronald Reagan's first term. Christian Coalition is also very pleased with support in the platform for the Federal Marriage Amendment. . . .
>
> Christian Coalition over the years has trained hundreds of thousands of activists, in both parties, who are active in the political process. Christian Coalition has many national delegates represented at the Republican Party National Convention including a number of Christian Coalition State Chairmen. Many activists are also on the Platform, Rules and Arrangements Committees.[24]

For these religious conservatives, the Republican Party's platform offered the desired signals. With this common cause spelled out, it is no surprise that, come election time, religious conservatives usually danced with the GOP.

## THE CHOSEN ISSUES

Not all symbolic issues are created equal, of course. In particular, the political mobilization of religious conservatives has been powered of late by two engines: opposition to abortion and to same-sex relationships. Abortion was the first to emerge on a national scale. Religious conservatives did not immediately mobilize in response to the Supreme Court's *Roe v. Wade* decision in 1973, but abortion soon became a defining issue.[25] According to anthropologist Susan Friend Harding, in the early 1980s "preachers and lay leaders around the country 'biblicalized' total opposition to abortion," a process by which they "pulled opposition to abortion into the very heart of what it meant to be a born-again Christian, made it a sign of faith and a gospel that must be preached far and wide." It has remained that way ever since. Consider the view of Rick Warren, the pastor of an evangelical megachurch in southern California and author of the bestseller *The Purpose Driven Life*. In 2004, Warren in his e-mail newsletter, distributed weekly to more than 130,000 ministers, declared that a political candidate's opposition to abortion rights was the number one consideration for conservative Christian voters. Warren said that "for those of us who accept the Bible as God's Word and know that God has a unique, sovereign purpose for every life," opposition to abortion rights is "non-negotiable"—indeed it is "not even debatable because God's Word is clear." The conservative organization Catholic Answers advised exactly the same "non-negotiable" opposition to abortion in a 2004 voters' guide distributed to millions.[26]

Absolute certainty is embedded in these outlooks. Evidence suggests that Republicans displayed a similar confidence in their abortion outlook, whereas Democrats struggled to do the same. For example, in Figure 5.5, we calculated the number of words that each party devoted to their respective sides of the abortion debate in platforms from 1980 through 2004, with a positive direction indicating congruence with religious conservatives and a negative direction indicating the opposing viewpoint. The figure shows that Democrats and Republicans consistently came down on opposite sides of the abortion debate, with the GOP always taking the antiabortion, prolife position favored by religious conservatives. Just as important, Republicans did so emphatically. The GOP in its platforms never devoted fewer than 100 words to abortion, and in four of seven platforms it devoted well over 200 words to the issue. In contrast, the Democrats over the same period devoted fewer than 100 words to abortion three times and only twice devoted more than 200 words to it. The result is that, beginning in 1984, Republicans outpaced Democrats in addressing this key issue in every party platform. That's a posture suggestive of a true believer.

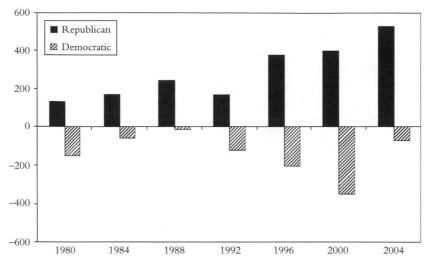

FIGURE 5.5. Total Word Counts and Congruence with Religious Conservatives in Platform Language about Abortion, 1980–2004

Figure 5.5 shows another important trend: Democrats were uncertain in how much to say about abortion. In 1980, the Democratic platform devoted 156 words to the topic, but in 1984 it was 60 words, and in 1988 the platform had a single, 15-word sentence about the issue. Then, during the 1990s, Democrats went the opposite way: they noticeably increased their discussion of abortion in each platform. By 2000, they gave the issue its own heading—a lengthy section on "choice"—and discussed it for a full 354 words. But in 2004, Democrats reversed course once more, cutting back to 74 words on the issue. Democrats seemingly could not decide whether to play up or play down the abortion issue. In contrast, the Republican strategy since 1980 was a portrait of consistency and simplicity: the more emphasis on abortion, the better. The approach to this issue offered by the two parties could hardly have been more different. Democrats spoke of abortion sometimes in a whisper and sometimes in full voice. Meanwhile, Republicans shouted about abortion through a megaphone, turning up the volume almost every year. Both of these were important signs about party commitments.

Further, closer examination of the platforms shows that Republicans also were far more consistent than Democrats in *what* they said about abortion. From the outset, the GOP focused on religious conservatives' central goals: passage of new laws and installation of new judges to uphold them. The Republican Party platform addressed abortion for the first time in 1976, immediately connecting policy, the Constitution, and the judiciary:

There are those in our Party who favor complete support for the Supreme Court decision which permits abortion on demand. There are others who share sincere convictions that the Supreme Court's decision must be changed by a constitutional amendment prohibiting all abortions. Others have yet to take a position, or they have assumed a stance somewhere in between polar positions. We protest the Supreme Court's intrusion into the family structure through its denial of the parents' obligation and right to guide their minor children. The Republican Party favors a continuance of the public dialogue on abortion and supports the efforts of those who seek enactment of a constitutional amendment to restore protection of the right to life for unborn children.

In 1976, then, the GOP took the middle road with a lean toward the right. In 1980, the lean became an embrace: "While we recognize differing views on this question among Americans in general—and in our own Party—we affirm our support of a constitutional amendment to restore protection of the right to life for unborn children. We also support the Congressional efforts to restrict the use of taxpayers' dollars for abortion." Later in the platform came these words: "We will work for the appointment of judges at all levels of the judiciary who respect traditional family values and the sanctity of innocent human life." This language urged judicial reform and did so based on rich moral and religious themes: family values and life itself. The 1980 platform could not have appealed more to religious conservatives if they had written it—which they might have.[27] An alliance was taking shape.

In 1984, the party added a potent one-two message that was the epitome of a narrowcast signal. The GOP platform declared support for a "human life" constitutional amendment, the first time the proposed law was given a name, and endorsement of "legislation to make clear that the Fourteenth Amendment's protections [of life, liberty, and property] apply to unborn children." Connection of a new amendment with the Fourteenth was a deliberate move. The Fourteenth Amendment was passed following the Civil War to guarantee former slaves the full privileges of U.S. citizenship, and marked an epic achievement for the antislavery movement. It has great symbolism for today's antiabortion activists. Historian Randall Balmer notes that fundamentalists and conservative evangelicals in the 1980s "sought to portray themselves as the 'new abolitionists,' drawing a parallel between their pro-life agenda and the nineteenth-century campaign against slavery." This connection of the antiabortion cause with the Fourteenth Amendment suggested that the GOP's stance was as much a moral and religious position as a political one. Since 1984, the push for a new amendment and invocation of the Fourteenth, in conjunction with the 1980-installed language of support for judges who uphold the "family" and "innocent human life," have anchored the GOP's platform plank on abortion. In 1996, when late-term, "partial birth" abortions entered the platform, the morally charged rhetoric escalated even further: the GOP said the practice was "rightly branded as four-fifths infanticide."[28] With Republicans' antiabortion position made crystal clear, religious conservatives had found a home—and the GOP had an electoral base.

This alliance was helped along by the Democratic Party, which was inconsistent in its platform language about abortion. In 1980, the party's platform plank said this: "The Democratic Party supports the 1973 Supreme Court decision on abortion rights as the law of the land and opposes any constitutional amendment to restrict or overturn that decision." That's about as plain as can be. In the next two platforms, however, the word "abortion" and discussion of the amendment disappeared. In their place, Democrats emphasized "the fundamental right of a woman to reproductive freedom" in 1984 and a "fundamental right of reproductive choice" in 1988. Then, in 1992, the Democratic platform brought back "abortion" and introduced potential legislation of its own, invoking the Constitution as it did so:

> Democrats stand behind the right of every woman to choose, consistent with *Roe v. Wade*, regardless of ability to pay, and support a national law to protect that right. It is a fundamental constitutional liberty that individual Americans—not government—can best take responsibility for making the most difficult and intensely personal decisions regarding reproduction. The goal of our nation must be to make abortion less necessary, not more difficult or more dangerous.

This plank was repeated verbatim in 1996 and was underscored by a brief statement about respect for differing viewpoints: "The Democratic Party is a party of inclusion. We respect the individual conscience of each American on this difficult issue, and we welcome all our members to participate at every level of our party."

This consistency did not last, though. In 2000, the Democrats dropped their calls for new legislation and emphasized their differences with Republicans. In introducing their statement about respect for differing viewpoints about abortion, the Democrats said, "[W]e are proud to put into our platform the very words which Republicans refused to let Bob Dole put into their 1996 platform and which they refused to even consider putting in their platform in 2000." In 2004, the Democrats again avoided new legislation and separated themselves from Republicans: "We will defend the dignity of all Americans against those who would undermine it. Because we believe in the privacy and equality of women, we stand proudly for a woman's right to choose, consistent with *Roe v. Wade*, and regardless of her ability to pay. We stand firmly against Republican efforts to undermine that right."

From 1980 through 2004, then, Democrats' platform language was inconsistent and increasingly positioned the party as reactive to Republicans. Both imply uncertainty—a surefire recipe for disaster when it comes to morality politics. And indeed, in mid-2005, Democratic Party chair Howard Dean called a meeting with Jim Wallis, editor of the religiously liberal *Sojourners* magazine and author of the bestselling book *God's Politics*. Dean's goal was to figure out how his party could talk about abortion without turning away citizens, especially religious citizens who oppose the practice.[29] It is no coincidence that Democratic platforms were most consistent, confident, and Constitution-invoking in their language on abortion in 1992 and 1996, the only two years since 1976 that the party won the White House. If you want to be seen as a political true believer, don't waver and do escalate the rhetoric.

Further, do it again if the opportunity arises—which is exactly what Republicans did with same-sex marriage. In recent decades, this issue became so symbolic for religious conservatives that Gary Bauer—a former Reagan administration adviser, GOP presidential candidate, and now president of the organization American Values—called it "the new abortion." In other words, it came to be widely seen as nonnegotiable for conservative Protestants and Catholics *and* is thought to have the potential to politically unite these groups for decades on end. In 1980, Paul Weyrich declared, "Homosexuality is explicitly condemned in Scriptures, so if you're for gay rights, you're violating a specifically articulated tenet of Holy Scripture." In the years since, this perspective has undergirded concerns about education curricula, hiring policies, military service, and most recently, marriage. In 2003, James Dobson of Focus on the Family said:

> [T]he Holy Scriptures set forth the Creator's plan for marriage and family. To deviate from that model is to invite disaster. As early as the second chapter of Genesis, we learn that God created Eve as a "suitable companion" for Adam who would complement him physically, spiritually and emotionally. This "marriage" was the very first institution that God created, and it continues to be the primary institution of society to this day. God designed marriage between a man and a woman as the first system of interdependent human relationships, as well as the means by which spiritual teaching is passed down through the

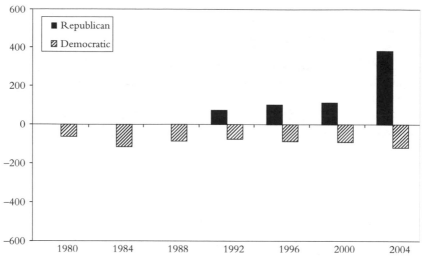

FIGURE 5.6. Total Word Counts and Congruence with Religious Conservatives
in Platform Language about Same-Sex Relationships, 1980–2004

generations. God and history will judge us on how we handle
this crisis.[30]

In the words of historian Randall Balmer, opposition to same-sex relationships
provided evangelicals with "a new enemy" against which to mobilize.[31] All
that was needed was a symbol to rally around. This arrived in due time.

Figure 5.6 parallels the previous one on abortion, by showing word count
and congruence with religious conservatives. We see that Democrats were the
first to address same-sex relationships. They did so in their 1980 platform,
including this antidiscrimination statement: "We must affirm the dignity of all
people and the right of each individual to have equal access to and participation
in the institutions and services of our society. All groups must be protected
from discrimination based on race, color, religion, national origin, language,
age, sex or sexual orientation." This type of language remained a fixture in
Democratic platforms from 1980 through 1992. After this first move, the party
did not amplify its voice or significantly expand its vision. Meanwhile, the
Republican Party platform was silent on this matter: the GOP often had
antidiscrimination language, but it did not include either religion or sexual orientation. Without a specific rallying symbol, Republicans were content to be at peace with religious conservative voters and to provide space
for moderate Republicans who might hold different views. This changed in
1992.

That year, Republicans introduced the topic of same-sex *marriage* into their platform, with a one-sentence plank on the matter: "We oppose any legislation or law which legally recognizes same-sex marriages and allows such couples to adopt children or provide foster care." As with abortion, the party went with the message, fueled by religious conservatives' mounting electoral importance after the party's 1994 takeover of Congress. The party's agenda on same-sex marriage crystallized further in 1996 with support for the passage of "the Defense of Marriage Act, which defines 'marriage' for purposes of federal law as the legal union of one man and one woman and prevents federal judges and bureaucrats from forcing states to recognize other living arrangements as 'marriages.'" The 2000 platform plank was almost identical, but added a moral rationale for the GOP's position: "We support the traditional definition of 'marriage' as the legal union of one man and one woman. . . . We rely on the home, as did the founders of the American Republic, to instill the virtues that sustain democracy itself." Then in 2004, the Republican platform elevated its rhetoric to a new level, with a plank titled "Protecting Marriage" and a message that paired the Constitution and the courts:

> We strongly support President Bush's call for a Constitutional amendment that fully protects marriage, and we believe that neither federal nor state judges nor bureaucrats should force states to recognize other living arrangements as equivalent to marriage. . . . Attempts to redefine marriage in a single state or city could have serious consequences throughout the country, and anything less than a Constitutional amendment, passed by the Congress and ratified by the states, is vulnerable to being overturned by activist judges. On a matter of such importance, the voice of the people must be heard. The Constitutional amendment process guarantees that the final decision will rest with the American people and their elected representatives. . . . President Bush said, "We will not stand for judges who undermine democracy by legislating from the bench and try to remake America by court order."

And, to drive home the message for religious voters, the platform again appealed to the virtue of the family: "[T]he well-being of children is best accomplished in the environment of the home, nurtured by their mother and father anchored by the bonds of marriage." It was a reprise of the GOP's approach to abortion: incorporate a key agenda item of religious conservatives, elevate the rhetoric by pushing for a constitutional amendment, pummel the courts, and use moral and religious language. It worked with abortion, and it worked with same-sex marriage.[32]

119

As with abortion, the Democratic Party's response to same-sex marriage was slow to take shape. The party expanded its platform language in 1992 to include a commitment to "provide civil rights protection for gay men and lesbians," and in 1996 the party expressed a desire "to end discrimination against gay men and lesbians and further their full inclusion in the life of the nation." In 2000, the Democrats increased their language on same-sex relationships by a total of three words, but one of them was crucial: "We support the full inclusion of gay and lesbian *families* in the life of the nation."[33] In none of this Democratic platform language, however, did the word "marriage" appear. This absence was pronounced in 1996, when party leader and president Bill Clinton had announced months earlier that he would sign the Defense of Marriage Act should it pass the Republican Congress—a controversial position among party supporters.[34] As a result, the matter was left out of the platform. Not until 2004 did Democratic discussion of same-sex relationships include the word "marriage." When it did, its full statement was: "In our country, marriage has been defined at the state level for 200 years, and we believe it should continue to be defined there. We repudiate President Bush's divisive effort to politicize the Constitution by pursuing a 'Federal Marriage Amendment.' Our goal is to bring Americans together, not drive them apart."

Just as had occurred with abortion, on the issue of same-sex marriage Democrats struggled in party platforms to find a consistent volume, voice, and vision. Proactive in the 1980s, they came to sound reactive by the 2000s. The conclusion of opponents and even some supporters was to question the Democratic Party's moral compass.[35] Such a perception might have been unfair. It might have been spot-on. Either way, it was exactly what the Republican Party wanted. The GOP's God strategy was in overdrive, and the Democrats had been run over.

## JUSTICE SUNDAYS

Religious conservatives in early 2005 were within arm's reach of the holy grail of U.S. politics: the chance to remold the U.S. Supreme Court. Chief Justice William Rehnquist was ill, suffering from thyroid cancer, and other Court vacancies appeared likely during George W. Bush's second term. The stars—or heavens—seemed to be lining up. The Republican Party controlled the White House and the Senate, clearing the way for conservative justices to be confirmed to the Court. Only one obstacle remained. Democrats were a minority in the Senate, but they could still block a nominee by engaging in a filibuster— a maneuver by which 41 of its members can gridlock debate. Religious conservatives had been disappointed time and again by Supreme Court justices nominated by GOP presidents: Sandra Day O'Connor, Anthony Kennedy, and David Souter all were more liberal than religious conservatives wished. Another Republican nominee, Robert Bork, was the dream candidate of these voters, but he was defeated in a bruising, Democratic Party–led Senate vote in 1986. So close to the promised land, religious conservatives would not brook another disappointment. James Dobson, head of Focus on the Family, promised "a battle of enormous proportions from sea to shining sea" if he and his allies were denied the justices they wanted.[36]

If ever there were a moment for Republicans and religious conservatives to work in close alliance, this was it. When the Senate convened in January, GOP leaders engineered a showdown with Democrats over the ability to filibuster *any* of Bush's judicial nominees, at any court level. Republican majority leader Bill Frist threatened to invoke a Senate procedure through which the filibuster could be suspended—the so-called nuclear option. The timing of the showdown was deliberate: if Democrats agreed not to filibuster the president's nominees, the path would be clear when a Supreme Court vacancy opened; if Democrats did not back down, Republicans said they would eliminate the filibuster. For months on end, party leaders squabbled, with polls showing public support leaning toward the Democratic Party. Into the breach came conservative religious leaders, who mobilized their followers to support the GOP's machinations. Specifically, conservative religious leaders organized and invited Republican Party officials to join them in three carefully orchestrated, nationwide rallies on behalf of the party's judicial tactic. Each event was titled Justice Sunday, and their shared objective was unabashed: to "mobiliz[e] people of faith for one of the most important challenges of our time."[37]

Justice Sundays I, II, and III were organized by Focus on the Family and the Family Research Council. Each rally was timed to correspond to a major judicial event. The first, subtitled "Stopping the Filibuster against People of Faith," was held in April 2005 as the Senate showdown over filibusters of nominees loomed. A compromise eventually was reached, but the stakes grew much higher when Supreme Court justice Sandra Day O'Connor announced her retirement in July. O'Connor had been a crucial swing vote for decades, siding often with liberals on school prayer, abortion, and other issues. Her retirement had vast implications. As Tony Perkins, head of the Family Research Council, put it: "This is the moment that social conservatives have been awaiting for more than a decade—a real chance to change the philosophical balance of the Supreme Court." The alliance went to work again, producing "Justice Sunday II: May God Save This Honorable Court," which took place shortly before the Senate began confirmation hearings for John Roberts, who had been nominated to replace O'Connor. Then Chief Justice Rehnquist died in September, opening another seat and ensuring another round of Senate hearings—and prompting a third rally by religious conservatives. The day before the Senate began confirmation hearings in January 2006 on new nominee Samuel Alito, there was "Justice Sunday III: Proclaim Liberty throughout the Land."[38]

If timing is everything, these events had everything and more, including a veritable who's who of conservative religious leaders: Dobson and Perkins, Jerry Falwell, National Association of Evangelicals president Ted Haggard, Catholic League for Religious and Civil Rights president Bill Donohue, Southern Baptist Theological Seminary president Albert Mohler, Prison Ministries Fellowship founder Charles Colson, Eagle Forum president Phyllis Schlafly, and minister Wellington Boone. Each rally was held in a church on a Sunday evening, simulcast in other churches around the nation, and transmitted live via Christian broadcasting networks to more than 60 million U.S. households. Despite this vast reach, these events were not intended for the general public. No, these were aimed specifically at religious conservatives. For the Republican Party, these rallies presented a near-perfect narrowcasting opportunity: a chance to speak directly to the GOP's electoral base on a matter of epic importance, with less concern about placating moderate voters. It was a dream come true for Republicans, and they capitalized: Senate majority leader Bill Frist spoke via videotape at Justice Sunday I, House majority leader Tom DeLay and former Georgia governor and senator Zell Miller spoke in person at the second event, and Pennsylvania senator Rick Santorum did the same at the third.[39]

From the get-go these events were the zenith of today's religious politics, with overt mixing of faith, nation, policy agendas, and public activism. For example, the first broadcast began with a voiceover that said:

> Our prayers and our involvement will shepherd well-qualified judges onto benches across this great land. Our children will best be served by judges who appreciate America's Godly heritage and can interpret the United States Constitution exactly as it is written. Our Founding Fathers, many of whom were great men of faith themselves, would expect nothing less.

Albert Mohler, in Justice Sunday I, reminded the audience of the key issues at stake—and the expected positions of the audience:

They're saying that this [event] is partisan. Well, let me say something clearly: I long for the day when we have to choose as candidates between a pro-life Republican and a pro-life Democrat, between a Republican who understands what marriage is and a Democrat who understands what marriage is. Then they can compete for our votes.

That same evening, Bill Donohue said, "We've got traditional Catholics, we have evangelical Protestants, we have Orthodox Jews, and those people on the secular left they say, 'Well, we think you're a threat.' You know what, you're right." James Dobson appeared via videotape in Justice Sunday II, and called out several Democrats and liberals as the enemy:

Now, we do know that [John] Roberts is a man of unquestioned competence and expertise, a man who has been described as having a brilliant legal mind, and now it's up to us. We need to defend his nomination from the likes of, goodness, Ted Kennedy, and Patrick Leahy, and Joseph Biden, and Dick Durbin, and George Soros, and Ralph Neas, and all the other minions on the left who want to preserve the majority on this Court, [because] it's done their bidding for so very long.

Phyllis Schlafly offered a similar perspective during the same evening:

The biggest threat facing America today is the out-of-control judges who are banning our acknowledgment of God in schools and public places, overturning marriage and morality, and imposing their social views on us. I call these judges supremacists because they advocate the supremacy of judges over Congress, the president, state legislatures, and the will of the American people. The battle cry of the liberals is we have to have an independent judiciary, but what they really mean is independent of the Constitution, and we absolutely cannot allow that.

And during Justice Sunday III, Jerry Falwell brought the point home once more: "What we have done through these years is coming to culmination, to consummation right now. We were able to hold off Michael Moore and most of Hollywood and most of the national media and George Soros and [Ted] Kennedy and other crowds who fought so fiercely against the re-election of George Bush. That was just a year ago." He continued:

And now we're looking at what we really started over 30 years ago—a reconstruction of a court system gone awry. John Roberts is now on the Court, he's chief justice and everybody thinks he's wonderful. But these same guys were calling him bad names just a few months ago. And now, today on the talk shows, everywhere, poor Judge Alito, didn't know how bad he was, how dishonest he is. He heard that today. But the fact is that he is a qualified justice and all the president is trying to do is keep his promise to put on the court men like [Antonin] Scalia and [Clarence] Thomas, who will stand for a strict constructionist application of the Constitution and stand for faith and family and all the things that this nation under God has for plus 200 years been. . . . Go to the telephone. Write your letters. Get to your U.S. senators. Let's confirm this man, Judge Alito, to the U.S. Supreme Court, and let's make one more step towards bringing America back to one nation under God.

Speaker after speaker across the rallies looked upon religious politics and declared it to be good. These events were political rallies draped in religious robes. They were religious revivals draped in judicial robes. They were both.

For Republican Party leaders, being part of these events sent an unequivocal signal. But there were some risks. Foremost was that overt religiosity by GOP politicians could raise eyebrows among journalists, who were watching. Bill Frist faced the most difficult situation. His status as Senate majority leader—along with the novelty of the event—led to media scrutiny of his decision to participate in Justice Sunday I. But the event was crucial for Frist: he was considering a 2008 presidential bid, which would require these voters' support. So he took a middle path, opting to participate via a taped message and focusing his comments on the Senate showdown over Bush's Court nominees.[40] For Frist, though, his presence was enough: simply by participating he positioned himself as a man of these people. Indeed, in introducing Frist, Tony Perkins made this clear: "He is a friend of the family in this country." Frist did offer a veiled cue with these words, "When we think judicial decisions are outside mainstream American values, we will say so," and he took one other subtle step to connect with the audience. As he spoke on videotape, behind him on a bookshelf in clear view sat a small replica of the statue of Abraham Lincoln at this president's memorial in Washington, DC. It was the only item on the shelf other than books, and it was a meaningful choice. Lincoln is a key figure for religious conservatives because, as noted earlier, they see their moral causes to be modern-day equivalents of the anti-slavery movement, which Lincoln capped with the freeing of the slaves.[41]

From the outside looking in, Frist's participation in the event came off as subdued. But to those on the inside, Frist made clear that he and his party were with them.

House majority leader Tom DeLay and Senator Rick Santorum, who spoke at subsequent Justice Sundays, were less hamstrung than Frist because both have long been known as allies of religious conservatives. For example, Perkins introduced DeLay as "one of the strongest friends of the family that I know in Washington, D.C. He is a true patriot. He is a great American. He is a friend of mine."[42] For his part, DeLay made sure to highlight both of the central symbols of morality politics. The event itself was about the judiciary, and DeLay invoked the U.S. Constitution 13 times in an address of less than eight minutes, beginning with his very first words after thanking the hosts and the audience: "The ideals of our nation were first written into our Declaration of Independence and Constitution more than 200 years ago. The durability of these founding documents is due in equal part to the wisdom and moral force behind the ideas they contain." DeLay then built on his point, claiming that the problem with the courts is that "[l]ongstanding traditions are found to be unconstitutional. Moral values that have defined the progress of a human civilization for millennia are cast aside in favor of those espoused by a handful of unelected lifetime-appointed judges." To make sure this message struck a chord, he invoked the bellwether issues: "The American people have heard the arguments in favor of state-sanctioned same-sex marriage, in favor of partial-birth abortion, in favor of raiding the public square of any mention of our nation's religious heritage. We've heard the arguments. We just disagree." Later, in concluding, DeLay said, "I just thank you for loving your country and your fight to sustain it. God bless you. Thank you for having me." And then he tacked on the Bush family's signature closing line: "And may God continue to bless the United States of America."

Santorum, like his GOP colleagues before him, received an insider's welcome from Perkins: "I want to introduce someone to you who knows a lot about religious liberties and freedom. He's here tonight because he has been the defender of religious liberty and freedom around the globe. He also happens to be a senator from the state of Pennsylvania. Please welcome my friend." Santorum then started in a fashion similar to DeLay, by invoking the nation's founding ideals: "There is no better place to have an event that highlights the importance of religious freedom in this country than here in Philadelphia. William Penn more than any other American planted the seed for religious freedom and our founders drafted a Constitution here that is the manifestation of Penn's ideal." With that said, Santorum explicitly linked God and country: "The ideas born in this city have resulted in a society full of people of deeply held faith who are at the same time respectful and tolerant of people of different faith. This freedom, this freedom is what makes America one of the most religious countries in the world, a fact at the core of the success of America in this experiment." And then came the hammer: "But that freedom is at risk today because of the actions of liberal activist judges on the Supreme Court." This state of events, Santorum went on to suggest, highlighted the importance of getting Samuel Alito confirmed, because Alito was "the kind of jurist our founders hoped for to preserve the principles of our great Constitution." Santorum eventually came full circle, tying Alito to the nation's founding: "Are we going to stand by and allow the destruction of Penn's great experiment and of the Constitution given to us some 219 years ago here in Philadelphia? If your answer is no, then join me to make sure the answer is yes on judge Sam Alito. Thank you, and God bless you."

And then there was Zell Miller, the one other high-profile politico who spoke at these events. Miller had been a Democrat while serving as governor of Georgia and then as a senator but crossed over to support George W. Bush in 2004, even giving the keynote address at the Republican convention. One other circumstance put Miller in a unique position when he spoke at Justice Sunday II: he was no longer in office. He had not sought reelection in 2004 and therefore had the greatest freedom among the political set to elevate his religious and moral language. In all ways, he was the perfect messenger to signal that the GOP understood religious conservatives. And he was up to the task, pulling together all of the key themes in one dramatic address. Miller began, like DeLay and Santorum, by grounding his call for judicial reform in history:

> Sometimes in the life of a nation, a time comes when men and women
> of conscience and courage have to stand up, be counted, and say,
> enough, no more, this cannot continue. . . . That was the way it was
> with Abraham Lincoln, when he was defeated after only one term
> in Congress and thought he was through with politics forever. But
> then, the Dred Scott decision came down from the Supreme Court and
> Lincoln knew he could not live with the highest court in the land
> saying slavery was legal. It set him on fire and he knew he could not
> remain silent and neither can we.

Miller followed up this allusion to one of religious conservatives' favorite historical figures with a pointed attack on the Supreme Court:

> For too long, way too long, the Supreme Court has been handing
> down decisions that people of faith simply cannot accept. It has ignored

our Constitution, made rulings without precedent, using psychobabble and the latest foreign fads. It has removed prayer and the Bible from schools. Each Christmas, it kidnaps the baby Jesus, halo, manger, and all from the city square. It has legalized the barbaric killing of unborn babies and is ready to discard like an outdated Hula Hoop, the universal institution of marriage between a man and a woman. It will even put you in jail if you dare to put up a copy of the Ten Commandments in a public place.

Miller maintained a similar tone throughout the address, making religion his most prominent theme:

[R]emember when our oppressed pilgrim forefathers came to this dangerous new world for, in their words, the glory of God and the advancement of the Christian faith, and then literally, with a Bible under one arm and a musket under the other, they carved out of this nation a nation under God. Our country's birth certificate, the Declaration of Independence, mentions our Creator not once, but five times, and so it was down through our glorious, Godly history, until in the 1960s, when the hostile enemies of religion found that they could win battles with appointed judges that they could not win with elected representatives and then, with that, the original intent of the United States Constitution was hauled off in a garbage truck.

In the end, Falwell, Perkins, and Dobson would have been hard-pressed to more potently articulate religious conservatives' core outlook: the courts had failed to uphold the Constitution and the ideals of the Declaration of the Independence, thereby stripping the nation of a perceived Christian heritage. Miller then concluded by declaring, in an unvarnished example of the prophetic speaking style we saw earlier, that the mission at hand was divinely decreed:

Today, there is another great task assigned by Providence to us. [The] Founding Fathers did not shirk their duty when they pledged their lives, their fortunes, and their sacred honor against the oppression of their day, and we can do no less in ours. Now is the time. This is our chance. Call and write your senators and organize your friends to do the same. Cover this confirmation process with a blanket of prayer. When they make it harder for us to pray, we just pray harder—for this is our chance. This is our chance to be doers of the word and not hearers only. Thank you and God bless you.

It was the God strategy in unfettered form. Republicans had found the ultimate narrowcast delivery mechanism to reach religious conservatives—simulcasts originating from churches on Sunday evenings, hosted by religious leaders, and beamed to Christian audiences via the Internet and satellite television. It was an information-age version of the *Old Time Gospel Hour* that Jerry Falwell had used to catapult religious conservatives' moral revolution in the late 1970s. Presented with this opportunity, Republicans not only brought their heavyweights to spread a message of national morality, but they also called upon a former Democratic Party leader who had undergone a political conversion. On behalf of the GOP, Miller preached to the choir and they loved it. His message echoed the officeholding Republicans who participated in the events, yet Miller took morality politics to a rhetorical plane that only a former politician could dare approach. The result represented a new frontier of faith and partisan politics. Even Tony Perkins, himself no stranger to the public eye and spreading his version of the political good news, was left speechless. As he followed Miller onto the stage, he said: "Well, how do you top that? I don't think you can." The Republican Party could not have scripted a better response, and for their part religious conservatives could not have crafted a better agenda. By early 2006, the Supreme Court had been remolded in the image of both. The promised land was at hand.

# CHAPTER SIX

❊

## RELIGIOUS POLITICS AND

## DEMOCRATIC VITALITY

With the reelection of George W. Bush in 2004 and the transformation of the Supreme Court secured shortly thereafter, Republican Party leaders envisioned an era of political dominance. GOP strategist Karl Rove talked of an enduring Republican majority, one with the impact of FDR's New Deal coalition. In that case, Democrats built an alliance of liberal Protestants and Catholics that lasted for generations and produced decades of success for the party. Now the shoe was on the other foot—and had been increasingly since the late 1970s, when fundamentalists and many conservative evangelicals came off the political sidelines. To capitalize on this collection of newly engaged voters, Republicans formulated the God strategy. It was a stunningly successful move: it enticed both conservative Protestants and Catholics and, by 2004, had delivered to the GOP control of the White House, the Congress, the Supreme Court, and a majority of state governorships. In the view of Rove and company, everything was working perfectly. But it was not to last. Instead of a cementing of the revolution that he had helped to fuel decades earlier, conservative leader Paul Weyrich experienced in 2006 what he called "the most disappointing race in my political lifetime": a Democratic sweep of the midterm elections.[1]

The fall from the mountaintop of U.S. politics can be sudden, but in this case there were signs it was coming. For almost three decades, the Republican Party had used calculated religiosity to transform American politics. But this approach is not foolproof. Like any political tactic, it can be adopted by the opposition—as Bill Clinton demonstrated—and it can be mishandled. Both of these dynamics were at work in 2006. Further, there are close parallels between this campaign and the one in 1992, when Democrats won the White House and retained majorities in both chambers of Congress. In this chapter, we reflect upon the workings and implications of America's new religious politics, beginning with the patterns common to these elections.

## THE GOLDEN RULE

The God strategy requires walking a fine line. Politicians must signal to devout religious believers that they share and appreciate these citizens' faith, but do so without pushing away religious moderates or secular-minded voters, the latter of whom are particularly important for Democrats. Hence, the golden rule of today's U.S. politics: exhibit faith, but don't be too strident or nakedly partisan in doing so. Deviation from this rule in either direction leads to precarious electoral territory. Politicians who veer left and send few religious signals, send the wrong ones, or send none at all often are unable to attract sufficient support among the many Americans whose faith is important to them. In the words of Al From, chair of the centrist Democratic Leadership Council, in 2003: "We went for years in the Democratic Party without recognizing God and we pay a high price for that." Just as damaging is for political leaders to veer right and suffuse their public activities with too much overt religiosity. Doing so turns a political agenda into a faith-based crusade that alienates moderate voters. Consider that among conservatives it is politicians sending religious signals who have won the presidency, not religious leaders—such as Pat Robertson and Gary Bauer—attempting to enter the political arena.[2] The God strategy's raison d'être may be the rise of religious conservatives as a political force, but the success of this approach hinges just as much on religious moderates. If a Democrat attracts them or a Republican holds them, that candidate wins. Whoever fails to woo them delivers a concession speech.

This electoral technique is far from the whole story, but it did much to help the GOP dominate U.S. national politics from the election of Ronald Reagan to George W. Bush's second term. There are two notable exceptions over this span of time: Bill Clinton's presidential victories in 1992 and 1996, and the Democratic Party's recapture of Congress in 2006. Republicans pushed their religious politics too far in these instances, while at the same time Democrats offered their own faith overtures. The result was a swing of religious moderates from the Republican camp, where they have usually resided, to the Democrats. This pattern is apparent in Table 6.1, which shows the support for Democratic Party candidates among religious voting blocs in four contexts since 1980: presidential elections 1980 through 1988; presidential elections in 1992 and 1996; presidential elections in 2000 and 2004; and the 2006 elections

Table 6.1. Percentage of Two-Party Electoral Support for Democratic
Candidates in Key Presidential and Congressional Elections, 1980–2006

| | Presidential | | | Congressional |
|---|---|---|---|---|
| | 1980–1988 | 1992–1996 | 2000–2004 | 2006 |
| Evangelical Protestants | 35 | 43 | 34 | 41 |
| Mainline Protestants | 34 | 52 | 45 | 51 |
| Catholics | 48 | 60 | 49 | 56 |
| No religious affiliation | 55 | 73 | 55 | 77 |

Note: Results derived from National Election Studies data for presidential elections, national exit polls for House of Representatives election.

for the House of Representatives.[3] These trends show the vital role of two groups of moderates: mainline Protestants and Catholics. The only electoral contexts in which Democrats won more than half of these voters were 1992, 1996, and 2006. In each case, Democrats also attracted a greater-than-usual share of evangelicals and increased their traditional advantage among "no religious affiliation" voters—outcomes which suggest that Democrats more carefully adhered to the golden rule than did Republicans. Close analysis of these electoral contexts affirms exactly that.

In 1992, Republicans gathered in Houston for their national convention. During the Persian Gulf War President George H. W. Bush had received the highest approval ratings ever recorded, but he was now trailing Democratic challenger Bill Clinton.[4] A choice was at hand: the party could reach out to political moderates, whom Bush had secured in 1988, or it could seek to mobilize the base of religious conservatives that had been built over the previous 12 years. The GOP took the latter approach—emphatically so. When the Christian Coalition hosted a God and Country rally, complete with "God Is Pro-Life" buttons and a Pat Boone performance, Vice President Dan Quayle was there to praise their values. When Jerry Falwell needed a place to sit in the convention hall, a seat with the Bush family was provided. When the party platform was formulated, it contained plenty of religious language, references to the Bible adhered strictly to the King James version, and Republicans took what many felt were their most socially conservative stances in decades— including, for the first time, explicit opposition to same-sex marriage. And most important, religious conservative favorites Pat Robertson and Pat Buchanan were given prime slots in the speaking lineup and were allowed to bypass the vetting process required of other speeches. Buchanan responded by declaring: "There is a religious war going on in our country for the soul of

America. It is a cultural war, as critical to the kind of nation we will one day be as was the Cold War itself."[5] Had this been a Justice Sunday narrowcast, Buchanan's words would have been pitch-perfect. But this was a broadcast, with millions of Americans tuning in—and many moderates were turned off.

These developments were indicative of the force that religious conservatives had become in the Republican Party. Long-time antiabortion crusader and Eagle Forum founder Phyllis Schlafly declared "total victory," and Christian Coalition director Ralph Reed, Jr., said: "We are here to celebrate a victory. . . . [T]he Republican Party passed a pro-life, pro-family platform! The feminists threw everything they had at us! We won and they lost!" Moderates had a different response: they resented the ascendance of religious conservatives. Some were so upset that they left the convention early, and they grumbled afterward that the Republican leadership was, as one convention volunteer put it, "out of touch with the way things are." Party pollster William McInturff said of GOP moderates, "[T]his platform doesn't do anything for them," and Republican National Committee member Richard Rosenbaum made this observation: "I remember saying [in the late 1970s] this right-wing drift couldn't get much worse. But it did." One unnamed former Reagan cabinet member put it more simply, telling the *Boston Globe* that kowtowing to religious conservatives had "devastated" the Republican Party.[6]

Facing this smoldering fire, the God strategy's golden rule directed Bush to reach for the water; instead, he grabbed the gasoline. Rather than modulating the approach, within days of the convention Bush spoke to a national meeting of conservative religious leaders that included Robertson, Buchanan, Schlafly, and Falwell. There Bush declared that the Democratic platform had "left out three simple letters, G-O-D"—a remark that prompted the *New York Times* to editorialize that Bush had "crossed a line" by "questioning the religious convictions of his opponents." The *Times* went on:

> In the short term, such rhetoric threatens to divert attention from Topic A, the economy. But the graver danger is that the fundamentalist impulses at large in the Republican Party could divide the nation along religious lines. The President owes it to the country not to exploit such an explosive division. Beyond that, it's up to moderate Republicans to assert themselves and pull their party back to moderation. . . . They have every reason to worry about the drift of their party into the hands of those who would use faith as a cudgel.[7]

Journalists ran with this frame. The national media turned comments by Robertson in opposition to an Iowa equal rights measure into a symbol of the

GOP's shift to the right. In a fundraising letter Robertson said: "The feminist agenda is not about equal rights for women. It is about a socialist, anti-family political movement that encourages women to leave their husbands, kill their children, practice witchcraft, destroy capitalism and become lesbians." Several major newspapers around the nation jumped on this story, with headlines such as "Pat Robertson Says Feminists Want to Kill Kids, Be Witches."[8] Due to the convention fallout, the national media were now scrutinizing even the campaign's narrowcast messages. At this point, the smart move for Bush was to distance himself from religious conservative leaders. Instead, he cozied up: within weeks Bush made a pilgrimage to speak to Robertson and his Christian Coalition. Say this for the Bushes: they don't change course easily once they've made their stand.

But many didn't like where Bush stood. In his zeal to embrace the base, he had broken the golden rule, and those in the middle of the political spectrum noticed. By the end of August, nearly 6 in 10 self-identified moderates agreed with the proposition that "George Bush does not share the values of most Americans." One citizen, speaking at a question-and-answer session with the president, put it this way:

> Good evening, Mr. President. I voted for you, sir, in 1988 because I thought you were a moderate. I'm voting for Governor Clinton in '92 because he's the moderate. And the thing is, your convention—Pat Buchanan, Pat Robertson, extreme right-wing jargon—I mean, it didn't seem to fit with George Bush and the George Bush we knew in 1988.[9]

The further Bush went, the more untoward his actions seemed—even to those in the Republican fold. Consider the view of conservative luminary George Will, writing in late August 1992:

> Today honorable conservatives feel the sort of fury felt by honorable conservatives 40 years ago when Joe McCarthy was giving anti-communism a bad name. . . . [S]erious people flinch from being associated with the intellectual slum that is the Bush campaign, with its riffraff of liars and aspiring ayatollahs. Bush calls his campaign "a crusade to bring back values." His campaign is powerful evidence of the need for such a crusade.

And the National Council of Churches, the largest ecumenical organization in the nation, wrote Bush a letter expressing their dissatisfaction with his charge that Democrats were neglecting God: "We believe it is blasphemy to invoke the infinite and holy God to assert the moral superiority of one people over another or one political party over another." As Bush's strident faith-based politics pushed voters away, Clinton's comfortable religiosity pulled them in.[10] On the day Bush spoke to the Christian Coalition, Clinton went to Notre Dame courting Catholics, a moderate voting bloc that would prove central to his success. Clinton's emphasis on faith was more subtle than Bush's, but no less sure. Bush overreached in 1992 while Clinton played it straight down the middle. The combination netted large electoral rewards for Democrats.

More than a decade later, the Republican overreach on religious politics began at an unexpected moment—a few months after their success in the 2004 elections—and in a most unlikely place: a Florida hospice. There, Theresa Marie Schiavo lay in a persistent vegetative state, with her family divided about the next course of action. Schiavo's name began to appear in national news stories in late January 2005, and by March the battle between her husband and her parents had become a national spectacle. For religious conservatives, it was a symbolic moment: the "fight for Terri." In this environment, GOP leaders saw an opportunity. Senate Republicans circulated a memo calling the Schiavo case "a great political issue" that would excite "the pro-life base." Led by Senate leader Bill Frist and House leader Tom DeLay, Congress held a special session over Easter recess and passed what legislators called a "Palm Sunday compromise." This bill transferred jurisdiction of Schiavo's case from Florida courts to federal courts. In so doing, it thrust Republican leaders into the spotlight of what had been a personal, judicial, and state matter. George W. Bush was vacationing at his ranch in Texas, but he made a dramatic return to Washington on *Air Force One* to sign the legislation in the middle of the night.[11] As religious signals go, this one exceeded a broadcast: this was a red alert.

Despite these efforts, a federal judge ultimately ruled that Schiavo's feeding tube was not to be reinserted, and she died on March 31. Religious conservatives were outraged and directed their anger at a familiar enemy: the judicial system. Focus on the Family founder James Dobson, for example, said the judges were "guilty not only of judicial malfeasance—but of the cold-blooded, cold-hearted extermination of an innocent human life." Frist, DeLay, and other conservatives echoed these criticisms, and DeLay even suggested retribution: "The time will come for the men responsible for this to answer for their behavior, but not today." GOP leaders were speaking to the base, but just as in 1992 many more Americans were hearing it—and again most didn't like the message. In a widely circulated op-ed piece in the *New York Times*, John Danforth, a moderate former GOP senator and ordained Episcopal minister, wrote:

I do not fault religious people for political action. Since Moses con-
fronted the pharaoh, faithful people have heard God's call to political
involvement. Nor has political action been unique to conservative
Christians. Religious liberals have been politically active in support of
gay rights and against nuclear weapons and the death penalty. In
America, everyone has the right to try to influence political issues,
regardless of his religious motivations. The problem is not with people
or churches that are politically active. It is with a party that has gone
so far in adopting a sectarian agenda that it has become the political
extension of a religious movement.[12]

Much of the public seemed to agree: 76% said they disapproved of Congress
getting involved in the Schiavo case, and 74% said Congress intervened "to
advance a political agenda" rather than "because they really care about what
happens in this case." A year later, these numbers were unchanged and an ABC
News poll showed that fully 73% of white Catholics felt that removing
Schiavo's feeding tube was the "right thing." After Democrats gained control
of Congress, right-leaning radio host Michael Smerconish cited the Schiavo
case as a key reason, saying it "was a national debacle for the GOP, and we
never got beyond it."[13]

Things then went from bad to worse for Republicans: the Iraq War bogged
down, scandals in Congress erupted, and the president's popularity declined.
As a result, Frist—having learned his lesson—and party colleagues began to
seek the political center. In May 2005, the House of Representatives passed a
bill easing restrictions on federal funding for stem cell research, and in July
2006 it passed the Senate with Frist's support. The move cost Frist points with
religious conservatives and may have sealed his decision not to enter the 2008
presidential field, but was consistent with the views of most U.S. citizens: 68%
said they favored his position.[14] The bill still required the president's signature,
though. Bush could have made a conciliatory gesture to moderates, but Karl
Rove was convinced that mobilizing the party's base was the right electoral
move. So Bush issued the first veto of his presidency. He had gone from
January 2001 to July 2006 without vetoing a bill, the longest of any president
since Thomas Jefferson. In breaking that string, the White House hosted a
televised event in which Bush was surrounded by families with children born
from frozen embryos. Religious conservatives applauded this move, but for
moderates it was another slap in the face: 73% of mainline Protestants and
almost 60% of white Catholics told pollsters they supported expanding stem
cell research. Months later, after the 2006 elections, the *National Catholic Reporter* attributed the GOP losses, in part, to "a religiosity owing to the most

extreme and conservative brand of Christianity," and former presidential adviser David Gergen blamed Rove: "He went off to hardliners, and that left an awful lot of moderates . . . feeling alienated."[15] Enter the Democrats, stage left.

Just as Bill Clinton had done, several Democrats in 2006 infused faith into their campaigns. They got an assist from an unlikely source: Howard Dean. A former governor of Vermont, Dean ran for the 2004 Democratic Party presidential nomination. Throughout, his discomfort with faith was palpable. Early on, Dean told southern campaign crowds, "We've got to stop voting on guns, God, and gays"—a line of argument that fellow Democrats and liberal religious leader Jim Wallis rebuked as antireligious. Dean later reversed course and told Iowa caucus audiences that faith was an important part of his life, a shift that drew yet more criticism from people who saw it as disingenuous. If anyone symbolized Democrats' uncertainty about religious politics, it was this northeastern liberal whom the *New Republic* called "one of the most secular candidates to run for president in modern history." Just about the time Terri Schiavo was entering the national consciousness in early 2005, Dean was elected chair of the Democratic National Committee. As Republicans veered right on matters of faith, Democrats seemed poised to crash and burn on the left. But then Dean put into motion a "50-state strategy" to revitalize his party, with a commitment to field candidates across the country regardless of how conservative an area might be.[16] Dean's plan wasn't religious in aim, but it was in result. Democrats who wanted to make inroads in heavily Republican districts faced voters who expected candidates to make faith public and political.

Some Democrats did so immediately. In November 2005, Democrat Tim Kaine won the Virginia governor's race. Kaine, a devout Catholic, spoke early and often about his overseas missionary work while in college, quoted the apostle Paul in his stump speeches, and defended his opposition to the death penalty on religious grounds. Other Democrats soon took more dramatic steps. In 2006 in Pennsylvania, for instance, Catholic Bob Casey, Jr., took on GOP senator Rick Santorum, another Catholic and the only member of Congress included in a *Time* magazine list of the "25 most influential evangelicals in America" in 2005. Casey spoke of his faith, had an informal advisory group of Catholics, and neutralized a key wedge issue by emphasizing his opposition to abortion. In September, Casey made a pilgrimage to Catholic University in Washington, DC, where he delivered an address titled "Restoring America's Moral Compass: Leadership and the Common Good." Casey handily defeated Santorum, garnering roughly 60% of mainline Protestant and Catholic votes.[17] Further, there was symbolism to Casey's victory: a decade earlier his father was a prolife Democratic governor of Pennsylvania who had refused to endorse Bill Clinton, and he had been denied a chance to speak at his party's national convention. In 2006, the younger Casey, who held the same position on this bellwether issue, was *recruited* by Democrats to run for the Senate—and he knocked off a high-ranking Republican who represented the intimate ties of political and religious conservatives.[18]

But Casey was far from the lone Democrat engaging in religious politics. Ohio gubernatorial candidate Ted Strickland, an ordained Methodist minister and congressional representative, regularly invoked his favorite Bible verse during his campaign. His aides distributed across Ohio 15,000 copies of his kickoff speech, in which he emphasized the two most important influences in his life: his mother and the church. "Over and over, people in churches would say there's something here for me after they read his speech," said a Strickland campaign consultant. "They'd say, 'He's one of us.'" The reelection campaign of Michigan governor Jennifer Granholm included meetings with religious leaders around her state and a pilgrimage speech at her alma mater, evangelical Hope College. Both Strickland and Granholm won by large margins on the strength of religious moderates.[19] In a wide range of other states as well, Democrats engaged the faithful. For example, Democrats in Oregon ran advertisements on Christian radio stations, and in Tennessee, Senate candidate Harold Ford, Jr., ran a campaign with Ronald Reagan–like precision. Ford filmed a commercial in a church, was fond of saying "I love Jesus," and concluded his final debate by invoking Reagan's vision of America as a "shining city up on a hill"—with Ford adding the word "up" to make it his own.[20] Ford lost, but only after nearly becoming the first African American since Reconstruction to win a U.S. Senate seat in the South. By 2006 the die was cast, and many Democrats were betting on faith.

The patterns across these election contexts more than a decade apart highlight the Achilles heel of the God strategy: push too hard with this approach and it will fail. Republicans entered the 1992 and the 2006 campaign cycles riding high, with historic presidential approval ratings in the former and back-to-back-to-back electoral affirmations of GOP leadership in the latter. The result among Republicans was confidence, perhaps even certainty, that their religious politics would work again. But success with this method means adhering to the golden rule. In these instances the GOP did not, and severe rhetoric and partisan ploys turned off religious moderates. Perhaps in more favorable electoral contexts Republicans could have held on despite their missteps, but 1992 and 2006 were hardly favorable: the former was marked by recession, the latter by a controversial war and multiple scandals. Further, Democrats were adept with their own faith-based politics, which impelled the GOP to push harder and, ultimately, too far. There was one notable difference between these elections, though. Bill Clinton in 1992 carried the religious politics banner for the Democrats. In 2006, a range of Democratic senators, representatives, and governors were on board. It was a sea change. Northerners and southerners, Republicans and Democrats: the God strategy had become the norm on both sides of the partisan aisle.

## THE INTEGRATION OF CHURCH AND STATE

In the United States today, it is hard to know where religion ends and politics begins. Or where politics ends and religion begins. There is a resounding emphasis on God and faith in the public communications of political leaders, especially of presidents and presidential candidates. God and country have been fused, mixing citizens' understandings of America with claims about divine wishes. Presidents have entered into public communion with religious leaders, by making pilgrimages, issuing proclamations, and embracing holy rituals. And morality politics are ubiquitous, with issues turned into symbols, the Constitution and the courts persistently invoked, and religious and moral rhetoric the norm. Beginning with the campaign of Ronald Reagan in 1980, successful political leaders have used these techniques in ways never before seen in the modern presidency.

One might be tempted to view these developments as a reasonable outgrowth of the Judeo-Christian heritage common to many Americans.[21] Michael Gerson is the former head speechwriter for George W. Bush—from Bush's presidential candidacy through his second Inauguration—and a graduate of evangelical Wheaton College, and he put it this way: "[W]e sometimes employ religious language to talk about the historic influence of faith on our country. We argue that it has contributed to the justice of America, that people of faith have been a voice of conscience." This perspective has more than a tinge of veracity to it—so much so that two-thirds of Americans consistently say they conceive of the United States as a "Christian nation."[22] Indeed, when modern presidents emphasize religion in their public communications they are echoing, in some significant way, the nation's founding fathers. Embedded deeply in America's self-image is the Declaration of Independence, in which the founders declared that "the Laws of Nature and of Nature's God" compelled them to pen these famous words: "We hold these truths to be self-evident: that all men are created equal; that they are endowed, by their Creator, with certain unalienable rights; that among these are life, liberty, and the pursuit of happiness." Near the close of this document, the founders added that their actions were undertaken with "firm reliance on the protection of Divine Providence."[23] Given this beginning, it is not surprising that religious words and ideas have long been part of American politics.

But this tradition masks a stark transformation in recent decades. In September 1960, John F. Kennedy addressed the Houston Ministerial Association, a collection of conservative southern clergy who were concerned about Kennedy's adherence to Catholic teachings should he become president. On that day, Kennedy pledged a commitment to an "absolute" separation between his religious beliefs and the presidency. He promised a nation where a president's "views on religion are his own private affair," where White House decisions would be made "without regard to outside religious pressure or dictates," and where the presidency would not be "limited or conditioned by any religious oath, ritual, or obligation." Kennedy's speech was a forceful articulation of a precept nearly as old as the country itself: there should be, as Thomas Jefferson styled it, a "wall of separation" between church and state. Of course, both Kennedy and Jefferson were expressing an ideal rather than an on-the-ground reality. It is an ideal, though, that lasted for nearly two centuries. It is startling, therefore, that in the United States today *even the ideal itself* has lost much of its traction. Consider that nine days after his Inauguration in 2001, George W. Bush issued a presidential executive order establishing the Office of Faith-Based and Community Initiatives. In defending the constitutionality of the program, Bush declared that there is an "important bridge between church and state."[24] From a wall of separation to a bridge of integration: that's the new religious politics in America.

This shift has been fueled by the desire of U.S. political leaders to appeal to the faithful. Since the late 1970s, religious conservatives have decreed that a convergence of religion and politics is a necessary calling card if a politician, particularly one running for national office, wants their votes. The result has been the profound shift in political communications documented in this book. In the words of Martin Medhurst, a distinguished scholar of political language:

> [O]ne thing is clear: this is not the rhetoric of civic piety or of traditional civil religion. This is not the religion of the Republic as described by scholars of American history nor is it the bland Deism of the Founders. Here we find no references to "Nature and Nature's God," or the hand of the "Creator," or the agency of "Divine Providence." Instead, we find particular beliefs, articulated within the framework of a campaign for public office, and offered as either the motivation for or the value structure underlying specific public policies.[25]

What America now has is an integration of church and state in its public discourse. For many religious conservatives, this is literally an answer to prayers. In the view of Concerned Women for America, for instance, separation of church and state is a "myth." The Alliance Defense Fund claims to be an organization that "God raised up" with a clear goal: "to tear down the 'wall of separation.'" These voices are not trees falling silently in a forest; they are being heard. The Texas Republican Party is a bellwether for relations between religious conservatives and the national GOP, and its 2004 platform said: "Our party pledges to exert its influence to . . . dispel the 'myth' of the separation of church and state."[26] Such perceptions have been fostered and furthered by the God strategy. When the political environment is dominated by religious language, symbolism, and concerns, church-and-state separation begins to feel foreign. At best, this principle soon seems a noble but impractical notion; at worst, it appears a mistaken illusion. Either of these outcomes puts at grave risk the American experiment in democracy.

History has shown with tragic consistency that too intimate a relationship between religion and politics can do irreparable damage to both—from the crusades of medieval times to the terrorism of modern times. Constant use of the God strategy by political leaders encourages just such a relationship. When George W. Bush justifies the Iraq War by saying that liberty is "God's gift to humanity" and that America's "calling" is to deliver that gift to the Iraqi people, he is offering something quite like a divine vision for U.S. foreign policy. It is precisely this conflation of abstract claims about God with the concrete goals of the state that led esteemed religion scholar R. Scott Appleby to call the administration's rhetoric about spreading freedom and liberty "a theological version of Manifest Destiny." At a minimum, this approach risks repeating the errors of the original manifest destiny: unduly emphasizing the norms and values of white, conservative Protestants at the expense of those who will not or cannot conform.[27] Just as important, pairing religious doctrine with public policy encourages citizens to conclude that the U.S. government's actions are the will of God—or at least congruent with such wishes—and therefore beyond question. Dogmatic political voices and hints of divinely inspired policy are not the ingredients of a robust republic; they're the recipe for hubris, jingoism, and the decline of democracy. These are disquieting possibilities, but the words of our political leaders in recent decades have moved America toward them. Both the Gospel of John and the record of evils past teach one thing: in the beginning, always, are words.

The founding fathers understood this potentiality and took steps to prevent it. Many of these men were devoutly religious, but they were also eminently aware of the problems with faith-driven politics. They were only an ocean removed from the religious strife that had plagued Europe for centuries—the very strife that had compelled their ancestors to seek religious freedom in a new world. And they were familiar with the sectarianism that characterized the early development of that new world.[28] It was because of this shared history and their appreciation of honest faith that the founders sought something different for America. They envisioned a nation that would protect the church from the state and the state from the church. The Declaration of Independence signaled the birth of that nation, but it was the Constitution that codified the law of America. In formulating this document, the founders didn't include a single mention of God. Instead, they included a Bill of Rights which began with a guarantee that Congress could neither establish religion nor prohibit its free exercise. The founders understood that in getting down to the business of governing, of creating policy and keeping democracy vital, citizens do well to keep religious doctrines at a distance.

This was an astonishing position at the time, virtually unprecedented in world history. But it defined the nation and has served it well.[29] The United States today is one of the most religiously diverse nations in the world: millions of citizens freely practice the faiths of their choice, while millions of others are free to observe no faith at all. Further, Americans have lived relatively free of the religious turmoil common in other parts of the world. The United States has never had a formal state religion, an anti-Jewish pogrom, much sustained conflict between Protestants and Catholics, nor any large-scale sectarian violence within its borders.[30] These outcomes are the direct product of the founders' unique vision for the nation. Today that vision is at serious risk. The evidence shows that American politics are now characterized not by the occasional use of religious language as an expected function of political office. Instead, religion is employed over and over in a calculated and partisan manner. It is faith used as a political weapon, and it is fatal to this nation's future. The founders realized this more than two centuries ago, and we ignore their wisdom at our peril. Religion and politics should both be celebrated as integral parts of the fabric of America, but the two must be woven in distinctly different colors.

The First Amendment is not the only constitutional principle that the God strategy has compromised. Article VI, section 3, stipulates that "no religious test shall ever be required as a qualification to any office or public trust under the United States." In the contemporary political climate, candidates who hope to win do face a de facto religious test: are they willing to make their faith demonstrably public? If they aren't, they fail—particularly those running for national offices. Consider the Republican Party presidential primaries of 2000, when George W. Bush and John McCain were the frontrunners for the GOP nomination. Bush made faith a dominant theme of his campaign, highlighted early on by his "Christ moment" in an Iowa debate. McCain wanted no part of it. After Bush's declaration in that debate set off a series of religious testimonies, McCain talked about Teddy Roosevelt, not Jesus. Later in the campaign, McCain made a stop at a Virginia high school. There he criticized Jerry Falwell and Pat Robertson—in their backyards, no less—as "agents of intolerance" who "shame our faith, our party and our country."[31] It was a bold declaration of independence, and McCain's unwillingness to play politics with faith may have cost him the GOP nomination. Six years later, he adopted a different tune. In May 2006, as he positioned himself for a 2008 presidential run, McCain made another stop in Virginia. This time he went to Falwell's home: Liberty University. But rather than deliver a critique, McCain delivered the commencement address. It was an act of both contrition and communion, in one shot.

For U.S. politicians today, having faith isn't enough; it must be displayed, carefully and publicly. McCain learned this lesson the hard way, and four years later John Kerry did as well. In a 2006 speech at religiously grounded Pepperdine University, Kerry reflected on his experience as the 2004 Democratic presidential nominee:

> I learned how important it is to make certain people have a deeper understanding of the values that shape me and the faith that sustains me. Despite this New Englander's past reticence of talking publicly about my faith, I learned that if I didn't fill in the picture myself, others would draw the caricature for me. I will never let that happen again—and neither should you, because no matter your party, your ideology, or your faith, we are all done a disservice when the debate is reduced to ugly and untrue caricatures.

Imposing a test of public religiosity on a candidate is more than a disservice to that individual; it is a disservice to the nation.[32] Democracy is at its best when good candidates run for office and the finest of those candidates has a chance to win. When the God strategy is a necessity, candidates who can't or won't employ its tactics will not run, let alone win.

Who might this exclude? Some of the most revered among America's modern presidents, judging by the patterns of communications identified in our data. Franklin Roosevelt, Harry Truman, and Dwight Eisenhower had some highly religious moments, but none of them approached the sustained and partisan public religiosity that defines today's presidential politics. Kennedy's call for an "absolute" separation of church and state, were he to issue it today, would doom his candidacy. This is especially unfortunate, for Kennedy well understood the dangers of a religious test for public office. Being a religious outsider will do that for you. As he neared the conclusion of his address to the Houston Ministerial Association, Kennedy said: "[I]f this election is decided on the basis that 40 million Americans lost their chance of being President on the day they were baptized, then it is the whole nation that will be the loser, in the eyes of Catholics and non-Catholics around the world, in the eyes of history, and in the eyes of our own people." Similar words must be said today. If modern American politics systematically excludes those who feel that faith is a deeply private matter, those who believe that religion can be practiced without being preached, those who observe a faith other than Christianity, and those who choose not to believe in a higher power, it is our democracy that will be the loser.

None of this means that religious sentiment should be excised from public life. Doing so is neither possible nor desirable. Rather, the depth and breadth of faith among Americans—nine of every ten say they believe in a higher power—ought to motivate politicians to attain a kind of "religious literacy."[33] Understanding the diverse range of religious and spiritual beliefs that exist within the United States can help leaders to meet the needs of their constituents and, when appropriate, celebrate the cultural significance of faith. The use of the God strategy since the late 1970s has done nothing to engender such literacy. In contrast, public religiosity has been made beholden to partisan goals and often restricted to conservative faith. American politics in the twenty-first century demands a broader outlook. Consider that the Congress elected in the autumn of 2006 includes two Buddhists, one Muslim, and, for the first time ever, an openly atheistic member. The Muslim member, Minnesota Democrat Keith Ellison, during his oath of office laid his hand on the Koran rather than the Bible. Ellison's decision led Representative Virgil Goode, a Virginia Republican, to call for stricter immigration laws to prevent more Muslims from gaining office. Syndicated radio host and columnist Dennis Prager declared that Ellison's decision "undermines American civilization." Such attitudes betray the founders' promise of religious freedom—which, notably, was on full display at Ellison's swearing in: the Koran he used for his oath once belonged to Thomas Jefferson.[34] On matters of faith and politics, Jefferson and the rest of America's forefathers who sought a more perfect union would have expected better. Today, the responsibility lies with us.

## INSTITUTIONAL DUTIES

The future pathways of religion and politics in the United States will require thoughtful contributions from many sectors. Local, state, and national political officials will be influential, as always: their words do much to set the parameters for public debate. Citizens have the power to push for changes, if they have the will; public pressure could provide a tipping point toward a new political dynamic. In the end, though, the greatest impact may be exerted by formal institutions and organizations—an often overlooked force in a society that trumpets the power of the individual. In America, the words and actions of specific men and women tend to dominate news stories and fill history books, but it is the everyday practices within social institutions that commonly establish how deeply held matters such as faith, nation, and politics are understood and lived out.[35] Consider how the internal values and habits of Fortune 500 companies shape the national sensibility. Attitudes about profit, philanthropy, the balance of career and family, and even what qualifies as appropriate retirement age are all shaped by the practices of business organizations. In a similar manner, several important institutions are in position to shape the interplay of religion and politics in the United States. Some of them were caught off guard by the rise of religious politics in recent decades and, as a result, they were all but run over by a moral revolution not of their making. Nevertheless, three of these institutions are still in position to make a difference in the years ahead.

The first is the news media. For too long, journalists at mainstream media have inadequately covered the religious dimensions of American politics. This is so for several reasons. For one, political journalists underestimate the importance of religious values to the U.S. public, in part because reporters at leading news outlets tend to be less religious than other Americans. Consider that more than one-third of U.S. full-time journalists in 2002 said they did not practice any religion, more than double the percentage among the full U.S. population. Further, only 36% of journalists rated their religious faith as "very important," roughly half as many as in the broader citizenry.[36] Second, political journalists seem to view faith as hallowed ground, in the sense that they rarely question religious positions in the way that they do standard political fare. For a journalist to openly critique politicians' religious claims and practices vis-à-vis their political activities was almost unheard of until recent years. But if faith is to be a political weapon, then it requires the scrutiny of the press. Third, mainstream journalists are entrenched in the political establishment, often relying upon people in power to frame their news stories. In the words of *Washington Post* reporter Karen DeYoung: "We are inevitably the mouthpiece for whatever administration is in power."[37] In combination, these factors have often allowed religious politics to receive a free pass from news organizations. This needs to change. Democracy is a fiction without a vibrant press that helps citizens to make sense of the world.

Journalists have a responsibility to ponder, explain, critique, and meaningfully understand today's religious politics. A half-century ago, broadcast journalist Edward R. Murrow risked his career to challenge Senator Joseph McCarthy's claims about communism in the United States. A few years later, in 1958, Murrow addressed leaders of the radio and television industries. His words included these:

> I would just like to see [television] reflect occasionally the hard, unyielding realities of the world in which we live. . . . The responsibility can be easily placed, in spite of all the mouthings about giving the public what it wants. It rests on big business, and on big television, and it rests at the top. Responsibility is not something that can be assigned or delegated. And it promises its own reward: good business and good television. . . . This instrument can teach, it can illuminate; yes, and it can even inspire. But it can do so only to the extent that humans are determined to use it to those ends. Otherwise it is merely wires and lights in a box.[38]

The same can be said today about the entirety of the U.S. news media: coverage of faith in politics can be both good journalism and good business. It can also teach, illuminate, and even inspire. When a politician imbues a speech with invocations of God and faith, news media should assess what this means and why it was done. When a political party ignores a "moral issue" for months but makes it a priority as an election nears, journalists should dissect the machinations at work—and do so not merely by relying on the voices of vested interests. When a political leader speaks of the nation or its objectives as divine, journalists should take up the theological and ideological implications. On the religious side of this coin, news media need to develop a Rolodex of sources who live—literally and figuratively—outside the Beltway of Washington, DC. As new religious voices such as Rick Warren, T. D. Jakes, and Brian McLaren replace the old guard of Jerry Falwell, Pat Robertson, and Jim Wallis, the press needs to adapt. And it shouldn't just be Christian leaders who make the news. Journalists must seek out competing perspectives to provide a richer, more accurate representation of faith in America.

To their credit, some leading news organizations have begun to do just this. For example, in the spring of 2005, the *New York Times*—widely regarded as the nation's premier news organization—identified the need to conduct more reporting on the role of religion in American life as a top way to improve the newspaper. In making this case, the *Times*'s leadership said, "Our news coverage needs to embrace unorthodox views and contrarian opinions and to portray lives both more radical and more conservative than most of us experience." In the autumn of 2006, the *Washington Post* and *Newsweek* jointly launched *On Faith*, an online forum that takes as its starting point this perspective: "Religion is the most pervasive yet least understood topic in global life." With this in mind, these news outlets collected religious leaders, journalists, and scholars to "engage in a conversation about faith and its implications in a way that sheds light rather than generates heat." This is good; even better would be for other news organizations to follow their lead. A cynic would note that these news outlets are merely responding to the marketplace, particularly the dialogues on faith and culture occurring online at places such as www .beliefnet.com, which opened shop in 1999 and has since won awards for its journalism.[39] The cynic would be at least partly right, but the benefits for the citizenry of these small steps are as great as the financial ones accruing to the media's ownership. The opportunity is at hand for the press to better serve the public interest.

A second key social institution is the public education system. Children in the United States spend thousands of formative hours in school, yet in many cases the role of religion in historical and social developments receives scant attention in the curriculum. There may be no other issue so substantial in many Americans' lives that receives so little discussion in U.S. public schools. The separation of church and state must be an ironclad principle, and educators need to take great care to ensure that discussions of religion never devolve into proselytizing. But this does not preclude social studies curricula from exploring the roots, social and political implications, and cross-cultural challenges of religious world views. The emotions that arise in public educational circles at any hint of discussing faith engender defensiveness and confusion among both parents and educators. The result, too often, is that religion becomes the elephant in the room that no one feels comfortable discussing, regardless of one's views. This is a dangerous outcome. The solution to conflict-laden topics should be more discussion, more conversation, more opportunities for learning—never less. When topics of great magnitude become radioactive in the classroom, human nature dictates that their energy will be channeled elsewhere. Without knowledge of diverse perspectives, this energy might fuel myopia, fear, division, even hatred. America cannot afford this risk. The public educational system has a responsibility to be part of a solution, for its own good and for the good of the nation. Two matters in particular merit attention.

School prayer has been a flashpoint in the culture wars since the 1960s. However, this issue is only part of a broader debate over what forms of religious expression should be allowed within public schools. Often, conflict in this conversation arises from a faulty or incomplete understanding of what is permissible under current U.S. law. Decisions frequently are made by individual school district administrators, school principals, or even teachers, and the result is a lack of consistency and clarity. This approach all but guarantees that students will sometimes have their religious freedoms unfairly limited, and other times encounter situations that run afoul of the First Amendment's establishment clause. The Department of Education has taken steps to clarify the role of religion in the public schools, but these guidelines vary by administration and have been criticized for taking on a partisan edge.[40] A better approach is offered by the "Joint Statement of Current Law on Religion in the Public Schools" endorsed by a diverse collection of more than 30 religious organizations and interest groups, running the gamut from the National Association of Evangelicals and the National Council of Churches, to the Anti-Defamation League and the American Civil Liberties Union, to the American Muslim Council and the National Sikh Center.[41] The statement describes the current laws and explains how they can be applied evenhandedly. By developing consistent models of applying these guidelines, educators can ensure that they are doing all they can to protect the rights of students under the Constitution.

Education might also highlight the convergence of faith and politics as a global phenomenon. Religion is now at ground zero of some of the most potent dynamics around the globe, and leaders must respond. Former U.S. secretary of state Madeleine Albright in 2006 put it this way: "Religion has to be considered as we look at various conflicts. Our diplomats have to understand the religious basis of these conflicts. In fact, they have to have training in religion."[42] This book has focused on American politics, but one need not look far to find variants of the God strategy at work. To the north and east of the United States in recent years have been vocally religious individuals heading the Canadian and English national governments—key allies both, of course. Moving east from the British Isles one finds overt religious politics in the Middle East, where theology and ideology intersect with uncommon force. Still farther east one encounters the conflicts between Hindus and Muslims in Southeast Asia. Almost anywhere one looks, from Africa to Ireland, religion and politics are intersecting in significant ways. In several cases, considerable loss of life has been a consequence. There are other simmering religious politics in play as well; even in secular-leaning Europe there are conflicts among traditionally Christian populations over the immigration of Muslims from North Africa and the potential entrance into the European Union of Turkey, a predominantly Muslim nation.[43] Perhaps never before in modern history has there been a greater need for young people to have a firm grasp of the complex relationships among faith, culture, and politics. Educators may not be able to solve these problems, but they have a responsibility to prepare the generations that might.

Finally, leading clergy and religious organizations have a significant role to play. Our focus has been the rising salience of religion in politics; it is also the case, though, that politics affect religion. Since the mid-1970s, God and faith have become deeply politicized in America, to the detriment of both. When religious institutions are perceived to be the extension of political movements, the outcome is never favorable for the faith. Consider the view of Cal Thomas and Ed Dobson, who worked for the Moral Majority before becoming a columnist and a pastor, respectively. They put it this way:

> [W]e affirm the right and responsibility of every person, religious or not, to participate in the political process. But we warn that when the clergy and other institutions of the church do so, they run the risk of being compromised and their central message obscured as they are often seduced by the siren song of temporal political power. . . . Does this mean conservative Christians should retreat into separatism and a catacomb-like existence? No. Believers should engage the world. They just should not marry it.

When houses of worship provide political campaigns with membership rosters, turn over their pulpits to political leaders, or endorse candidates implicitly or explicitly, it is the religious institutions that are sullied. When sacred teachings are used for political purposes, it is the faith that is tarnished. One might recall the words of Billy Graham in 1981: "It would disturb me if there was a wedding between the religious fundamentalists and the political right. The hard right has no interest in religion except to manipulate it."[44] Hard Right or hard Left, Graham makes a crucial point: when we render unto Caesar the things that are God's, religion suffers.

But this concern extends beyond domestic American politics and religion. Over the eight decades that this book covers, the Abrahamic faiths that have gone far to define Western civilization—Judaism, Islam, and Christianity—have in several instances been used for political purposes. Perhaps the most infamous example is the record in Germany in the 1930s and 1940s of Protestant leaders, many of whom struck Faustian bargains with the Nazi Party. A small number of German religious leaders resisted, however, and in 1934 created the Confessing church with a statement of separation from National Socialism. In so doing, theologians and activists such as Karl Barth, Martin Niemöller, and Dietrich Bonhoeffer lost careers and sometimes lives, but provided an example for those who would pursue the highest principles of their faith.[45] Today, there is a similar need for clergy and religious institutions to reclaim their faiths. For too many westerners, the face of Islam is a suicide terrorist. For too many people living in the Middle East, the face of Judaism is a West Bank settler or an Israeli soldier. And for too many people across the globe, the face of Christianity since the beginning of the Iraq War has been George W. Bush. In all of these instances, religion has been unfairly subjugated to politics. For the good of the faith, religious leaders and institutions must do all they can—as the ecumenical National Council of Churches did in 1992 with its public letter criticizing the religious politics of George H. W. Bush—to change this.

At its best, religion is the province of the ideal, a sphere in which sacred visions are extolled and upheld for inspiration and comfort. At their best, religious leaders act upon these visions to call people to more responsible citizenship and more noble endeavors. They do this by *speaking into* the political arena, not by forming alliances with its various factions. This was the position of Dorothy Day, Mahatma Gandhi, Martin Luther King, Jr., Mother Teresa, and countless others who shared their faiths in ways that uplifted humanity. In King's words, "The church must be reminded that it is not the master or the servant of the state, but rather the conscience of the state. It must be the guide and the critic of the state, never its tool." In America in recent years, believers—and particularly conservatives—have too often ignored this point. But, over time, a much-needed realization may have come as well. After the midterm elections in 2006, the *National Catholic Reporter* offered this reflection:

> [T]he electorate has recognized that what some once claimed was God-ordained-and-blessed is merely a matter of ambition gone bad. Our faint hope is that religion, in all its forms, has also learned from the past six years. What we may be coming to understand is that acting out of faith is a complex matter, that God doesn't sign off on political parties, strategies or wars. That in the end, with God's grace, we are left, human to human, to puzzle out, humbly if with determination, the great issues of the day.

Faith is a complex matter, but since the mid-1970s it has been simplified into a no-holds-barred political calculus. David Kuo, a former high-ranking official in the Bush administration's Office of Faith-Based and Community Initiatives, proposed in 2006 that evangelical Christians take a two-year "fast" from political involvement.[46] The sentiment is compelling but we are concerned that in a participatory democracy a self-imposed political exile for any group of citizens may lead to other problems. Our preference would be for Americans to do what we rarely do: engage in a robust societal conversation.

That discussion must begin now. The growing nexus of religion and politics merits as much attention as did slavery in the nineteenth century, women's suffrage in the early 1900s, the economy in the 1930s, fascism in the 1940s, and civil rights in the 1950s and '60s. Like these issues, its resolution will forever alter the character of our democracy. When British troops finally scored their first significant victory in World War II, after more than three years of fighting, Winston Churchill said: "Now this is not the end. It is not even the beginning of the end. But it is, perhaps, the end of the beginning."[47] That is where we stand today: at the end of the beginning of a new religious politics. Act I has concluded. This Act saw the development of a powerful alliance between religious and political conservatives that worked for decades—with occasional fractures—to transform the nation, its political communications, and its public policies. The Democratic Party fully entered the fray just before the curtain came down, and along the way few stones were left unturned or unthrown. Our greatest hope as we go forward is that Americans of all persuasions—religious and secular, liberal and conservative— might author new declarations of independence from the political powers that be. For the nation's institutions and leaders, their credibility and vitality are at stake. For citizens worldwide who must learn to live together despite their differences, the stakes are even higher.

# EPILOGUE

✳

# ACT II

There was a day in 2006 when America's religious politics changed. It occurred at the behest of Rick Warren, who had emerged as a leading voice of a new generation of religious conservatives in the previous decade. Warren is the affable pastor of Saddleback Church—an influential southern California congregation known for its laid-back style and emphasis on small-group fellowship—and author of the highest-selling nonfiction book in the history of U.S. publishing, *The Purpose Driven Life*. Warren's words are the basis for sermons and Bible studies in countless churches, he is a regular on talk shows, and he is respected both inside and outside of religious circles. As Philadelphia pastor Herbert Lusk put it, Warren is "the leading evangelical in the world, unquestionably." Inevitably, Warren was drawn into the orbit of religious politics, and in 2004 he decreed that five issues—opposition to abortion, same-sex marriage, cloning, euthanasia, and research on stem cells—should drive the voting decisions of Christians, an outlook that firmly aligned him with the Republican Party. But Warren's political world view had been expanding ever since. In early 2006, he said, "I'm worried that evangelicals be identified too much with one party or the other. When that happens, you lose your prophetic role of speaking truth to power. And you have to defend stupid things that leaders do."[1] By late 2006, Warren had turned his star power toward a broader range of issues, including poverty and global warming. On December 1, designated as World AIDS Day, he and his church hosted a Global Summit on AIDS and the Church.

It was the kind of event that merited pilgrimages from politicians considering runs for higher office. And indeed, Sam Brownback of the Republican Party was on hand. Brownback, a U.S. senator from Kansas and a devout Catholic, is beloved by Christian conservatives for his staunch opposition to abortion and same-sex relationships. For Brownback, this event served as a launching pad for his aspirations for the presidency in 2008: three days later, he filed the papers to take the first formal step toward becoming a candidate. The God strategy was firing on all cylinders.

The day's focus was relatively new for the nation's religious politics, though. Brownback was slated to speak because he had worked to stop human sex trafficking, starvation, and genocide in the Sudan and had visited Rwanda and Darfur in 2006. He had seen Africa's AIDS pandemic up close and personal. In his speech on that December day, he sought partners in the cause. He quoted Scripture at length and declared that Christians, particularly in America, had a moral calling to make a difference, and concluded with "You're wonderful. I appreciate you. I love you. And together we're going to change the world. God bless you all."[2] It was a moment worthy of Ronald Reagan or either President Bush, occurring in exactly the type of setting that GOP politicians had dominated for years. By all rights, Brownback should have been the political headliner for this event. On this day, however, he was the warm-up act.

Two years earlier, Barack Obama was a little-known Illinois state senator when he delivered a stirring keynote address at the Democratic Party's national convention, speaking of unity and challenging the divisions—religious and otherwise—between red and blue America. He proclaimed, "We worship an 'awesome God' in the blue states" and criticized those who "use faith as a wedge to divide us." He invoked the Declaration of Independence's promise "that all men are created equal, that they are endowed by their Creator with certain inalienable rights, that among these are life, liberty and the pursuit of happiness," and declared that what "makes this country work" is a "fundamental belief: I am my brother's keeper. I am my sister's keeper." And, as he brought his message home to an electrified audience, he spoke of hope: "Hope—hope in the face of difficulty. Hope in the face of uncertainty. The audacity of hope! In the end, that is God's greatest gift to us, the bedrock of this nation. A belief in things not seen. A belief that there are better days ahead." He became a political star overnight, and the press talked of "Obama fever," an "Obama buzz," and "Obamania." His profile only grew in the following months. In November 2004, he became the third African American to be elected to the U.S. Senate since Reconstruction. By November 2006, he had delivered the keynote address at a major conference on religion and politics, graced the cover of *Time* magazine, appeared on *The Daily Show* and *Oprah*, and become the hottest Democratic speaker on the campaign trail.[3]

Along the way, Obama struck up a friendship with Rick Warren. Obama asked Warren to review a chapter on faith in his book *The Audacity of Hope*, and their relationship brought Obama—who had recently traveled to Africa to observe the AIDS situation there—to Saddleback Church. Obama's presence was notable in several ways. For starters, he also was eyeing a potential run for the presidency in 2008. Just as noteworthy, here was a Democratic politician addressing evangelical ministers at a meeting hosted by one of the nation's most prominent religious conservatives.[4] Indeed, several religious leaders had publicly criticized Warren for inviting the prochoice Obama to speak at his church. A group of antiabortion leaders, including Phyllis Schlafly of the Eagle Forum and Tim Wildmon of the American Family Association, issued a statement, saying, "You cannot fight one evil while justifying another." Rob Schenck, president of the National Clergy Council, charged, "Senator Obama's policies represent the antithesis of biblical ethics and morality" and expressed his hope that Warren would "find the courage to rescind his invitation to Senator Obama." Warren affirmed his disagreement with Obama's position on abortion, but refused to exclude him. Instead, he stood with Obama and Brownback on that December day and offered a sentiment that in previous years had been unthinkable from someone in his position: "I've got two friends here, a Republican and a Democrat. Why? Because you've got to have two wings to fly."[5] To amplify his point, Warren and the senators later clasped hands and prayed.

When Brownback sat down after speaking, Obama stood up and won over the audience. He began with these words: "Giving all praise and honor to God for bringing me here today, let me send greetings from my church, Trinity United Church of Christ on 95th Street on the South Side of Chicago." It was an I'm-one-of-you opening that echoed New Testament letters by the apostle Paul. Obama went on to speak warmly about Brownback, established his own gravitas on AIDS by highlighting the trip he had taken to Africa, and emphasized his faith. He said, for instance:

My faith reminds me that there are times where I have fallen and made mistakes. My faith tells me, as Pastor Rick has said, that it's not a sin to be sick. My Bible tells me that when God sent His only son to Earth it was to heal the sick and comfort the weary and feed the hungry and clothe the naked, to befriend the outcast and redeem those who had strayed from righteousness. Living His example is the hardest kind of faith, but it's surely the most rewarding. It is a way of life that can [not] only light our way as people of faith, but guide us also to a new and better politics as Americans.

Obama later turned again to biblical teachings: "Corinthians says that we are all of one spirit, and that if one part suffers, every part suffers with it. But it also says if one part is honored, every part rejoices with it." And he closed with "God bless you all. God bless Pastor Rick." The audience response was unabashed: a standing ovation and shouts of "Amen."[6] Obama had delivered a political sermon, one worthy of Bill Clinton, and to those listening it was as good as gospel.

The day's events had only begun for Obama, though. His talk at the AIDS summit functioned as a perfect narrowcast signal, and when he was done he turned his attention to a broadcast message: he headed to the television studios of NBC to appear that evening on *The Tonight Show with Jay Leno*. There, speaking to a much larger, younger, and more diverse audience, Obama again tied himself to Warren and talked about their shared objective. Asked by Leno what had brought him to town, Obama responded:

Today is World AIDS Day, and there is a pastor, a wonderful pastor, Rick Warren of Saddleback Church in Orange County, and he had an AIDS conference where he was bringing experts together from all various fields. And he asked me to speak at the conference, and it was wonderful, and I think people are, I think, getting educated across the political spectrum about HIV/AIDS.

Later in the show, Obama made his appearance at Warren's event seem like the most common and natural thing in the world, saying: "Everybody was reporting on me going to this church. It was like, 'There's a Democrat in church!' " Leno got the joke and followed it up with feigned disbelief: "Right, right. Good Lord!"[7] But what had occurred that day *was* newsworthy. In the religious politics that has dominated the United States since the mid-1970s, rarely have Democrats been invited to speak with conservative believers. And almost never have officeholding Democrats and Republicans—soon-to-be adversaries in the 2008 presidential campaign, to boot—stood side by side speaking about faith-informed politics. For all of those involved, this was a powerful signal: something new was afoot.

The curtain on Act II of America's new religious politics was raised that December day in 2006, with hints offered about potential plot developments to come. A number of rising religious conservative leaders wish to expand the playing field to include more issues and broader ideological partnerships. In addition to working with politicians of differing stripes to address AIDS, Rick Warren has joined with celebrities Bono, Tom Hanks, Ellen DeGeneres, and P. Diddy on a global antipoverty initiative, the One Campaign. T. D. Jakes, a conservative pastor with a large ministry in Dallas and the only African

American on *Time*'s list of the "25 most influential evangelicals in America," in early 2005 said, "I think it's wrong for us to think that God can be franchised and owned by either party. I think that God transcends political alliances and allegiances."[8] In 2006, nearly 100 evangelical leaders—including the presidents of 39 colleges and a wide range of Protestant and Catholic clergy—signed an Evangelical Climate Initiative to address global warming. Their statement included this declaration: "Love of God, love of neighbor, and the demands of stewardship are more than enough reason for evangelical Christians to respond to the climate change problem with moral passion and concrete action." And National Association of Evangelicals vice president Richard Cizik lamented in 2006 that whenever business and religious interests come into conflict in the Republican Party, business wins "[e]very time. Every single time. . . . We need to stop putting all of our eggs in one basket—that's just not good politics."[9] A diversifying of the moral revolution, should it occur, would be a tectonic development.

It will not happen, however, without considerable pushback. In July 2006, the Christian Coalition hired as its president Joel Hunter, the pastor of a large church in Orlando, Florida, and an outspoken critic of conservative evangelicals' intimate ties to the Republican Party. Hunter brought plans to expand the organization's core issues of concern: he publicly vowed to "rebuild and rebrand" the Christian Coalition and to make it less focused on "below the belt" issues of sexuality. Hunter added, "This is a changing of the guard." As it turns out, it wasn't, as both sides soon realized. Hunter resigned in November 2006, saying that the coalition's board "pretty much said, 'These issues are fine, but they're not our issues; that's not our base.' " For its part, the organization's board accepted Hunter's resignation unanimously.[10] Similarly, even though it had been encouraging the faithful to engage in "creation care" since at least 2004, the National Association of Evangelicals did not sign the Evangelical Climate Initiative in 2006 because of vocal opposition by almost two dozen conservative religious leaders.[11] These disagreements came to a head in early 2007, with long-time power brokers James Dobson, Tony Perkins, Donald Wildmon, Gary Bauer, and Paul Weyrich calling publicly for the ouster of the NAE's Cizik because of his focus on global warming—which they said was "shift[ing] the emphasis away from the great moral issues of our time," most notably abortion and same-sex marriage. The NAE responded by affirming its commitment to Cizik and to combating global warming.[12] Nonetheless, this face-off is indicative of what may come: those who have led religious conservatives to the political promised land will not go quietly, if they go at all.

A tipping point may arrive nonetheless. Sociologists and political scientists emphasize the role of "generational change" in transforming cultural beliefs and practices. The idea is that it is psychologically easier for people to be brought up within a new world view than to alter one they have always had. As a result, changes in attitudes that are seeded by one generation commonly aren't cemented until years later, when new cohorts come of age with different assumptions about the world. For example, the civil rights movement worked for decades before support for racial equality became the norm among political leaders.[13] It is useful, then, to consider a Harvard University poll of U.S. college students in 2006, which found that 70% said religion is an important part of their lives and that they, by a 4:1 margin, had become more spiritual since entering college.[14] Just as notable is that one-fourth were "religious centrists" whose issue positions did not come close to lining up along traditional partisan lines. Across a wide range of issues, from abortion and same-sex marriage to health care, international trade, the environment, immigration, and the responsibilities of the federal government, these individuals were *independent*. They also were committed to the public arena: they were optimistic about the future, participated in high numbers in electoral politics, and were deeply concerned about the moral direction of America. As a result, the report's authors said, religious centrists were positioned to be "the critical swing vote" in the 2008 presidential contest and "will likely be the most influential group in American politics for years to come."

Such centrist, moderate citizens will do much to decide the path traveled by American religion and democracy in the years ahead. In 1980, Ronald Reagan launched a "crusade" to transform America, and in the decades since both Republicans and Democrats have done much to turn religion into a political weapon. It has been done deliberately, it has reaped partisan rewards for both parties, and it has turned U.S. campaigns and elections into divisive moral showdowns. But for politicians interested in utilizing the God strategy, the political equation will be more complicated in Act II. Greater attention to the merger of God and country by institutions such as the news media and public education make such an outcome likely; the entrance of a significant number of Democrats into the game and the desire of some new-generation Christian leaders to look broadly across the political spectrum ensure it. How to entice people of religious faith whose views do not neatly coalesce along familiar political lines is the challenge for the next Reagans, Bushes, and Clintons—some of whom may bear these same last names. One thing is certain: someone will figure it out. A candidate will emerge to offer a finely calibrated, twenty-first-century message that appeals both to devout believers and the broader citizenry. And when this occurs, the public will be electrified anew. Whether religious or political, Americans are always looking for a savior. Our hope is that the nation doesn't lose its soul along the way.

# ACKNOWLEDGMENTS

✳

We are grateful to the many people who contributed to this project.

Staff at the University of Washington libraries, the University of Illinois libraries, the Lyndon Baines Johnson Presidential Library and Museum, the Richard Nixon Presidential Library and Museum, the University of Oklahoma Political Communication Center, the Television News Archive at Vanderbilt University, and the University of Maryland library's Archive and Manuscripts Department responded to requests and helped us fill gaps in our evidence. Jessica Albano at the University of Washington and Sahr Conway-Lanz at the Nixon Library and Museum, in particular, went beyond the call of duty in their assistance.

This research was supported by several grants. The University of Washington's Royalty Research Fund and William Test Fund in the Department of Communication provided time and research assistance. The Ernest Becker Foundation offered generous support at a crucial point in the project. Without all of this support, the book would still be in the works.

Clem Brooks and Jeff Manza were true scholars, taking time to aid our understanding of their research and sharing their data and analytic techniques. Scott Keeter and research associates at the Pew Research Center similarly were generous with their time, answering questions and sharing their data. Jay Childers and Julilly Kohler-Hausmann provided resources that facilitated our analysis.

W. Lance Bennett, Andre Billeaudeaux, James Caswell, Kenneth Clatterbaugh, Robert Eleveld, Jr., Anna Fahey, Greg Goodale, Michelle Hals, Allen Hilton, Dan Larson, Tom Sine, Mark Smith, Laura Stengrim, and Barbara Warnick offered valuable insights by reading drafts and talking with us. Clara Chaney, Mary Higdon, Madhavi Murty, Michele Poff, Penelope Sheets, and John Winters provided accurate and timely research assistance, and Julia Anderson assisted with data entry. Special thanks are due to Mike Coe, whose uncommonly thorough readings of multiple drafts of the manuscript improved it considerably.

# ACKNOWLEDGMENTS

Our editor at Oxford, Theo Calderara, challenged us to think more deeply and more broadly, and to clarify our arguments and findings. We are grateful for his support and investment in the manuscript from beginning to end. We also appreciate Peter Labella's original interest in the research and his scrutinizing questions, and thank Stacey Hamilton for seeing the book through production.

Most important, this book would not have been possible without the support of Lisa, William, and Julia. Their unwavering confidence inspires us; their endless patience sustains us.

# NOTES

❋

## INTRODUCTION

1. A transcript of Reagan's address can be accessed at www.americanrhetoric.com. That journalists pay attention to a politician's departure from prepared remarks was a point made by David Kusnet, the chief speechwriter for Bill Clinton from 1992 to 1994, in a public talk given at the University of Washington on October 16, 2006. Indeed, the *Washington Post* printed the prepared text it had been given for Reagan's speech and noted Reagan's departure from it. See "The Republicans in Detroit: 'The time is now . . . to recapture our destiny' " (1980, July 18). *Washington Post.* Retrieved June 12, 2006, from Nexis database.

2. Regarding the strategic sophistication of Reagan's campaign and presidency, see Cannon, L. (1980, June 5). "Reagan adds to organization, prepares to meet Ford today." *Washington Post*, A-16; Hertsgaard, M. (1988). *On bended knee: The press and the Reagan presidency.* New York: Farrar, Straus and Giroux; Maltese, J. A. (1994). *Spin control: The White House Office of Communication and the management of presidential news* (2nd ed.). Chapel Hill: University of North Carolina Press; Raines, H. (1980, September 27). "Lyn Nofziger: Barometer in Reagan strategy shift." *New York Times.* Retrieved June 8, 2006, from Nexis database. In 1984, one Reagan aide made this observation about the strategy of mixing religion and politics: "It's a gamble, but it's a gamble we'll win." See Williams, J. (1984, March 6). "The religious merges with the political in Reagan's campaign." *Washington Post.* Retrieved March 7, 2007, from Nexis database. Regarding strategic communications at the highest levels of American politics, see Domke, D. (2004). *God willing? Political fundamentalism in the White House, the "war on terror," and the echoing press.* London: Pluto; Goldberg, J. (2006, February 13). "The believer." *New Yorker.* Retrieved July 4, 2006, from www.newyorker.com/fact/content/articles/060213fa_fact1; Kuo, D. (2006). *Tempting faith: An inside story of political seduction.* New York: Free Press; Rich, F. (2006). *The greatest story ever sold: The decline and fall of truth from 9/11 to Katrina.* New York: Penguin. Regarding the drafts of Reagan's speech, see Willis, D. (1980, July 17). "Reagan acceptance speech six weeks in making." *Associated Press.* Retrieved May 20, 2006, from Nexis database.

3. See Goldman, P., with Doyle, J., Lubenow, G. C., Lindsay, J. J., Borger, G., & Clift, E. (1980, July 28). "Reagan's 'crusade' begins." *Newsweek.* Retrieved March 2,

2007, from Nexis database; Shales, T. (1980, July 18). "Tailored to TV: The prime-time polish of Reagan's speech." *Washington Post*. Retrieved July 28, 2005, from Nexis database. Shales noted that Republicans were ahead of the scheduled speaking times that evening, so much so that ABC and NBC missed Reagan's entry into the convention hall; CBS interrupted a commercial so as to avoid the same fate. Shales added: "Obviously, Reagan was in a rush so that his speech would be placed as strategically as possible in the midst of prime viewing time. Vice presidential candidate George Bush's acceptance speech was kept to a spartan six minutes, clearly in pursuit of the same goal, maximum exposure for Reagan." Poll information was retrieved May 22, 2006, from the Roper poll center at the University of Connecticut, available in Nexis database. See ABC News (1980, July 18, Roper accession number 0003979). Regarding the importance of evangelicals for Reagan's election, pollster Louis Field determined that, without the support of evangelical Protestants in the 1980 presidential election, Reagan would have lost to Jimmy Carter by 1% of the popular vote. See Balmer, R. (2006). *Thy kingdom come: How the religious Right distorts the faith and threatens America*. New York: Basic, xvii.

4. Quote about Democratic Party convention in O'Neill, M. (1992, July 19). "Democrats hail the hero Clinton." *Herald Sun*. Retrieved May 22, 2006, from Nexis database. Regarding Southern Baptists, this community had generally supported the Republican Party since the late 1970s. See Barnes, F. (1992, November 9). "The new covenant." *New Republic*, 32–33. Barnes noted that a Southern Baptist publication, the "*Associated Baptist Press*, has ballyhooed Clinton and Gore as 'the first all-Baptist ticket for the nation's two highest offices.' The Clintons and the Gores 'are as engaged in religion as any four people we've ever had running for office,' says James Dunn of the Baptist Joint Committee in Washington. 'They're not superficial churchies.'" See also Turner, D. (1992, July 18). "How will Baptists vote?" *St. Petersburg Times*. Retrieved May 22, 2006, from Nexis database.

5. A transcript of Clinton's address can be accessed at www.americanrhetoric.com. Clinton had launched his campaign in the autumn of 1991 by delivering three speeches at Georgetown University in which he talked of a "new covenant" on social policy, economic policy, and national security. His speech at the Democratic Party convention in 1992 was his introduction of the idea to the mass U.S. public. Clinton's speeches at Georgetown were noted by David Kusnet, personal interview, October 16, 2006.

6. For the news reactions, see Toner, R. (1992, July 19). "The bounce: Blunt reminders that it's not over until Nov. 3." *New York Times*. Retrieved May 22, 2006, from Nexis database; Greenfield, J. (1992, July 19). "Clinton pushes emotional buttons as party bids yesterday farewell." *Chicago Sun-Times*. Retrieved May 22, 2006, from Nexis database. For Quayle's comments, see Power, S. (1992, July 18). "Quayle says Clinton, Gore adopted GOP emphasis on family values." *Boston Globe*. Retrieved May 22, 2006, from Nexis database. For the Falwell and Robertson quotes, see "Evangelists blast Clinton speech." (1992, July 21). *USA Today*. Retrieved May 22, 2006, from Nexis database. For Clinton's appearance on the Vision Interfaith Satellite Network, see Gonzalez, C. (1992, July 20). "Clinton is queried on values: Addresses issues via religious TV." *Boston Globe*. Retrieved May 22, 2006, from Nexis database. See also Loth, R. (1992, July 26).

"Democrats use old-time religion." *Boston Globe*. Retrieved March 3, 2007, from Nexis database.

7. Washington delivered his address on April 30, 1789. A transcript can be accessed at www.americanpresidency.org. On the centrality of religion in the founding of the nation and throughout U.S. history, see Johnson, P. (1999). *A history of the American people.* New York: Harper Perennial. (Original work published in 1997). See also Noll, M. (2002). *America's God: From Jonathan Edwards to Abraham Lincoln.* New York: Oxford University Press; Wolfe, A. (2005). *Return to greatness: How America lost its sense of purpose and what it needs to do to recover it.* Princeton, NJ: Princeton University Press. On religion and the presidency, see Alley, R. S. (1972). *So help me God: Religion and the presidency, Wilson to Nixon.* Richmond, VA: John Knox; Hart, R. P. (1977). *The political pulpit.* West Lafayette, IN: Purdue University Press; Hutcheson, R. G., Jr. (1988). *God in the White House: How religion has changed the modern presidency.* New York: Macmillan; Meacham, J. (2006). *American gospel: God, the founding fathers, and the making of a nation.* New York: Random House; Smith, G. S. (2006). *Faith and the presidency: From George Washington to George W. Bush.* New York: Oxford University Press. Bellah quotes drawn from Bellah, R. (1967). "Civil religion in America." *Daedalus, 96,* 1–21; Bellah, R. (1975). *The broken covenant: American civil religion in time of trial.* New York: Seabury. In addition to Bellah's writings, see Marty, M. E. (Ed.). (1992). *Modern American Protestantism and its world: Civil religion, church and state.* New York: KG Saur; Parsons, G. (2002). *Perspectives on civil religion.* Burlington, VT: Ashgate; Pierard, R., & Linder, R. (1988). *Civil religion and the presidency.* Grand Rapids, MI: Academie.

8. Kennedy delivered his address on September 12, 1960, to the Greater Houston Ministerial Association. A transcript can be accessed at www.americanrhetoric.com. For the Falwell quote, see Kirkpatrick, D. D. (2004, November 1). "Evangelicals see Bush as one of them, but will they vote?" *New York Times.* Retrieved February 8, 2005, from Nexis database. On Dobson, see Gilgoff, D. (2007). *The Jesus machine: How James Dobson, Focus on the Family, and evangelical America are winning the culture war.* New York: St. Martin's Press. On the Catholic church's positions, see U.S. Conference of Catholic Bishops (2004). *Catholics in political life.* Retrieved June 7, 2005, from www.usccb.org/bishops/catholicsinpoliticallife.htm. On John Kerry's attempts to show fealty to the Catholic church, see Farrell, J. A. (2004, October 19). "Kerry cites Catholic-vote record: The Democrat says an analysis shows his strong support for church issues outside of abortion rights." *Denver Post.* Retrieved March 4, 2007, from Nexis database; Finer, J. (2004, July 5). "Kerry says he believes life starts at conception." *Washington Post.* Retrieved March 4, 2007, from Nexis database; Kranish, M. (2004, September 26). "GOP urges Catholics to shun Kerry." *Boston Globe.* Retrieved March 4, 2007, from Nexis database; Kirkpatrick, D. D., & Goodstein, L. (2004, October 9). "Group of bishops using influence to oppose Kerry." *New York Times.* Retrieved March 4, 2007, from Nexis database.

9. A copy of the "theology of war" statement was accessed on August 10, 2006, at www.sojo.net/index.cfm?action=action.election&item=confession_signers. On the Network of Spiritual Progressives founding, see Dolbee, S. (2005, July 28). "Left to

Right: Heeding last November's lesson, a new launch for liberals." *San Diego Union-Tribune*. Retrieved August 31, 2005, from Nexis database; Lerner, M. (2006). *The left hand of God: Taking back our country from the religious right*. San Francisco: Harper. Information on the U.S. Conference of Catholic Bishops' actions was accessed on January 30, 2007, at www.justiceforimmigrants.org. See also Gencer, A., & Padilla, S. (2006, April 6). "Mass draws on 'Justice for Immigrants' program." *Los Angeles Times*. Retrieved June 10, 2006, from Nexis database; Watanabe, T. (2006, March 4). "Catholic leaders hope to sway immigration debate." *Los Angeles Times*. Retrieved June 10, 2006, from Nexis database. On the voter guides, the *Washington Post* wrote, "Secular groups such as the NAACP, the League of Women Voters and the Sierra Club have long published election-year guides to issues and candidates' positions. Since the conservative Christian Coalition began distributing voter guides in 1992, however, it has faced little or no competition from liberal or moderate religious organizations." See Cooperman, A. (2006, September 29). "Religious-Right voter guides facing challenge from Left." *Washington Post*. Retrieved January 30, 2007, from Nexis database. See also Steinfels, P. (2006, October 14). "Voters' guides define moral compromises to take to polls." *New York Times*. Retrieved January 30, 2007, from Nexis database.

10. On the electoral implications of religious factors, see Green, J., & Silk, M. (2003). "The new religion gap." *Religion in the News*, 6(3, supp.), 1–3, 15; Green, J., & Silk, M. (2004). "Gendering the religion gap." *Religion in the News*, 7(1), 11–13; Green, J., & Silk, M. (2005). "Why moral values did count." *Religion in the News*, 8(1), 5–8. On the metaphor of dog-whistle communications, see Safire, W. (2005, April 24). "Dog whistle." *New York Times*. Retrieved March 7, 2007, from Nexis database.

11. On Bush's strategic mixing of religion and politics, see Wead, D. (2004, April 29). Interview for *The Jesus factor* (Television broadcast). Boston: Public Broadcasting Service; Dubose, L., Reid, J., & Cannon, C. M. (2003). *Boy genius: Karl Rove, the brains behind the remarkable political triumph of George W. Bush*. New York: Public Affairs; Fineman, H. (2003, March 10). "Bush and God." *Newsweek*, 22–30; Moore, J., & Slater, W. (2006). *The architect: Karl Rove and the master plan for absolute power*. New York: Crown. On the political dimensions of the faith-based initiative, see Kuo, *Tempting faith*.

12. The 16 words in Bush's address that captured public notoriety were these: "The British government has learned that Saddam Hussein recently sought significant quantities of uranium from Africa." A small sampling of the news focus on this statement includes Balz, D., & Pincus, W. (2003, July 24). "Why commander in chief is losing the war of the 16 words." *Washington Post*. Retrieved September 1, 2005, from Nexis database; Kristof, N. (2003, July 15). "16 words, and counting." *New York Times*. Retrieved September 1, 2005, from Nexis database; Marquis, C. (2003, July 20). "The world: How powerful can 16 words be?" *New York Times*. Retrieved September 1, 2005, from Nexis database.

13. Bush delivered this address on January 28, 2003, in front of a joint session of Congress. A transcript can be accessed at www.americanpresidency.org. Polls were retrieved August 5, 2005, from the Roper poll center at the University of Connecticut, available in Nexis database. See ABC News (2003, January 28, Roper accession number 0419796); Fox News (2003, January 29–30, Roper accession number 0420224); Gallup/

CNN/USA Today (2003, January 28, Roper accession number 0422485); and CBS News (2003, February 24–25, Roper accession number 0421534).

## CHAPTER 1

1. Quote from de Tocqueville, A. (1966). *Democracy in America.* J. P. Mayer & M. Lerner (Eds.). G. Lawrence (Trans.). New York: Harper & Row. (Original work published in 1835), 271. Information on Pew's 44-nation survey of religious beliefs, part of the Pew Global Attitudes Project, was accessed May 31, 2006, from http://pewglobal .org/reports/display.php?ReportID=167. The exact percentages of adults saying that religion was "very important" were United States, 59; Canada, 30; Great Britain, 33; Italy, 27; Germany, 21; France, 11; Japan, 12; Korea, 25.

2. Gallup quote in Bishop, G. (1999). "The polls: Americans' belief in God." *Public Opinion Quarterly, 63,* 421–434. Survey data drawn from Gallup, National Election Studies, and the General Social Survey. All surveys are random samples of U.S. adults, with sample sizes of more than 1,000 respondents in almost every poll.

3. Tocqueville quote from *Democracy in America,* 271. For a general discussion of the centrality of religion in the founding of the nation and throughout U.S. history, see Johnson, P. (1999). *A history of the American people.* New York: Harper Perennial. (Original work published in 1997). For more focused treatments of religion and politics in U.S. history, see Noll, M. (2002). *America's God: From Jonathan Edwards to Abraham Lincoln.* New York: Oxford University Press; Smith, G. S. (2006). *Faith and the presidency: From George Washington to George W. Bush.* New York: Oxford University Press; Wolfe, A. (2005). *Return to greatness: How America lost its sense of purpose and what it needs to do to recover it.* Princeton, NJ: Princeton University Press. On religion and the abolition movement, see McKivigan, J. R., & Snay, M. (Eds.). (1998). *Religion and the antebellum debate over slavery.* Athens: University of Georgia Press. On religion during Reconstruction and into the civil rights movement, see Chappell, D. L. (2004). *A stone of hope: Prophetic religion and the death of Jim Crow.* Chapel Hill: University of North Carolina Press; Harvey, P. (2005). *Freedom's coming: Religious culture and the shaping of the South from the Civil War through the civil rights era.* Chapel Hill: University of North Carolina Press. On religion and the Social Gospel movement, see White, R. C., Jr., & Hopkins, C. H. (1976). *The Social Gospel: Religion and reform in changing America.* Philadelphia, PA: Temple University Press. On religion and the temperance movement, see chapter 4 in Israel, C. A. (2004). *Before Scopes: Evangelicalism, education, and evolution in Tennessee, 1870–1925.* Athens: University of Georgia Press. On religion during the Cold War, see Oakley, R. (1986). *God's country: America in the fifties.* New York: Pantheon.

4. On the cultural place of Roosevelt and the presidency, see Greenstein, F. I. (2004). *The presidential difference: Leadership style from FDR to George W. Bush* (2nd ed.). Princeton, NJ: Princeton University Press; Leuchtenburg, W. E. (1988). "Franklin D. Roosevelt: The first modern president." In F. I. Greenstein (Ed.), *Leadership in the modern presidency* (7–40). Cambridge, MA: Harvard University Press. On the importance of modern

mass media in the presidency and U.S. politics more generally, see Jamieson, K. H. (1988). *Eloquence in an electronic age: The transformation of political speechmaking*. New York: Oxford University Press; Schudson, M., & Tifft, S. E. (2005). "American journalism in historical perspective." In K. H. Jamieson & G. Overholser (Eds.), *Institutions of American democracy: The press* (17–47). New York: Oxford University Press. On Inaugural and State of the Union addresses, see Campbell, K. K., & Jamieson, K. H. (1990). *Deeds done in words: Presidential rhetoric and the genres of governance*. Chicago: University of Chicago Press. On diversity and multiculturalism throughout U.S. history, see Takaki, R. (1993). *A different mirror: A history of multicultural America*. Boston: Back Bay. On the changing demographic and cultural realities in the United States leading up to and in the early stages of the modern era, see parts 6 and 7 in Johnson, *A history of the American people*. For an overview of the trends in American citizens' political participation, see Conway, M. M. (2000). *Political participation in the United States* (3rd ed.). Washington, DC: Congressional Quarterly Press. The quote on the escalation of American civil religion is drawn from Hart, R. P. (1977). *The political pulpit*. West Lafayette, IN: Purdue University Press, 12. See also Canipe, L. (2003). "Under God and anti-communist: How the Pledge of Allegiance got religion in Cold-War America." *Journal of Church and State, 45*, 305–324.

5. *The Fundamentals* volumes were published between 1910 and 1915. On the origins and influence of fundamentalism in the United States, see Marsden, G. M. (1980). *Fundamentalism and American culture*. New York: Oxford University Press. See also Beale, D. (1986). *In pursuit of purity: American fundamentalism since 1850*. Greenville, SC: Bob Jones University Press; Carter, P. A. (1968). "The fundamentalist defense of the faith." In J. Braeman, R. H. Bremner, & D. Brody (Eds.), *Change and continuity in twentieth-century America*. Columbus: Ohio State University Press; Furniss, N. (1954). *The fundamentalist controversy, 1918–1931*. New Haven, CT: Yale University Press; Sandeen, E. R. (1970). *The roots of fundamentalism*. Chicago: University of Chicago Press. On the Scopes trial, the issues at stake for fundamentalists, and the national news coverage, see Armstrong, C., & Wacker, G. (2000). "The Scopes trial." *National Humanities Center*. Retrieved February 22, 2007, from www.nhc.rtp.nc.us/tserve/twenty/tkeyinfo/tscopes.htm; Harding, S. F. (2000). *The book of Jerry Falwell: Fundamentalist language and politics*. Princeton, NJ: Princeton University Press (especially chapter 2, 61–82); Larson, E. J. (1998). *Summer for the gods: The Scopes trial and America's continuing debate over science and religion*. Cambridge, MA: Harvard University Press.

6. Ammerman, N. T. (1991). "North American Protestant fundamentalism." In M. E. Marty & R. S. Appleby (Eds.), *Fundamentalisms observed* (1–65). Chicago: University of Chicago Press, 27.

7. Quote from Harding, *The book of Jerry Falwell*, 76. The cultural empire that religious conservatives have developed over the past 75 years is vast and influential. For a thorough tracking of these developments, see Moore, R. L. (1994). *Selling God: American religion in the marketplace of culture*. New York: Oxford University Press; Wuthnow, R. (1988). *The restructuring of American religion: Society and faith since World War II*. Princeton, NJ: Princeton University Press, chapter 8. On the substantial amount of money generated by conservative religious organizations, see Boston, R. (2006). "Religious Right power

brokers: The top ten." *Church & State, 59*, 130–134. For a broader analysis of the impact of conservative religious organizations, see Diamond, S. (1998). *Not by politics alone: The enduring influence of the Christian Right*. New York: Guilford. Perhaps the most recognizable feature of religious conservatives' cultural presence is their use of mass media. On this point, see Blake, M. (2005, May–June). "Stations of the cross: How evangelical Christians are creating an alternative universe of faith-based news." *Columbia Journalism Review, 44*, 32–39. For a broader analysis of what scholars have called the "electronic church," see Hoover, S. M. (1998). *Mass media religion: The social sources of the electronic church*. Newbury Park, CA: Sage.

8. The characterization of the governing philosophy of Roosevelt and Truman is taken from Gustafson, M. (1993). "Franklin D. Roosevelt and his Protestant constituency." *Journal of Church and State, 35*, 285–297. On FDR, the New Deal, and religious groups see Creed, J. B. (2001). "Freedom for and freedom from: Baptists, religious liberty, and World War II." *Baptist History and Heritage, 36*, 28–43; Isetti, R. (1996). "The moneychangers of the temple: FDR, American civil religion, and the new deal." *Presidential Studies Quarterly, 26*, 678–693; Meyerson, H. (2004, December). "God and the New Deal." *American Prospect, 15*, 41–44; Woolner, D. B., & Kurial, R. G. (Eds.). (2003). *FDR, the Vatican, and the Roman Catholic church in America, 1933–1945*. New York: Palgrave Macmillan. On the emergence of "evangelicals" as a societal group, see Marsden, G. M. (1984). *Evangelicalism and modern America*. Grand Rapids, MI: Eerdmans; Sweeney, D. A. (2005). *The American evangelical story: A history of the movement*. Grand Rapids, MI: Baker Academic.

9. Polls retrieved May 31, 2006, from the Roper poll center at the University of Connecticut, available in Nexis database. See National Opinion Research Center (1954, January 1–13, Roper accession number 0100573); National Opinion Research Center (1954, January, Roper accession number 0096297); and Gallup and National Opinion Research Center (1954, May–July, Roper accession number 0034289). See also Aiello, T. (2005). "Constructing 'godless communism': Religion, politics, and popular culture, 1954–1960." *Americana: The Journal of American Popular Culture 1900 to Present, 4*(1). Retrieved November 6, 2006, from www.americanpopularculture.com/journal.

10. See H.R. 1693, 83rd Cong., 2nd sess. (1954), and H.R. Rep. No. 83–1693 (1954). For more on the Pledge of Allegiance, see Ellis, R. J. (2005). *To the flag: The unlikely history of the Pledge of Allegiance*. Lawrence: University Press of Kansas. Eisenhower issued his statement on June 14, 1954. A transcript can be accessed at www.american presidency.org. The phrase "In God We Trust" is reminiscent of a line near the end of Francis Scott Key's "Star-Spangled Banner," which reads: "And this be our motto—'In God is our trust.' " The now-familiar phrasing began to appear on some coins in 1864, in response to religious concerns during the Civil War. The Department of the Treasury maintains a history of the phrase at www.treasury.gov/education/fact-sheets/currency/in-god-we-trust.shtml.

11. See Harding, *The book of Jerry Falwell*, 77–78. On developments in the 1960s and 1970s, see Marty, M. E. (1987). *Religion and republic: The American circumstance*. Boston: Beacon; Reichley, A. J. (1987). "The evangelical and fundamentalist revolt." In R. J.

Neuhaus & M. Cromartie (Eds.), *Piety and politics: Evangelicals and fundamentalists confront the world* (69–95). Washington, DC: Ethics and Public Policy Center. On the early development of the conservative movement more broadly, see McGirr, L. (2001). *Suburban warriors: The origins of the new American Right.* Princeton, NJ: Princeton University Press.

12. Ammerman, "North American Protestant fundamentalism," 40.

13. On the response to *Brown v. Board of Education*, see Chappell, *A stone of hope*; Harvey, *Freedom's coming*. In the 1960s, slightly more than 70% of southern white evangelical Protestants who were "highly committed" to their faith identified as Democrats. This number declined to 58% by the 1970s, to 53% by the 1980s, 32% by the 1990s, and 27% by the turn of the twenty-first century. At the same time, identification with the GOP among this group increased just as dramatically—from 20% in the 1960s to 63% in 2000. A similar but slightly less dramatic trend was observed for lower-commitment evangelical Protestants and for mainline Protestants. See Green, J. C., Kellstedt, L. A., Smidt, C. E., & Guth, J. L. (2003). "The soul of the South: Religion and southern politics at the millennium." In C. S. Bullock & M. J. Rozell (Eds.), *The new politics of the old South: An introduction to southern politics* (283–298). Lanham, MD: Rowman & Littlefield. See also Leege, D. C., Wald, K. D., Krueger, B. S., & Mueller, P. D. (2002). *The politics of cultural difference: Social change and voter mobilization strategies in the post–New Deal era.* Princeton, NJ: Princeton University Press, who find similar trends. They attribute the early movement almost entirely to evangelicals' concerns about racial issues and the later movement (after 1988) to evangelicals' concerns about broader "moral" issues, such as abortion and school prayer.

14. On religion and politics under Richard Nixon, see Byrnes, T. A. (1991). *Catholic bishops in American politics.* Princeton, NJ: Princeton University Press; King, R. E. (1997). "When worlds collide: Politics, religion, and media at the 1970 East Tennessee Billy Graham crusade." *Journal of Church and State, 39*, 273–295; Wimberley, R. C. (1980). "Civil religion and the choice for president—Nixon in 72." *Social Forces, 59*, 44–61. According to Byrnes, Nixon's opposition to abortion helped him to attract Catholics who had been part of the Democratic Party's coalition since the New Deal. The *Newsweek* cover on October 25, 1976, proclaimed "Born again! The evangelicals," and the cover story dubbed it "the year of the evangelicals." On the voting patterns of evangelical Protestants in 1976 and 1978, see Brooks, C., & Manza, J. (2004). "A great divide? Religion and political cleavage in U.S. national elections, 1972–2000." *Sociological Quarterly, 45*, 421–450. The movement among evangelicals away from the Republican Party and toward Democratic Party presidential nominee Carter in 1976 also is apparent in surveys by the American National Election Studies, the premier nonpartisan resource for information on the U.S. electorate. NES data indicated that in the presidential contest of 1972, evangelical Protestants voted for Republican Richard Nixon over Democrat George McGovern at a ratio of roughly 4:1. In 1976, evangelical Protestants split their votes almost evenly between Carter and Republican Gerald Ford. Further, Southern Baptists in 1976 gave 51% of their votes to Carter. See Phillips, K. (2006). *American theocracy.* New York: Viking, 185.

15. Dorning, M. (2005, July 17). "Evangelicals out for a justice." *Chicago Tribune* (reprinted in *Seattle Times*), A5. See also Reichley, "The evangelical and fundamentalist revolt."

16. See Harding, *The book of Jerry Falwell*; Lienesch, M. (1993). *Redeeming America: Piety and politics in the new Christian Right*. Chapel Hill: University of North Carolina Press; Falwell, J. (1979). *America can be saved*. Murfreesboro, TN: Sword of the Lord Publishers. Exactly how many people watched *Old Time Gospel Hour* is unclear. Falwell and others claimed different audience sizes. That the audience was into the millions is undisputed. The *New York Times*, in 1980, put the audience size at 18 million, while *Newsweek*, upon Falwell's death in 2007, put the 1980 audience at 1.2 million. See Alter, J. (2007, May 15). "Don't believe the Falwell hype." *Newsweek* online. Retrieved May 16, 2007, from www.msnbc.com; Lewis, A. (1980, September 18). "Abroad at home: Religion and politics." *New York Times*. Retrieved March 6, 2007, from Nexis database.

17. Falwell quotes in Sawyer, K., & Kaiser, R. G. (1980, July 16). "The Republicans in Detroit: Evangelicals flock to GOP." *Washington Post*. Retrieved July 20, 2005, from Nexis database. On the Moral Majority, see Bruce, S. (1987). "The Moral Majority: The politics of fundamentalism in secular society." In L. Caplan (Ed.), *Studies in religious fundamentalism* (177–194). London: Macmillan; Falwell, J. (1987). "An agenda for the 1980s." In R. J. Neuhaus & M. Cromartie (Eds.), *Piety and politics: Evangelicals and fundamentalists confront the world* (111–123). Washington, DC: Ethics and Public Policy Center; Webber, R. E. (1981). *The Moral Majority: Right or wrong?* Westchester, NY: Cornerstone.

18. Polls retrieved August 30, 2005, from the Roper poll center at the University of Connecticut, available in Nexis database. See Gallup (1976, August 27–30, Roper accession number 0047015); Gallup (1979, December 7–10, Roper accession number 0028819); and Gallup (1980, August 15–18, Roper accession number 0029292).

19. See Wead, D. (2004, April 29). Interview for *The Jesus factor* (Television broadcast). Boston: Public Broadcasting Service. A chicken-and-egg issue arises when one attempts to identify the causal direction of the changes that have led to today's religious politics. Without the political mobilization of religious conservatives in the late 1970s, the God strategy almost certainly would have never developed. And if political leaders never adopted the God strategy, the mobilization of religious conservatives might have stalled early on. Therefore, both political leaders' use of this approach and the continued mobilization of religious conservatives are trends that respond to, but also *constitute*, America's new religious politics.

20. Bush's lengthy no-veto streak stands in contrast to Bill Clinton's 37 vetoes during his eight years in office, the 44 issued by George H. W. Bush during his single term, and the 78 issued by Ronald Reagan over eight years. See Abrams, J. (2004, January 6). "Bush may get through term with no vetoes." *Associated Press*. Retrieved January 16, 2004, from Nexis database; Benedetto, R. (2006, March 23). "1,889 days and no vetoes: Bush gaining on Jefferson." *USA Today*. Retrieved June 13, 2006, from Nexis database; "Bush's first veto." (2006, July 20). *Los Angeles Times*. Retrieved July 25, 2006, from Nexis database.

Another interpretation of this trend is that, in order to maintain unity in the GOP ranks, Bush was hesitant to confront his fellow Republicans; this is also likely part of the story. See Stolberg, S. (2006, July 23). "Bush's record: One veto, many no's." *New York Times*. Retrieved July 24, 2006, from www.nytimes.com.

21. Of course, with any topic, not only religious belief, it is impossible to know for certain what political leaders actually believe. We have only their words and their actions to provide clues. Consider again the perspective of Republican political operative and Bush family friend Doug Wead. When asked by the *Frontline* news program if George W. Bush's faith was "genuine," Wead replied:

> There's no question that the president's faith is real, that it's authentic, that it's genuine, and there's no question that it's calculated. I know that sounds like a contradiction. But that will always be the case for a public figure. . . . Gandhi once said, "He who says that religion and politics don't mix understands neither one." I would say that I don't know when he's sincere and when he's calculated, and a reporter for *Frontline* doesn't know. George Bush doesn't know when he's operating out of a genuine sense of his own faith, or when it's calculated, and there must be gray areas in between. I think he operates instinctively.

See Wead, Interview for *The Jesus factor*. Similarly, the Reverend Don Jones, a Methodist minister and long-time mentor of Hillary Clinton, had this to say about Clinton's faith as she entered the 2008 presidential contest: "She's not using the language of prayer and God for the first time. While there may be a political dimension, it's authentic." Quote in Meadows, S. (2007, February 12). "Hillary's religious roots." *Newsweek*, 30.

22. Wead, Interview for *The Jesus factor*.

23. For circulation of newspapers, see "FAS-FAX circ numbers for the top 25 dailies and Sunday papers." (2007, April). *Editor and Publisher*. Retrieved May 4, 2007, from www.editorandpublisher.com. See also "The state of the news media 2006: An annual report on American journalism." Retrieved June 6, 2006, from www.stateofthenewsmedia .org/2006.

24. On the dynamics of talk radio, see Campo-Flores, A., & Thomas, E. (2006, May 8). "Rehabbing Rush." *Newsweek*, 26–29; Kurtz, H. (2005, June 13). "On radio, more laughter from the Left." *Washington Post*. Retrieved August 30, 2005, from Nexis database. Air America filed for bankruptcy in October 2006 and was purchased by Stephen Green in early 2007. See Story, L. (2007, January 30). "Air America radio agrees to be acquired by a New York real estate investor." *New York Times*. Retrieved February 3, 2007, from Nexis database. On the public's usage of the Internet, see Pew Research Center (2006, July 30). "Online papers modestly boost newspaper readership." Retrieved November 5, 2006, from http://people-press.org/reports. On the importance of new technologies, blogs, and other online sites in today's U.S. politics, see also Finnegan, M. (2007, January 29). "2008 candidates, foes rush to roll Web video: Messages can be shaped, gaffes can be spread, at little cost." *Los Angeles Times*. Retrieved February 3, 2007, from Nexis database; Howard, P. N. (2006). *New media campaigns and the managed citizen*. New York: Cambridge University Press, 20–23; Lizza, R. (2006, August 20). "The

YouTube election." *New York Times*. Retrieved February 3, 2007, from Nexis database; Robinson, E. (2007, January 23). "Throwing their blogs into the ring." *Washington Post*. Retrieved February 3, 2007, from Nexis database.

25. See Chaiken, S. (1980). "Heuristic versus systematic information processing and the use of source versus message cues in persuasion." *Journal of Personality and Social Psychology, 39*, 752–766; Fiske, S. T., & Taylor, S. E. (1991). *Social cognition*. New York: McGraw-Hill; Kuklinski, J. H., & Hurley, N. L. (1994). "On hearing and interpreting political messages: A cautionary tale of citizen cue-taking." *Journal of Politics, 56*, 729–751; Mondak, J. (1993). "Source cues and policy approval: The cognitive dynamics of public support for the Reagan agenda." *American Journal of Political Science, 37*, 186–212; Petty, R. E., & Cacioppo, J. T. (1986). *Communication and persuasion: Central and peripheral routes to attitude change*. New York: Springer-Verlag; Shah, D. V., Watts, M. D., Domke, D., Fibison, M., & Fan, D. P. (1999). "News coverage, economic cues, and the public's presidential preferences: 1984–1996." *Journal of Politics, 61*, 914–943; Watts, M. D., Domke, D., Shah, D. V., & Fan, D. P. (1999). "Elite cues and media bias: Explaining public perceptions of a liberal press." *Communication Research, 26*, 144–175; Zaller, J. (1994). "Elite leadership of mass opinion: New evidence from the Gulf War." In W. L. Bennett & D. L. Paletz (Eds.), *Taken by storm: The media, public opinion and U.S. foreign policy in the Gulf War* (186–209). Chicago: University of Chicago Press.

26. Indeed, news media, sometimes to their own detriment, facilitate the public's reliance on such cues by increasingly looking for ways to package information in an easy-to-digest form. This is done for several reasons: the public is thought to desire it, traditional media follow new media which tend toward this style, news focuses on the "game" of politics, which has led to less issue coverage and more strategy coverage (which requires less depth), and advertisements shrink the space that can be allotted for news content, which encourages news to be presented as concisely as possible. See Bennett, W. L. (2003). *News: The politics of illusion* (5th ed.). New York: Longman; Hallin, D. C. (1992). "Sound bite news: Television coverage of elections, 1968–1988." *Journal of Communication, 42*, 5–24; McChesney, R. W. (1999). *Rich media, poor democracy: Communication politics in dubious times*. Urbana: University of Illinois Press; Patterson, T. E. (1993). *Out of order*. New York: Knopf.

27. These anecdotes can be found in Ivie, R. L. (2004). "The rhetoric of Bush's 'war' on evil." *K.B. Journal, 1*(1). Retrieved January 11, 2005, from www.kbjournal.org; Egan, T. (2006, June 4). "All polls aside, Utah is keeping faith in Bush." *New York Times*. Retrieved June 4, 2006, from www.nytimes.com.

28. Domke, D., Shah, D. V., & Wackman, D. (1998). " 'Moral referendums': Values, news media, and the process of candidate choice." *Political Communication, 15*, 301–321; Domke, D., Shah, D. V., & Wackman, D. (2000). "Rights and morals, issues, and candidate integrity: Insights into the role of the news media." *Political Psychology, 21*, 641–665; Monroe, K. (1995). "Psychology and rational actor theory." *Political Psychology, 16*, 1–21; Shah, D. V., Domke, D., & Wackman, D. (1996). " 'To thine own self be true': Values, framing, and voter decision-making strategies." *Communication Research, 23*, 509–560.

29. On the marketplace of religion in America, see Kosmin, B. A., & Keysar, A. (2006). *Religion in a free market: Religious and non-religious Americans: Who, what, why, where.* Ithaca, NY: Paramount Market Publishing; Finke, R., & Stark, R. (2005). *The churching of America, 1776–2005: Winners and losers in our religious economy.* New Brunswick, NJ: Rutgers University Press. The estimated percentages of religious identification for 1972–2000 are reported from American National Elections Studies data by Brooks and Manza, in "A great divide?" The 2004 estimates were derived following their analytical approach. Other identified religious groups include black Protestants (on average, 6–8% of the population, according to NES data 1972–2004), Jews (on average, 2–3% of the population), and "other religion" (on average, 2–4% of the population). For information on how NES survey participants were assigned to these religious categories, see Brooks and Manza, "A great divide?" and Steensland, B., Park, J. Z., Regnerus, M. D., Robinson, L. D., Wilcox, W. B., & Woodberry, R. D. (2000). "The measure of American religion: Toward improving the state of the art." *Social Forces, 79*(1), 291–318. On changes in religious identification among Americans, see Green, J. C., & Guth, J. L. (1993). "From lambs to sheep: Denominational change and political behavior." In D. C. Leege & L. A. Kellstedt (Eds.), *Rediscovering the religious factor in American politics* (100–117). Armonk, NY: Sharpe; Green et al., "The soul of the South"; Layman, G. (2001). *The great divide: Religious and cultural conflicts in American party politics.* New York: Columbia University Press; Leege et al., *The politics of cultural difference*; Marlin, G. J. (2004). *The American Catholic voter: 200 years of political impact.* South Bend, IN: St. Augustine's; Wuthnow, *The restructuring of American religion.*

30. Each partisan grouping in Figures 1.1 and 1.2 consists of people who identified with a particular party in a "strong" or "weak" fashion, or were independents who "leaned" toward a particular party. Each of these levels of party identification could have been separated, but the trends are largely consistent across them. Similar patterns of political party identification as those presented in Figures 1.1 and 1.2 can be observed in surveys conducted by the Pew Research Center since 1987. See Pew Research Center (2003, November 5). "The 2004 political landscape: Evenly divided and increasingly polarized." Retrieved December 16, 2003, from http://people-press.org/reports; Pew Research Center (2005, January 24). "Politics and values in a 51%–48% nation." Retrieved July 27, 2005, from http://people-press.org/reports. NES data offer longer time trends and also are valuable for several other reasons. First, they have consistently used the same mode of interviewing—in this case, face to face. Survey responses to poll questions about religion show a sensitivity to whether people are interviewed in person or via telephone; see Bishop, "The polls: Americans' belief in God." NES data are primarily collected face to face, and for the data we present in this book we eliminated any NES interviews that were conducted via telephone. Second, NES surveys tend to have high response rates, usually at least 60% and often much higher. Third, the NES developed a sophisticated approach to measuring people's religious identification, which allows for a robust examination of distinctions among religious groups (e.g., evangelical Protestants versus mainline Protestants). See Leege, D. C., & Kellstedt, L. A. (Eds.). (1993). *Rediscovering the religious factor in American politics.* Armonk, NY: Sharpe. On public opinion

polling more generally, see Asher, H. (2004). *Polling and the public: What every citizen should know* (6th ed.). Washington, DC: Congressional Quarterly Press.

31. Colson, C. (2000, March 2). "Dividing the faithful won't work." *New York Times.* Retrieved August 3, 2005, from Nexis database.

32. Keeter, S. (2006, May 2). "Will white evangelicals desert the GOP?" Retrieved May 26, 2006, from http://pewresearch.org/obdeck.

33. Part of the increases in electoral size of the "no affiliation" category may be due to a change in question wording in the NES data, which was implemented in 1990. However, an increase among secular citizens in recent decades can be observed in the General Social Survey, another leading nonpartisan body of survey data on American social and political life. See Brooks and Manza, "A great divide?" 447. Notably, Brooks and Manza use the term "no religion" to refer to the same bloc of voters that we label as "no affiliation."

34. Pew Research Center (2004, August 24). "GOP: The religion friendly party." Retrieved July 7, 2006, from http://people-press.org/reports.

## CHAPTER 2

1. All quotes from the debate come from the FDCH eMedia transcript of the event. See "Republican presidential candidates participate in political debate." (1999, December 13). *FDCH Political Transcripts.* Retrieved July 19, 2006, from Nexis database. In addition, a videotape of this debate was obtained from the archives of the Political Communication Center at the University of Oklahoma.

2. On the general media response, see "In God we trust." (1999, December 25). *Economist.* Retrieved July 18, 2006, from Nexis database; Rosin, H. (1999, December 19). "Bush's 'Christ moment' is put to political test by Christians: Act of faith or partisan ploy, it draws faithful's attention." *Washington Post.* Retrieved July 18, 2006, from Nexis database. For quote, see Dionne, E. J., Jr. (1999, December 28). "Religion and politics." *Washington Post.* Retrieved July 18, 2006, from Nexis database. For criticisms of Bush's words, see, for example, Berke, R. L. (1999, December 15). "Religion center stage in presidential race." *New York Times.* Retrieved July 18, 2006, from Nexis database; "Religion on the hustings." (1999, December 17). *Christian Science Monitor.* Retrieved July 18, 2006, from Nexis database. For the percentage of evangelicals among likely caucus participants, see Buttry, S. (1999, December 15). "Candidates focus on Christian beliefs." *Des Moines Register.* Retrieved March 11, 2007, from http://archives.cnn.com/1999/ALLPOLITICS/stories/12/15/religion.register. For the comments of Dee Stewart, see Wilkie, C. (2000, January 10). "Bush puts faith in Iowa: Religious message appeals to state's conservatives." *Boston Globe.* Retrieved July 18, 2006, from Nexis database.

3. Graham quote in "Graham rejects Farrakhan as 'unifying force.' " (2000, January 3). *Ottawa Citizen.* Retrieved July 18, 2006, from Nexis database. Richard Land quotes in Rosin, "Bush's 'Christ moment' is put to political test by Christians." Interestingly, Bill O'Reilly, host of Fox News Channel's *The O'Reilly Factor,* had exactly the reaction Land predicted. On his program the day after the debate, O'Reilly said: "I myself would have

171

pointed to Jesus Christ as a philosopher who's most influenced me." See "Impact: George W. and Jesus Christ." (1999, December 14). *The O'Reilly Factor.* Retrieved July 18, 2006, from Nexis database. Quote from the debate observer in Dionne, "Religion and politics."

4. The 1933 Inaugural was the last to be scheduled for the date of March 4. In 1937, the date of presidential Inaugurations was moved to January 20, where it remains to this day. This shift was a product of the nation's adoption of the Twentieth Amendment to the Constitution, enacted in 1933. To be exact, we analyzed 358 speeches. A full list of the addresses can be found at this book's Web site, www.thegodstrategy.com. These speeches were selected and retrieved from *Public Papers of the Presidents,* available online at www.americanpresidency.org. We analyzed all addresses that met three criteria: they were addressed to the nation, were broadcast live (via radio for early dates, via television for later dates), and dealt substantively with domestic or foreign affairs. Those that met one or more of these criteria but not all three were surprisingly few: they were largely cele-bratory (e.g., a speech on a holiday that primarily marked the occasion), were a pre-election or election-night address (these types trumpeted the value of voting or marked electoral outcomes), were the weekly Saturday radio addresses delivered by presidents in recent years, or were addressed to the United Nations. Our sample is consistent with similar lists compiled by other scholars. See, for example, Hinckley, B. (1990). *The symbolic presidency: How presidents portray themselves.* New York: Routledge; Ragsdale, L. (1998). *Vital statistics on the presidency: Washington to Clinton* (Rev. ed.). Washington, DC: Congressional Quarterly Press.

5. On the media coverage of presidential addresses, see Farnsworth, S. J., & Lichter, S. R. (2006). *The mediated presidency: Television news and presidential governance.* Lanham, MD: Rowman & Littlefield; Graber, D. A. (2002). *Mass media and American politics* (6th ed.). Washington, DC: Congressional Quarterly Press; McDevitt, M. (1986). "Ideological lan-guage and the press: Coverage of Inaugural, State of the Union addresses." *Mass Comm Review, 13*(1), 18–24; Schaefer, T. M. (1997). "Persuading the persuaders: Presidential speeches and editorial opinion." *Political Communication, 14,* 97–111. For various perspec-tives on the manner in which presidential communications shape public opinion, see Edelman, M. (1977). *Political language: Words that succeed and policies that fail.* New York: Academic; Entman, R. M. (2004). *Projections of power: Framing the news, public opinion, and U.S. foreign policy.* Chicago: University of Chicago Press; McGee, M. C. (1980). "The 'ideograph': A link between rhetoric and ideology." *Quarterly Journal of Speech, 66,* 1–16; Zaller, J. R. (1992). *The nature and origins of mass opinion.* New York: Cambridge Uni-versity Press; Zarefsky, D. (2004). "Presidential rhetoric and the power of definition." *Presidential Studies Quarterly, 34,* 607–619.

6. Consider, for example, a Pew survey in 2005 which reported that 66% of Americans felt politicians discussed matters of faith and prayer either the "right amount" or "too little." See Pew Research Center (2005, August 30). "Public divided on origins of life." Retrieved July 20, 2006, from http://people-press.org/reports. In the words of Richard Cizik, vice president for governmental affairs for the National Association of Evangelicals: "I sleep better at night knowing he [George W. Bush] is a man who isn't afraid to say he prays, just like George Washington and many other presidents." See Cizik, R. (2004,

April 29). Interview for *The Jesus factor* (Television broadcast). Boston: Public Broadcasting Service. For more on the use of religious terminology in American political culture, see Hinckley, *The symbolic presidency*; Lincoln, B. (2003). *Holy terrors: Thinking about religion after September 11.* Chicago: University of Chicago Press; Shogan, C. J. (2006). *The moral rhetoric of American presidents.* College Station: Texas A&M University Press.

7. For the comments of Wead and Cizik, see interviews for *The Jesus factor* (Television broadcast). Boston: Public Broadcasting Service.

8. According to its leaders, the religious conservative movement's mobilization in the 1970s was significantly spurred by concerns about "secular humanism" in the United States. Tim LaHaye, one of the founders of the Moral Majority with Jerry Falwell in the late 1970s, said, "Secular humanism puts man at the center of all things.... They label it democracy, but they mean humanism, in all its atheistic, amoral depravity." Quoted in Blumenthal, S. (1987). "The religious Right and Republicans." In R. J. Neuhaus & M. Cromartie (Eds.), *Piety and politics: Evangelicals and fundamentalists confront the world* (271–286). Washington, DC: Ethics and Public Policy Center. See also Lienesch, M. (1993). *Redeeming America: Piety and politics in the New Christian Right.* Chapel Hill: University of North Carolina Press, 139–195. The call to arms against humanism was sounded most loudly and widely by LaHaye, who wrote the 1980 bestseller *The battle for the mind.* Old Tappan, NJ: Revell. See also Duncan, H. (1979). *Secular humanism: The most dangerous religion in America.* Lubbock, TX: Christian Focus on Government. Duncan calls humanism "Anti-God, Anti-Christ, Anti-Bible, and Anti-American" (15).

9. Quote in Geertz, C. (2002). "Religion as a cultural system." In M. Lambeck (Ed.), *A reader in the anthropology of religion* (61–82). Malden, MA: Blackwell. (Original work published in 1966), 63. See also Hicks, D. (1999). *Ritual and belief: Readings in the anthropology of religion.* New York: McGraw-Hill; Sherkat, D. E. (2003). "Religious socialization: Sources of influence and influences of agency." In M. Dillon (Ed.), *Handbook of the sociology of religion* (151–163). New York: Cambridge University Press; Wald, K. (1997). *Religion and politics in the United States* (3rd ed.). Washington, DC: Congressional Quarterly Press; Wuthnow, R. (1994). *Producing the sacred: An essay on public religion.* Urbana: University of Illinois Press; Zuckerman, P. (2003). *Invitation to the sociology of religion.* New York: Routledge.

10. The mechanisms at work in such instances are known as agenda setting and priming. See Iyengar, S., Peters, M. D., & Kinder, D. R. (1982). "Experimental demonstrations of the 'not-so-minimal' consequences of television news programs." *American Political Science Review, 76,* 848–858; Krosnick, J., & Kinder, D. R. (1990). "Altering the foundations of support for the president through priming." *American Political Science Review, 84,* 497–512. On elite influence and opinion change more broadly, see Zaller, J. R. (1992). *The nature and origins of mass opinion.* New York: Cambridge University Press.

11. Land, R. (2004, April 29). Interview for *The Jesus factor* (Television broadcast). Boston: Public Broadcasting Service. Land claimed that when he made this point to evangelical audiences, it was one of his "biggest applause lines."

12. To be specific, in identifying invocations of God, we included all direct references to a supreme being, including terms such as Him, Thy, and Your when they were used to refer to God. One person identified all God invocations in the sample of presidential

addresses. As a check of the accuracy of this analysis, a second person read approximately 25% of the speeches. Agreement between the readers was .92, which was .84 after accounting for agreement by chance. See Scott, W. A. (1955). "Reliability of content analysis: The case of nominal scale coding." *Public Opinion Quarterly, 19,* 321–325. Notably, presidents throughout history have relied on speechwriters, but presidential speeches are still very much a reflection of the president. Speechwriters attempt to craft language that the president would be likely to use, and presidents are typically involved in the speechwriting process. See Ritter, K., & Medhurst, M. J. (Eds.). (2003). *Presidential speechwriting: From the New Deal to the Reagan revolution and beyond.* College Station: Texas A&M University Press.

13. See Beasley, V. (2004). *You the people: American national identity in presidential rhetoric.* College Station: Texas A&M University Press; Campbell, K. K., & Jamieson, K. H. (1990). *Deeds done in words: Presidential rhetoric and the genres of governance.* Chicago: University of Chicago Press; Stuckey, M. E. (2004). *Defining Americans: The presidency and national identity.* Lawrence: University Press of Kansas.

14. One might wonder if this increase in God invocations can be explained by a parallel increase in the total number of words in the average address before and after 1981. In fact, the average number of words per address during these two periods was nearly identical. Across the 358 speeches analyzed, the average number of words per address was 2,948. For the period 1933–1980, presidents averaged 2,924 words; between 1981 and 2007, they averaged 2,991. Notably, in high-state speeches alone there was an increase of 25% in words per address in the latter period, rising from 3,879 before 1981 to 4,838 since. This increase was far smaller than the increase in presidential God invocations beginning with Ronald Reagan.

15. Ronald Reagan held a moment of silent prayer in his second Inaugural in 1985. Because he did not deliver this prayer through spoken words, we did not include it in our comparison of Eisenhower and Bush's prayers. The Pennell quote, along with religious conservatives' reaction to Carter more broadly, are in Evans, R., & Novak, R. (1980, July 4). "Belted in the Bible belt." *Washington Post.* Retrieved March 9, 2007, from ProQuest database. The quoted material of presidents, here and throughout the book (except where otherwise noted), comes from *Public Papers of the Presidents,* available online at www.americanpresidency.org. We follow the punctuation of these documents in the quoted material.

16. Quoted response to Bush's speech in Rainie, H., et al. (1989, January 30). "His moment arrives." *U.S. News & World Report.* Retrieved March 5, 2007, from Nexis database. On the prayer service that concluded the Inaugural events, see Lee, J. (1989, January 23). "The calm after inaugural storm: Some are skeptical of weekend's folksy tone." *USA Today.* Retrieved March 4, 2007, from Nexis database; "Look at closing events of the inaugural weekend partying." (1989, January 22). ABC's *World News Tonight.* Transcript retrieved March 5, 2007, from Nexis database.

17. Large numbers of the American public see these two events as comparable in magnitude. For example, in a 2006 Pew Research Center poll, 47% said that the attacks on September 11, 2001, were "about equal" to the attack on Pearl Harbor in 1941.

Another 35% said the September 11 attacks were the "more serious" of the two, while 14% said they were less serious. See Pew Research Center (2006, September 6). "Diminished public appetite for military force and Mideast oil." Retrieved September 28, 2006, from http://people-press.org/reports.

18. This December 8, 1941, address before Congress—which included FDR's famous line that December 7 was "a date which will live in infamy"—was not included in our sample because it was not broadcast to the nation. Had it been, this address would have yielded results very similar to the December 9 address to the nation that we do analyze. Roosevelt had one God reference in the congressional address.

19. For audience information, see "For ABC, a winning season, at least on paper." (2001, September 27). *Washington Post*, C-7.

20. In the 358 speeches analyzed here, these two references to Allah were the only ones made by any president.

21. Carnes, T. (2001, November 12). "Bush's defining moment." *Christianity Today*. Retrieved March 4, 2007, from EBSCO database. Noonan, P. (2001, September 28). "God is back." *Opinion Journal*. Retrieved March 4, 2007, from www.opinionjournal .com/columnists/pnoonan/?id=95001236. *Post* quote in Milbank, D. (2001, December 24). "Religious Right finds its center in Oval Office: Bush emerges as movement's leader after Robertson leaves Christian Coalition." *Washington Post*. Retrieved March 17, 2007, from Nexis database.

22. Appendix B at www.thegodstrategy.com contains a full list of the words included in this analysis. Our approach is modeled upon one used by political-communication scholar Roderick Hart. See Hart, R. P., & Childers, J. P. (2005). "The evolution of candidate Bush: A rhetorical analysis." *American Behavioral Scientist, 49*, 180–197. See also Hart, R. P. (1984). *Verbal style and the presidency: A computer-based analysis.* Orlando, FL: Academic. To track presidents' usage of faith terms, we used the Concordance computer content-analysis program. Details about this program can be found online at www .concordancesoftware.co.uk.

23. For this analysis, we included variants of these terms as well. Specifically, we counted the presence of "mission" and "missions," "crusade," "crusader," and "crusaders." (The terms "crusades" and "crusaded" did not appear in these speeches.)

24. In 1954, Republican Dwight Eisenhower was in the White House and in the midterm elections the GOP lost 18 seats in the House of Representatives and 1 in the Senate. This shift of a single Senate seat was enough to put the Democratic Party in control of that chamber, to go with the Democrats' new leadership position in the House. This election was far from a wipeout for Republicans, however, so we do not consider it to be in the same class as the shifts that occurred in the 1946, 1994, and 2006 midterm elections.

25. Although Clinton had not previously used the word church, he had once said "churches"—in his 1994 State of the Union address.

26. We used the following speeches to mark the beginning and end of the five wartime contexts: Roosevelt's December 9, 1941, address to Truman's September 1, 1945, address for World War II; Truman's July 19, 1950, address to Eisenhower's July 26, 1953, address for Korea; Johnson's August 4, 1964, address to Nixon's March 29, 1973, address for

Vietnam; G. H. W. Bush's August 8, 1990, address to his March 6, 1991, address for the Persian Gulf; and G. W. Bush's September 11, 2001, address to his final address on January 10, 2007, for Afghanistan and Iraq. To examine which presidents were facing an election, we counted all addresses delivered during the first term as being in an "election" context. We also counted all of Roosevelt's addresses as being in an election context because he was never term limited. It was not until the nation's adoption of the Twenty-Second Amendment to the Constitution, enacted in 1951, that presidents were limited to a maximum of two election victories. Johnson was another unique case: he announced on March 31, 1968, that he would not seek reelection, even though he was eligible for another term. We counted this address and the four that followed it as not occurring in an election context.

27.  Among the past four presidents, party membership was the only one of the three factors to produce noteworthy differences in invocations of God and faith. Republican presidents Reagan, Bush, and Bush invoked God 46% more than did Democrat Clinton; conversely, Clinton invoked faith 9.8% more than his Republican counterparts. These differences are reflected in Figures 2.2 and 2.3. The presence of war and facing reelection increased God and faith invocations only modestly, between 4% and 7% in all cases.

28.  On the presence of television at the 1952 party nominating conventions, see "TV as a political force." (1952, June 8). *New York Times*. Retrieved August 28, 2006, from ProQuest database. The *Times* article said:

> This year's Presidential campaign will differ from all others that have preceded it in that television will take the voter everywhere, and put him face to face with the candidate. . . . The TV audience is now nation-wide for the first time in a national campaign, and the camera is also newly ubiquitous. . . . Never before has the voter had such widespread opportunity to get the "feel" of the man he may or may not vote for to sit in the White House. Never before has he been able, with his own eyes, to take measure repeatedly of the sincerity, the goodwill and the intelligence of a candidate for high office.

Further, the Museum of Broadcast Communications had this to say about television at the 1952 conventions: "The impact of the medium, only recently networked into a truly national phenomenon, was immediate. After watching the first televised Republican convention in 1952, Democratic party officials made last minute changes to their own convention in attempts to maintain the attention of viewers at home." See "Presidential nominating conventions and television." *Museum of Broadcast Communications*. Retrieved August 28, 2006, from www.museum.tv/archives/etv/P/htmlP/presidential/presidential.htm.

29.  Neuhaus, R. J. (1984). *The naked public square: Religion and democracy in America*. Grand Rapids, MI: Eerdmans. See also Dionne, E. J., Jr., Elshtain, J. B., & Drogosz, K. M. (Eds.). (2004). *One electorate under God? A dialogue on religion and American politics*. Washington, DC: Brookings Institution; Heclo, H., & McClay, W. M. (Eds.). (2003). *Religion returns to the public square: Faith and policy in America*. Baltimore, MD: Johns Hopkins University Press.

## CHAPTER 3

1. The quote from Jimmy Carter's pollster, Patrick Caddell, is drawn from the Public Broadcasting Service's *American Experience*. "People & events: Carter's 'crisis of confidence' speech." Retrieved August 21, 2006, from www.pbs.org/wgbh/amex/carter/peopleevents/e_malaise.html. On the genesis and development of Carter's speech, see this PBS documentary and also Goldman, P., with DeFrank, T., Doyle, J. A., Borger, G., & Hubbard, H. W. (1979, July 23). "To lift a nation's spirit." *Newsweek*. Retrieved August 21, 2006, from Nexis database. A Gallup poll conducted in the days immediately following the address asked, "Did President Carter's speech make you feel more confident in him as a leader, less confident or didn't it affect your opinion?" Among randomly sampled U.S. adults who saw the speech, 41% said "more confident," 16% said "less confident," and 43% said it had "no effect." Poll retrieved August 21, 2006, from the Roper poll center at the University of Connecticut, available in Nexis database. See Gallup (1979, July 18–19, Roper accession number 0048771). For examples of criticism of Carter's address, see "Changing the way things are." (1979, July 15). *Washington Post*. Retrieved August 21, 2006, from Nexis database; Kennedy, E. (1979, August 5). "Carter agonistes." *New York Times*. Retrieved August 21, 2006, from ProQuest database; Morganthau, T., with Doyle, J. A. (1979, August 6). "The mood of a nation." *Newsweek*. Retrieved August 21, 2006, from Nexis database; Raines, H. (1979, August 3). "Citizens ask if Carter is part of the 'crisis.' " *New York Times*. Retrieved August 21, 2006, from ProQuest database.

2. Cherry, C. (Ed.). (1971). *God's new Israel: Religious interpretations of American destiny*. Englewood Cliffs, NJ: Prentice Hall, vii. This idea that America is a chosen nation was largely born out of British Pilgrims' belief in the "English national-religious myth," which held that they were "divinely appointed" to do God's work. On this point, see Johnson, P. (1999). *A history of the American people*. New York: Harper Perennial. (Original work published in 1997), 20–33. See also Bellah, R. N. (1975). *The broken covenant: American civil religion in time of trial*. New York: Seabury, 36–60; Hughs, R. T. (2003). *Myths America lives by*. Urbana: University of Illinois Press; Hunter, J. D. (1987). "The evangelical worldview since 1890." In R. J. Neuhaus & M. Cromartie (Eds.), *Piety and politics: Evangelicals and fundamentalists confront the world* (19–53). Washington, DC: Ethics and Public Policy Center; Madsen, D. L. (1998). *American exceptionalism*. Jackson: University Press of Mississippi. Consider Jerry Falwell's words in 1980:

> America has more God-fearing citizens per capita than any other nation on earth. There are millions of Americans who love God, decency, and biblical morality. North America is the last logical base for world evangelization. While it is true that God could use any nation or means possible to spread the Gospel to the world, it is also true that we have the churches, the schools, the young people, the media, the money, and the means of spreading the Gospel worldwide in our lifetime. God loves all the world, not just America. However, I am convinced that our freedoms are essential to world evangelism in this latter part of the twentieth century.

In Falwell, J. (1980). *Listen, America.* Garden City, NY: Doubleday, 213–214.

3. A transcript of Reagan's address can be accessed at www.reaganlibrary.com. Of Winthrop's words, U.S. historian Perry Miller said that "in relation to the principal theme of the American mind, the necessity laid upon it for decision, Winthrop stands at the beginning of our consciousness." See Miller, P. (1967). *Nature's nation.* Cambridge, MA: Harvard University Press, 6. See also Lienesch, *Redeeming America,* 197; Morgan, E. S. (1958). *The Puritan dilemma: The story of John Winthrop.* Boston: Little, Brown, 69–87. On the expense and careful promotion of Reagan's campaign announcement, see Bergholz, R. (1979, November 14). "Reagan enters race, lashes out at U.S. 'leaders.'" *Los Angeles Times.* Retrieved March 9, 2007, from ProQuest database. On the coalition of Christian professionals that organized in support of Reagan, see Dart, J. (1979, December 3). "50 Christians agree to raise Reagan funds." *Los Angeles Times.* Retrieved March 9, 2007, from ProQuest database. For Reagan's burnishing of the phrase, see Hendrickson, P. (1979, November 13). "Ronald Reagan: Rugged runner in the biggest race." *Washington Post.* Retrieved August 21, 2006, from Nexis database. Reagan was not the first president or presidential hopeful to invoke Winthrop's vision. In January 1961, for instance, President-elect John Kennedy delivered a speech to the Joint Convention of the General Court of the Commonwealth of Massachusetts in which he quoted Winthrop's "city on a hill." Notably, Kennedy invoked Winthrop in less overtly religious terms than did Reagan. A transcript of Kennedy's address can be accessed at www .jfklibrary.org.

4. See Anderson, B. (1991). *Imagined communities: Reflections on the origin and spread of nationalism* (Rev. ed.). New York: Verso. See also Bloom, W. (1990). *Personal identity, national identity and international relations.* New York: Cambridge University Press; Hutchinson, J. (1994). *Modern nationalism.* London: Fontana; Niebuhr, R. (1967). "The social myths of the Cold War." In J. Farrell & A. Smith (Eds.), *Image and reality in world politics* (40–67). New York: Columbia University Press; Rivenburgh, N. K. (2000). "Social identity and news portrayals of citizens involved in international affairs." *Media Psychology, 2,* 303–329; Schlesinger, P. (1991). "Media, the political order and national identity." *Media, Culture and Society, 13,* 297–308.

5. Hackney, S. (1997). "The American identity." *Public Historian, 19,* 13–22. Hackney was the chair of the National Endowment for the Humanities when he headed the conversation on American identity. For a similar perspective on the importance of national self-image from an opposing ideological perspective, see Huntington, S. P. (2004). *Who are we? The challenges to America's self-identity.* New York: Simon & Schuster. On the importance of presidential addresses in shaping public images of America, see Baker, W., & O'Neal, J. (2001). "Patriotism or opinion leadership? The nature and origins of the 'rally 'round the flag' effect." *Journal of Conflict Resolution, 45,* 661–687; Beasley, V. (2004). *You the people: American national identity in presidential rhetoric.* College Station: Texas A&M University Press; Calabrese, A., & Burke, B. (1992). "American identities: Nationalism, the media and the public sphere." *Journal of Communication Inquiry, 16*(2), 52–73; Coe, K., Domke, D., Graham, E. S., John, S. L., & Pickard, V. W. (2004). "No shades of gray: The

binary discourse of George W. Bush and an echoing press." *Journal of Communication, 54,* 234–252; Entman, R. M. (1991). "Framing U.S. coverage of international news: Contrasts in narratives of the KAL and Iran Air incidents." *Journal of Communication, 41*(4), 6–27; Hutcheson, J., Domke, D., Billeaudeaux, A., & Garland, P. (2004). "U.S. national identity, political elites, and a patriotic press following September 11." *Political Communication, 21,* 27–51; Manheim, J. B. (1994). "Strategic public diplomacy." In W. L. Bennett & D. L. Paletz (Eds.), *Taken by storm: The media, public opinion, and U.S. foreign policy in the Gulf War* (131–148). Chicago: University of Chicago Press; Zaller, J. (1994). "Strategic politicians, public opinion, and the Gulf crisis." In Bennett & Paletz, *Taken by storm* (250–274); Zaller, J., & Chiu, D. (1996). "Government's little helper: U.S. press coverage of foreign policy crisis, 1945–1991." *Political Communication, 13,* 385–405.

6. See Ammerman, N. T. (1991). "North American Protestant fundamentalism." In M. E. Marty & R. S. Appleby (Eds.), *Fundamentalisms observed* (1–65). Chicago: University of Chicago Press; Blumenthal, S. (1987). "The religious Right and Republicans." In R. J. Neuhaus & M. Cromartie (Eds.), *Piety and politics: Evangelicals and fundamentalists confront the world* (269–286). Washington, DC: Ethics and Public Policy Center; Hutter, G. H., & Storey, J. W. (1995). *The religious Right.* Santa Barbara, CA: ABC-CLIO; Phillips, K. (2006). *American theocracy.* New York: Viking, 174–193; Wilcox, C. (1992). *God's warriors: The Christian Right in twentieth-century America.* Baltimore, MD: Johns Hopkins University Press, 9–14.

7. Quotes from Falwell drawn from *Listen, America,* 217 and 6; and Falwell, J. (1987). "An agenda for the 1980s." In R. J. Neuhaus & M. Cromartie (Eds.), *Piety and politics: Evangelicals and fundamentalists confront the world* (109–123). Washington, DC: Ethics and Public Policy Center. Televangelist Pat Robertson founded the Christian Coalition in 1989 after running for the Republican Party presidential nomination in 1988. Although he lost to George H. W. Bush, he parlayed his campaign operations into an organization that succeeded the Moral Majority as the primary political arm of the U.S. religious conservative movement. Robertson hired rising political operative Ralph Reed, Jr., who created a sophisticated organization with a focus on strategic communications, grassroots mobilization, and close alliances with the Republican Party. See Green, J. C. (1996). "A look at the 'invisible army': Pat Robertson's 1988 activist corps." In J. C. Green, J. L. Guth, C. E. Smidt, & L. A. Kellstedt, *Religion and the culture wars: Dispatches from the front* (44–61). Lanham, MD: Rowman & Littlefield; Green, J. C., & Guth, J. L. (1996). "The Christian Right in the Republican party: The case of Pat Robertson's supporters." In Green et al., *Religion and the culture wars* (86–102); Moen, M. C. (1994). "From revolution to evolution: The changing nature of the Christian Right." *Sociology of Religion, 55,* 345–357.

8. Lienesch, M. (1993). *Redeeming America: Piety and politics in the new Christian Right.* Chapel Hill: University of North Carolina Press, 47. Robertson quote in Donovan, J. B. (1988). *Pat Robertson: The authorized biography.* New York: Macmillan, 152–154. See also Sine, T. (1995). *Cease fire: Searching for sanity in America's culture wars.* Grand Rapids, MI: Eerdmans; Webber, R. E. (1981). *The Moral Majority: Right or wrong?* Westchester, NY: Cornerstone, 33–39. Futher, Robertson, in *The turning tide* (1995, Dallas: Word), said:

As we review the history of the United States, it is clear that every one of those promises made to ancient Israel has come true here as well. There has never been in the history of the world any nation more powerful, more free, or more generously endowed with physical possessions. . . . But these things did not happen by accident, nor did they happen somehow because the citizens of America are smarter or more worthy than the citizens of any other country. It happened because those men and women who founded this land made a solemn covenant that they would be the people of God and that this would be a Christian nation. (293–294)

9. Reed, R., Jr. (1994). "What do religious conservatives really want?" In M. Cromartie (Ed.), *Disciples and democracy: Religious conservatives and the future of American politics.* Grand Rapids, MI: Eerdmans, 3. For Dobson's words, see Dobson, J. (1994, June). "The year was 1954 and we were all very young." *Focus on the Family Newsletter*; Dobson, J. (2000, September). "One nation under God?" *Focus on the Family Newsletter.* Retrieved August 23, 2006, from www.family.org/docstudy/newsletters/a0012735.cfm. For Lienesch's words, see Lienesch, *Redeeming America*, 157.

10. A Pew poll in 2002 asked this question: "Some people think that the United States has had special protection from God for most of its history. Other people think the United States has had no special protection from God. Which comes closer to your view?" A plurality, 48%, chose the "special protection" view, while 40% chose the "not had special protection" view. Among white evangelical Protestants, 71% chose the "special protection" position. See Pew Research Center (2002, March 20). "Americans struggle with religion's role at home and abroad." Retrieved November 3, 2006, from http://people-press.org/reports. On the power of naming the nation, see Ceaser, J. (1997). *Reconstructing America: The symbol of America in modern thought.* New Haven, CT: Yale University Press; Merritt, R. L. (1965). "The emergence of American nationalism: A quantitative approach." *American Quarterly, 17*(2), 319–335. On the general importance of language about faith and nation, see Harding, S. F. (2000). *The book of Jerry Falwell.* Princeton, NJ: Princeton University Press.

11. In this analysis, we grouped "United States of America" together with "United States." Thus references to "America" alone were considered to be distinct from the phrase "United States of America." (The phrase "USA" did not appear in these speeches.) References to an "American" or to "Americans" were not included because they are more centrally about citizens than about the nation. So momentous are Inaugurations as celebrations of the nation's self-image that historian Conrad Cherry considers them to be "the sacred scriptures of the [nation's] civil religion." See Cherry, *God's new Israel*, 21. See also Beasley, V. (2001). "The rhetoric of ideological consensus in the United States: American principles and American pose in presidential Inaugurals." *Communication Monographs, 68*(2), 169–183; Campbell, K. K., & Jamieson, K. H. (1990). *Deeds done in words: Presidential rhetoric and the genres of governance.* Chicago: University of Chicago Press. Notably, Gerald Ford did not give a formal Inaugural address because he replaced Richard Nixon midterm. However, Ford's address on taking the oath of office was comparable in

style and content to an Inaugural, and was therefore included in this analysis. See Hart, R. P. (1977). *The political pulpit.* West Lafayette, IN: Purdue University Press.

12. As an indication of the cultural resonance and political value of these kinds of phrases, Congress passed a resolution that proclaimed December 1985 to be Made in America Month. Ronald Reagan issued a presidential proclamation in accordance with this resolution, which can be accessed at www.americanpresidency.org.

13. Harry Truman also invoked the "United States" five times in his Inaugural in 1949. The references made up half of his total of ten national references. No other president had more than three invocations of the United States in their Inaugurals.

14. Mohler, R. A., Jr. (2005, January 20). "Inauguration day: The pageant of democracy." *Baptist Press News.* Retrieved March 6, 2007, from www.bpnews.net/bpnews .asp?ID=19955. Land quote in "President Bush promotes freedom abroad, character at home during inaugural speech." (2005, January 20). *Baptist Press News.* Retrieved March 6, 2007, from www.bpnews.net/bpnews.asp?ID=19948.

15. Appendix C at www.thegodstrategy.com contains a full list of the terms used in the analysis of these two themes.

16. Safire, W. (1993, January 22). "The inaugural address: Almost an A." *Oregonian.* Retrieved March 6, 2007, from Nexis database. The *St. Louis Post-Dispatch* commentator was Woo, W. F. (1993, January 24). "Summoning values from our past." *St. Louis Post-Dispatch.* Retrieved March 6, 2007, from Nexis database.

17. Here we also counted the truncated phrase "God bless the United States," which occurred once—in Bill Clinton's 1998 State of the Union. Another possible way to analyze this trend is to narrow the phrase and look simply for any reference to "God bless." Taking this approach reveals just as remarkable a pattern. Between 1933 and 1981, presidents said "God bless" in their national addresses a total of 15 times. Between 1981 and 2007, that number jumped to 137.

18. Two people read the entire sample of presidential addresses and identified all instances in which the president in his concluding paragraphs invoked a divine blessing of some kind. Agreement between the readers was .92, which was .84 after accounting for agreement by chance. See Scott, W. A. (1955). "Reliability of content analysis: The case of nominal scale coding." *Public Opinion Quarterly, 19,* 321–325. The conclusions of presidential addresses are almost exclusively where requests for divine favor tend to appear, so examining presidents' closing paragraphs provides a good representation of how much of this type of language presidents used.

19. For the opinion poll, see Cillizza, C. (2006, January 30). "The fix: Insider interview: Cornell Belcher talks values." *Washington Post.* Retrieved May 18, 2006, from http://blog.washingtonpost.com/thefix. On literal symbols of freedom in the United States, see Fischer, D. H. (2004). *Liberty and freedom: A visual history of America's founding ideas.* New York: Oxford University Press. See also Lakoff, G. (2006). *Whose freedom? The battle over America's most important idea.* New York: Farrar, Straus, and Giroux.

20. Quote from de Tocqueville, A. (1966). *Democracy in America.* In J. P. Mayer & M. Lerner (Eds.). G. Lawrence (Trans.). New York: Harper & Row. (Original work published in 1835), 39–40. On the centrality of freedom and liberty for Falwell, see

*Listen, America*, 25–43. On the history of Liberty University, see *Liberty University Alumni Newsletter* (2005, Summer), 3.

21. For the words of Richard Land, see Roach, D. (2005, September 30). "America 'the defender of freedom,' Land says in debate." *Baptist Press News.* Retrieved August 21, 2006, from www.bpnews.net. In regard to the importance of freedom and liberty among conservative Christians generally, see Ammerman, "North American Protestant fundamentalism"; Falwell, *Listen, America*; Webber, *The Moral Majority*, 11–32.

22. Lienesch, *Redeeming America*, 157; see also 19–22.

23. Specifically, we identified all explicit invocations of a supreme being when connected with any of these words: free, freed, freedom, freedoms, freeing, freely, freer, frees, freest, liberty, and liberties. Notably, our approach is a conservative estimate of presidential emphasis on freedom and liberty because we capture only the terms themselves, not abstract references to the ideas of freedom and liberty. Two people read every linkage of God with freedom and liberty in the sample of presidential addresses. Together, they evaluated whether the president had spoken from a petitioner or prophetic posture.

24. The decision to raise taxes was certain to hurt George H. W. Bush with fiscal conservatives. With this on the horizon, Bush may have sought to shore up his support among the religious wing of the Republican Party by adding a prophetic statement to his speech. It was not a bad move: religious conservatives did indeed largely stay loyal to Bush even when economic conservatives did not. The electoral data presented in Figure 1.3 show that in 1992 evangelical Protestants were, by a significant margin, the leading group among Republican voters. These data, derived from American National Election Studies, are consistent with claims by leading religious conservatives that their support for Bush was solid in 1992 and that Bush lost because fiscal conservatives deserted him. See Toner, R. (1992, November 11). "The transition: The Republicans: Looking to the future, party sifts through the past." *New York Times.* Retrieved August 26, 2006, from Nexis database. In this article, Ralph Reed, Jr., is quoted thus: "If everybody else had delivered their votes the way we delivered ours, George Bush would be getting measured for a tuxedo right now." See also Mannies, J. (1993, February 3). "Schlafly spurns scapegoat role." *St. Louis Post-Dispatch.* Retrieved August 26, 2006, from Nexis database. In this article, long-time religious conservative activist Phyllis Schlafly said, "A significant number of people who vote Republican are pro-life. The pro-life conservatives were faithful to George Bush when all the economic conservatives left."

25. Falwell, *Listen, America*, 18–19.

## CHAPTER 4

1. Buchanan delivered his address to the Republican convention on August 17, 1992. A transcript can be accessed at www.americanrhetoric.com. In a formal sense, the University of Notre Dame invited Bill Clinton to speak on campus. Universities have control of their facilities, so the campaign could use a room at Notre Dame only with the

university's support. David Kusnet, the primary speechwriter for Clinton's speech at Notre Dame, said the campaign was interested in speaking at the university and worked through Democratic Party and Catholic contacts to make it happen. According to Kusnet, the Notre Dame address was one of a handful of speeches on the schedule that the campaign had identified as "crucial," as "one he's got to do well." Personal interview with Kusnet, October 16, 2006. At the time, Notre Dame was ranked number three and Michigan number six in the Associated Press college football poll. During his trip to the campus, Clinton visited with Notre Dame coach Lou Holtz. The two had first met in the late 1970s when Holtz was coach at the University of Arkansas and Clinton entered public service. Later, as state attorney general, Clinton had represented Holtz and the university in a lawsuit brought by three members of the Arkansas football team. For insight into the choice of date and logistical challenges for this speech, see Walsh, E. (1992, September 12). "Clinton decries 'voices of intolerance': At Notre Dame, nominee recalls JFK struggle against religious bias." *Washington Post.* Retrieved September 29, 2006, from Nexis database; Hansen, L. (1992, September 13). "Clinton's Notre Dame visit and its set up." *Weekend Edition*, National Public Radio. Retrieved September 29, 2006, from Nexis database.

2. The words "mirror image" are those of David Kusnet, who was the primary speechwriter for the Notre Dame address. Personal interview with Kusnet, October 16, 2006. So important was this connection to Kennedy that Clinton's speechwriters gave him a copy of Kennedy's address beforehand (according to Kusnet). In Clinton's speech, the parallels between Clinton's and Kennedy's situations were made plain. Clinton discussed the anti-Catholic prejudice Kennedy had faced in 1960, tied it directly to the 1992 context, and even explicitly referenced Pat Buchanan's comment about religious war:

> Our freedom of conscience depends upon mutual respect. Each of us must never forget that as John Kennedy reminded the Baptist ministers in Houston in 1960, "When intolerance is turned loose," and I quote, "today I may be the victim but tomorrow it may be you. Until the whole fabric of our harmonious society is ripped." President Kennedy was right. To preserve our social fabric we must always appreciate the wonderful diversity of the American tapestry. That is why like so many Americans I have been appalled to hear the voices of intolerance raised in recent weeks, voices that have proclaimed that some families aren't real families, that some Americans aren't real Americans and one even said that what this country needs is quote, "a religious war." Well America does not need a religious war, it needs a reaffirmation of the values that for most of us are rooted in our religious faith.

Clinton also tied his own entrance into politics to Kennedy: "On a hot summer afternoon 29 summers ago, I met President Kennedy in the Rose Garden of the White House as a 16-year-old delegate to American Legion Boy's [sic] Nation. That afternoon turned me toward public service." All quotes from Clinton's address are taken from the CNN transcript of the event, retrieved October 8, 2006, from Nexis database.

3. On the importance of carrying Catholics in the election, see Walsh, "Clinton decries 'voices of intolerance.' " Throughout the address, Clinton emphasized the similarities between Baptists and Catholics. He said, for example:

> Both Baptists and Catholics in different ways are rooted in the spiritual richness of America's working people . . . people for whom life is a daily struggle in which they must sweat and sacrifice for themselves and their families, for whom life is made worthwhile not only through hard work and self-reliance but through opening their hearts to God and their hands to their neighbors.

On the ideological dynamics of the visit, see Barnes, F. (1992, November 9). "The new covenant." *New Republic*, 32–33; Crier, C., & Shaw, B. (1992, September 11). "Clinton appears before the University of Notre Dame." *Inside Politics*, Cable News Network. Retrieved September 29, 2006, from Nexis database; Ifill, G. (1992, September 12). "The 1992 campaign: Democrats: Clinton says foes sow intolerance." *New York Times*. Retrieved September 29, 2006, from Nexis database.

4. In the order in which they're cited in the text, the news reactions were drawn from the *Chicago Sun-Times*; CNN; *New Republic*; *St. Louis Post-Dispatch*; *Washington Post*; and ABC News. All articles retrieved September 29, 2006, from Nexis database. The Boston mayor's quote is drawn from Ifill, "The 1992 campaign: Democrats: Clinton says foes sow intolerance." The Barnes and Wofford quotes are in Barnes, "The new covenant," 33.

5. On the importance of "cultural resonance" in political messages, see Gamson, W. A. (1988). "The 1987 distinguished lecture: A constructionist approach to mass media and public opinion." *Symbolic Interaction, 11*, 161–174; Gamson, W. A., & Modigliani, A. (1989). "Media discourse and public opinion on nuclear power: A constructionist approach." *American Journal of Sociology, 95*(1), 1–37.

6. The contrast between broadcasting and narrowcasting has been drawn by scholars interested in mediated communications. Broadcast messages are those disseminated through mass media, such as newspapers, magazines, television, and radio. Narrowcast messages are those disseminated via focused technologies, such as direct mail, fax machines, e-mail, and niche advertising. The key distinction here is between broadly targeted messages and narrowly targeted messages. Political leaders engage in comparable dynamics with their public communications. Some messages are crafted with an expectation that they will be understood by millions of Americans—for example, presidential addresses to the nation—while others are expressed with an expectation that only certain segments of the American population will receive or fully understand them. In both cases, the communications are in the public arena. For narrowcast messages, though, the expectation is that they will be particularly noticed and recognized by certain constituencies. Sometimes this is accomplished through selection of the communication outlets, and sometimes this is accomplished through selection of the topics. See Friedenberg, R. V. (1997). *Communication consultants in political campaigns: Ballot box warriors*. Westport, CT: Praeger; Jacobs, L. R., & Shapiro, R. Y. (2000). *Politicians don't pander: Political manipulation and the loss of democratic responsiveness*. Chicago: University of Chicago Press; Jacobs,

L. R., & Shapiro, R. Y. (2005). "Polling politics, media, and election campaigns." *Public Opinion Quarterly, 69*, 635–642; Overby, L. M., & Barth, J. (2006). "Radio advertising in American political campaigns: The persistence, importance, and effects of narrowcasting." *American Politics Research, 34*, 451–478; Wattenberg, M. P. (2004). "The changing presidential media environment." *Presidential Studies Quarterly, 34*, 557–572; West, D. M., Maisel, L. S., & Clifton, B. M. (2005). "The impact of campaign reform on political discourse." *Political Science Quarterly, 120*, 637–652.

7. The Southern Baptist Convention's Web site at www.sbc.net has a section that addresses the issue of "How to Become a Christian." The answer begins: "You're not here by accident. Jesus loves you, and He wants you to have a personal relationship with Him." According to Amy Black, a professor at Wheaton College, "[O]ne of the things that makes an evangelical faith look different, perhaps, than others, [is] there's an emphasis on . . . a personal relationship with Jesus Christ." See Black, A. (2004, April 29). Interview for *The Jesus factor* (Television broadcast). Boston: Public Broadcasting Service. See also McGarvey, A. (2004, April). "Reaching to the choir." *American Prospect.* Retrieved October 8, 2006, from Nexis database. Similarly, the National Association of Evangelicals "promotes fellowship, cooperation, networking, and dialogue as means of evangelical witness." This according to its Web site at www.nae.net. Also see Kellstedt, L. A., Green, J. C., Guth, J. L., & Smidt, C. E. (1996). "Grasping the essentials: The social embodiment of religion and political behavior." In J. C. Green, J. L. Guth, C. E. Smidt, & L. A. Kellstedt (Eds.), *Religion and the culture wars: Dispatches from the front* (175–192). Lanham, MD: Rowman & Littlefield. Kellstedt et al. describe the social embodiment of belief as the " 'belonging' aspect" of religion, focusing on citizens' affiliation and involvement with a religious community. They point out that for "beliefs to be more than abstractions . . . they must be learned, applied, and practiced by individual believers in their daily lives" (175). See also Leege, D. C., Wald, K. D., & Kellstedt, L. A. (1993). "The public dimension of private devotionalism." In D. C. Leege & L. A. Kellstedt (Eds.), *Rediscovering the religious factor in American politics* (139–156). Armonk, NY: Sharpe.

8. Campo, J. E. (1998). "American pilgrimage landscapes." *Annals of the American Academy of Political and Social Science, 558*, 40–56. See also Chidester, D., & Linenthal, E. T. (Eds.). (1995). *American sacred places.* Bloomington: Indiana University Press. On religious pilgrimages generally, see Davies, J. G. (1988). *Pilgrimage yesterday and today: Why? where? how?* London: SCM; Eade, J., & Sallnow, M. J. (Eds.). (1991). *Contesting the sacred: The anthropology of Christian pilgrimage.* London: Routledge; Morinis, E. A. (1984). *Pilgrimage in the Hindu tradition: A case study of West Bengal.* Delhi: Oxford University Press; Turner, V. A., & Turner, E. (1978). *Image and pilgrimage in Christian culture: Anthropological perspectives.* New York: Columbia University Press.

9. For example, when George W. Bush was campaigning for the presidency in 2000, he delivered a speech at Bob Jones University, a conservative religious institution that, at the time, prohibited interracial dating. When Bush took some criticism for the visit, Ralph Reed, Jr., former director of the Christian Coalition, highlighted the visit's religious importance: "I don't think it was an endorsement of racial exclusion, it was an

endorsement of the inclusion of people of devout faith." See Ainsworth, B. (2000, February 4). "Bradley rips Bush for stop at Bob Jones U.: South Carolina school prohibits interracial dating." *San Diego Union-Tribune*. Retrieved October 11, 2006, from Nexis database.

10. This quote was retrieved October 7, 2006, from www.family.org/prayer. Further, prayer among religious conservatives also often has a clear political component. For example, the Family Research Council's Prayer Team organizes citizens to pray for specific political policies, and on the Web site of the Traditional Values Coalition one can send a prayer directly to the president. For more on the Family Research Council's Prayer Team, see www.frc.org. For more on the Traditional Values Coalition, see www.tra ditionalvalues.org. There also exists a nonprofit organization called the Presidential Prayer Team devoted to "mobilizing millions of Americans to pray daily for our president, our leaders, our nation, and our armed forces." See www.presidentialprayerteam.org. On the function and importance of prayer as a religious and cultural practice more generally, see Dallmann, W. (1999). "The wonder of prayer." *ETC.: A Review of General Semantics, 56,* 184–191; Moore, J. P. (2005). *One nation under God: The history of prayer in America.* Garden City, NY: Doubleday; Zaleski, P., & Zaleski, C. (2005). *Prayer: A history.* Boston: Houghton Mifflin.

11. See Cooper, P. J. (2002). *By the order of the president: The use and abuse of executive direct action.* Lawrence: University Press of Kansas; Mayer, K. R. (2001). *With the stroke of a pen: Executive orders and presidential power.* Princeton, NJ: Princeton University Press; Watts, J. F., & Israel, F. L. (2000). *Presidential documents: The speeches, proclamations, and policies that have shaped the nation from Washington to Clinton.* New York: Routledge. Groups with a stake in specific presidential proclamations take notice of these symbolic documents. For example, in February 1983, Ronald Reagan issued a proclamation on the Year of the Bible. Bill Bright of Campus Crusade for Christ had a hand in this procla-mation, and he said: "I believe the greatest spiritual awakening this country could ex-perience could grow out of this." In response, the American Civil Liberties Union brought a lawsuit on behalf of 16 plaintiffs, seeking a declaration that the proclamation was unconstitutional. The ACLU claimed that the proclamation "exalts Christianity" over other beliefs. The suit was eventually dismissed by a federal judge. See Herbut, P. (1983, February 12). "Bible year hailed with varying degrees of enthusiasm." *Washington Post.* Retrieved October 11, 2006, from Nexis database; Hyer, M. (1983, November 26). "Reagan's declaration on Bible spurs suit." *Washington Post.* Retrieved October 17, 2006, from Nexis database. Another example came in June 1999, when Bill Clinton issued a proclamation declaring June to be Gay and Lesbian Pride Month. Within days, the Southern Baptist Convention issued a resolution that "call[ed] upon the President to rescind his proclamation endorsing homosexuality." Paige Patterson, then president of the convention, said Clinton's proclamation was "entirely inconsistent with his confession as an evangelical Christian and certainly as a Southern Baptist." See Vara, R. (1999, June 15). "Baptist church urged to discipline Clinton: President's gay pride proclamation criti-cized." *Houston Chronicle.* Retrieved October 11, 2006, from Nexis database; White, G.

(1999, June 17). "Southern Baptists rebuke Clinton on gays." *Atlanta Journal-Constitution*. Retrieved October 11, 2006, from Nexis database. For other examples of presidential proclamations being noticed by targeted groups, see Bush, G. W. (2002). "National Bone and Joint Decade: 2002–2011: A proclamation by the president of the United States of America." *Journal of Bone and Joint Surgery, American volume, 84A*, 1297; Clinton, W. J. (1998). "President issues proclamation declaring April Cancer Control Month." *Journal of the National Cancer Institute, 88*, 580–581; Reagan, R. (1985). "Law Day statements: U.S. president Ronald Reagan: A proclamation." *New Jersey Law Journal, 115*, 1.

12. Quote from Geertz, C. (2002). "Religion as a cultural system." In M. Lambeck (Ed.), *A reader in the anthropology of religion* (61–82). Malden, MA: Blackwell. (Original work published in 1966), 26. On the importance of ritual in religion, see Bellah, R. N. (2003). "The ritual roots of society and culture." In M. Dillon (Ed.), *Handbook of the sociology of religion* (31–44). New York: Cambridge University Press; Rappaport, R. A. (1999). *Ritual and religion in the making of humanity*. New York: Cambridge University Press. On the importance of ritual more broadly, see Rothenbuhler, E. W. (1998). *Ritual communication: From everyday conversation to mediated ceremony*. Thousand Oaks, CA: Sage.

13. On the Alliance Defense Fund's actions, see Tucker, N. (2005, December 20). "Have a holly, jolly holiday: Conservatives, others angry over removals of word 'Christmas.'" *Washington Post*. Retrieved October 7, 2006, from Nexis database. The attention paid to presidential commemorations of Christmas became apparent in December 2005, when some religious conservatives voiced their displeasure about the White House Christmas card, which offered best wishes for the "holiday season" but did not mention Christmas. Notably, however, the card did contain a Bible verse. See Cooperman, A. (2005, December 7). "'Holiday' cards ring hollow for some on Bushes' list." *Washington Post*. Retrieved October 7, 2006, from Nexis database.

14. Quote from Campo, "American pilgrimage landscapes," 41. Campo writes, "Not only are pilgrimage themes and metaphors thus inscribed in our national narratives, explicitly and implicitly, but our country's territory has come to incorporate a variety of actual pilgrimage centers and routes." For a broader analysis of how presidential speeches are influenced by geography, see Hart, R. P. (1987). *The sound of leadership: Presidential communication in the modern age*. Chicago: University of Chicago Press.

15. Appendix D at www.thegodstrategy.com contains a list of identified remarks. The number 15,000 is a conservative estimate of the total formal presidential remarks made to public audiences between 1933 and early 2007. We generated this estimate by searching *Public Papers of the Presidents* (online at www.americanpresidency.org) for the term "remarks," which is the label usually given to public speeches made by presidents. To identify presidential pilgrimages, two people read through the titles of presidential public remarks outside the White House and compiled independent lists of addresses delivered at religious sites or to distinctly religious audiences. As a check on the remarks identified as pilgrimages, the entire body of titles was read a third time. Notably, when presidents made comments to the press after attending their home churches, we did not consider those to be pilgrimages. Such remarks were uncommon.

16. One might wonder if the increase in foreign religious pilgrimages beginning with Ronald Reagan in 1981 is the result of a general increase in foreign appearances by U.S. presidents. Scholar Lyn Ragsdale tracked foreign presidential appearances beginning with Harry Truman in 1945 through Bill Clinton's fifth year in the White House, 1997. From Truman through the end of Jimmy Carter's term in 1981, presidents averaged 14.6 foreign appearances a year. From Reagan in 1981 through Clinton in 1997, presidents averaged 24.8 foreign appearances a year—a 70% increase over pre-Reagan presidents. This increase pales relative to the rise in presidential foreign pilgrimages with a distinctly religious emphasis: the per-term increase in these pilgrimages, illustrated in Figure 4.2, shows a 766% increase beginning with Reagan's presidency. See Ragsdale, L. (1998). *Vital statistics on the presidency: Washington to Clinton* (Rev. ed.). Washington, DC: Congressional Quarterly Press, 173.

17. Bush spoke at Beijing's Gangwashi Protestant Church on November 20, 2005. The photograph appeared on the front page of the *New York Times* on the same date, which was possible due to the time-zone differences. One of the authors of this book was traveling by airplane that day, and he saw the same photograph on the front of several major U.S. newspapers. Richard Land said he was "delighted the president chose to highlight the cause of religious freedom while he was in China. He has done this before, and it does help to keep the issue on the front burner both in world opinion and with Chinese government officials." Strode, T. (2005, November 23). "Bush's visit to church in China applauded by Baptist leader." *Baptist Press News.* Retrieved March 6, 2007, from www.bpnews.net/bpnews.asp?ID=22145. In regard to the importance of Pope John Paul II, consider that after Reagan took office in 1981, presidents also met on U.S. soil with this pontiff four times during his visits: in 1987, 1993, 1995, and 1998.

18. In a few instances, a president spoke to an audience affiliated with an institution of higher education in an off-campus location. Jimmy Carter on December 9, 1979, spoke at a fundraising dinner for the Tip O'Neill Professor's Chair at Boston College. Ronald Reagan on September 23, 1986, spoke at a scholarship fundraising dinner for Eureka College, his alma mater. Both of these events were held at hotels. George W. Bush on January 17, 2005, and again on January 16, 2006, spoke at Georgetown University's Let Freedom Ring celebration; in both cases Bush spoke at the Kennedy Center for the Performing Arts, located in Washington, DC. All of these instances were considered to be pilgrimages to educational sites with religious symbolism.

19. Clinton's remarks at the Church of God in Christ in Memphis, where Martin Luther King, Jr., had given his final sermon, were delivered November 13, 1993. That these were extemporaneous is according to Clinton's chief speechwriter, David Kusnet (personal interview, October 16, 2006). In his address, Clinton quoted Martin Luther King, Jr., thus: "If Martin Luther King, who said, 'Like Moses, I am on the mountaintop, and I can see the promised land, but I'm not going to be able to get there with you, but we will get there'—if he were to reappear by my side today and give us a report card on the last 25 years, what would he say?" Notably, Clinton and George W. Bush were distinct from Reagan and George H. W. Bush in their public remarks at funeral and memorial services. Clinton spoke at 11 such services during his presidency, and the younger Bush

had spoken at six through the halfway point of his second term. No other president did so more than twice.

20. This prayer breakfast was first held on February 5, 1953, and Dwight Eisenhower spoke at its inaugural event. Eisenhower spoke at this breakfast one other time during his presidency, in 1956. Kennedy in 1961 spoke at the event at his first opportunity, and presidents have not missed the annual prayer breakfast since. It is held in late January or early February. On these breakfasts, see Kuo, D. (2006). *Tempting faith: An inside story of political seduction.* New York: Free Press, 21–24.

21. To assess whether the increases in presidential pilgrimages to religious educational institutions and to meetings with religious groups were simply reflective of a general increase in targeted presidential communications, we again turned to research by Lyn Ragsdale. She tracked what she calls "minor presidential speeches"—defined as "remarks made to a specific group or in a certain forum" and "[o]ften given at university commencements or various labor, business, or professional association conventions." These communications serve as a useful point of reference. From Harry Truman in 1945 through the end of Jimmy Carter's term in 1981, presidents averaged 9.9 minor presidential speeches a year. From Ronald Reagan in 1981 through Bill Clinton in 1997, presidents averaged 16 of these speeches a year—a 61% increase over pre-Reagan presidents. In contrast, presidential pilgrimages to religious educational settings and to meetings with religious groups, shown in Figure 4.2, increased by 176% beginning with Reagan's presidency. See Ragsdale, *Vital statistics on the presidency: Washington to Clinton,* 174–175.

22. The National Association of Evangelicals represents 60 denominations and 30 million citizens nationwide, according to its Web site (accessed on October 26, 2006) at www.nae.net. The National Religious Broadcasters Association, according to its Web site, is "an international association of Christian communicators with over 1400 member organizations representing millions of viewers, listeners, and readers. The Association exists to represent the Christian broadcasters' right to communicate the Gospel of Jesus Christ to a lost and dying world." The Web site (accessed on October 26, 2006) is located at www.nrb.org.

23. Blake, M. (2003, May/June). "Stations of the cross: How evangelical Christians are creating an alternative universe of faith-based news." *Columbia Journalism Review.* Retrieved July 4, 2007, from http://cjrarchives.org/issues/2005/3/blake-evangelist.asp.

24. On the distinctly political element of these meetings about the faith-based initiative, see Kuo, *Tempting faith.*

25. See Cooper, *By the order of the president,* 136–138. Cooper suggests that there are essentially three varieties of presidential proclamations:

> First, and by far the most numerous, are the hortatory proclamations that single out particular individuals, groups, or occasions for recognition and celebration. Second are those proclamations that are like presidential determinations and their domestic equivalent. These are used to invoke particular statutory or constitutional powers and can result in very significant actions. Third, there are policy

pronouncements issued to those outside government that have the force of law, often issued in conjunction with another policy instrument, such as an executive order or an executive agreement. (122)

We focus on religiously inclined proclamations, almost all of which fall within the first grouping. Notably, some presidential proclamations are issued in response to resolutions passed by Congress. In such cases, the proclamation notes that Congress "has authorized and requested the President to issue a proclamation" on a particular matter. Even in such instances, a president has the final say both in whether to issue a proclamation and in what that proclamation will say.

26. Stephen B. Chapman writes a regular column, "Living by the word," in *Christian Century* magazine. In the October 17, 2006, issue, he said, "I know that the church has many faithful voices, whose week-in, week-out proclamation of Christ continues courageously in spite of the smug apathy generated by the consumeristic wealth of our culture." Later, he added, "The Christian leader who belittles someone or puffs up himself or herself at another's expense cannot proclaim the gospel adequately because that leader no longer lives it." See Chapman, S. B. (2006, October 17). "Living by the word: Upside-down world." *Christian Century*, 21. See also Dickie, M. K. (2004). "Priestly proclamations and sacred laws." *Classical Quarterly, 54*, 579–591; Duling, D. C., & Perrin, N. (1994). *The New Testament: Proclamation and parenesis, myth and history.* Fort Worth, TX: Harcourt Brace; Ellingsen, M. (1990). *The integrity of biblical narrative: Story in theology and proclamation.* Minneapolis, MN: Fortress; McNeil, L. F. (2004). "Thinking of Christ: Proclamation, explanation, meaning." *Theological Studies, 65*, 662–663.

27. Appendix E at www.thegodstrategy.com contains a list of identified proclamations. Two people read the titles and compiled independent lists of proclamations deemed to be religious. Titles tended to be quite descriptive and highlighted religious emphases when present. In the small number of cases when there were questions, the proclamations were read and a final decision was reached. As with our analysis of presidential pilgrimages, we focused only on proclamations that emphasized the Christian faith.

28. Presidential issuance of proclamations has risen significantly since Franklin Roosevelt took office, with a considerable jump beginning with Ronald Reagan's presidency. From Roosevelt through Jimmy Carter in 1981, presidents issued 2,784 proclamations, an average of 232 per four-year term. From Reagan through the halfway mark of George W. Bush's second term, presidents issued 3,284 proclamations, an average of 505 per term. Once again, Reagan's entry into the White House was a defining moment. This increase in presidential proclamations among the past four presidents (more than a doubling of the issuance rate) was far outpaced, the data in Figure 4.3 show, by the increases of the two most notable categories of religious proclamations.

29. Harry Truman in 1948 issued the first proclamation that designated Memorial Day as a day of prayer for peace. He did so again in 1949, and then Congress passed a resolution in 1950 that Truman signed, making this an annual matter. Since then, presidents have annually issued a proclamation about Memorial Day as a day of prayer for peace, except in 1951, when Truman spoke about Memorial Day in this vein as part of a press conference,

but did not issue a proclamation. In 1952, Congress issued a joint resolution creating an annual National Day of Prayer, and that year Truman issued the first proclamation of this series. Every year since, presidents have issued a proclamation regarding this day. In 1988, the law was amended and signed by President Reagan, permanently setting the day as the first Thursday of every May. The National Day of Prayer Task Force Web site was accessed on March 17, 2007, at www.ndptf.org/press_room/index.cfm. Information about the organization's history was collected from this site, as was the quote regarding the organization's purpose. On the political ends of National Days of Prayer, see Kuo, *Tempting faith*, 230.

30. Many presidential proclamations are available at www.americanpresidency.org, which is the source of all of the quoted proclamations material in this section.

31. In the words of a spokesperson for the organization, "It would be a substantial setback for us if Ronald Reagan is not re-elected." Quotes in Associated Press. (1983, January 24). "Thousands rally against abortion." Retrieved October 17, 2006, from Nexis database.

32. See, for example, Christian Coalition (2007, January 20). "Washington weekly review." Retrieved March 12, 2007, from www.cc.org/content.cfm?id=380&srch= proclamation; "Pro-life marchers in Washington told they are winning the real-life battle." (2007, January 23). *Baptist Press News*. Retrieved March 12, 2007, from www .bpnews.net/bpnews.asp?id=24818.

33. John Gibson's book was published by Penguin Books in October 2005. Gibson makes clear his view that more is at stake in this "war" than a single holiday. As he puts it: "The war on Christmas is worse than I thought—and perhaps than you thought, because it's really a war on Christianity" (160). The Family Research Council's publication was released on December 20, 2005, and was retrieved October 18, 2006, from the Family Research Council Web site at www.frc.org. See also Gumbel, A. (2005, December 8). "Happy holidays? Not if the Christian Right has its way." *Independent*. Retrieved October 17, 2006, from Nexis database; Rutledge, R. (2005, December 3). "A crusade over Christmas: Christian group slams secularization; others call issue 'manufactured.'" *Milwaukee Journal Sentinel*. Retrieved October 7, 2006, from Nexis database; Thomas, E. (2005, November 18). "AFA founders urge pro-family holiday season shoppers to shun Target." *Agape Press*. Retrieved October 18, 2006, from http://headlines.agapepress.org/ archive/11/afa/182005b.asp. On the idea of a culture war generally, see Hunter, J. D. (1991). *Culture wars: The struggle to define America*. New York: Basic. See also Fiorina, M., with Abrams, S. J., & Pope, J. C. (2005). *Culture war? The myth of a polarized America*. New York: Pearson Longman; Sharp, E. B. (Ed.). (1999). *Culture wars and local politics*. Lawrence: University Press of Kansas.

34. See Pew Forum on Religion and Public Life (2006, December 12). "The Christmas wars: Religion in the American public square." Retrieved January 27, 2007, from http://pewforum.org/events/index. In 2006, for example, the Liberty Counsel continued its Friend or Foe Christmas Campaign and the Seattle-Tacoma Airport received national criticism for removing its Christmas trees after a local rabbi asked for a menorah display. It later restored the trees when the rabbi, after receiving hate mail and angry phone

calls, dropped his threat to sue the airport. See Martin, J. (2006, December 10). "Airport puts away holiday trees rather than risk being 'exclusive': Sea-Tac officials faced with legal threat." *Seattle Times*, A-1; Menon, V. (2006, December 13). "Foes of Christmas repelled." *Toronto Star*. Retrieved January 24, 2007, from Nexis database; "Rabbi feels wrath over removal of Yule trees." (2006, December 11). *Washington Post*. Retrieved January 24, 2007, from Nexis database. Notably, the campaign against a "war on Christmas" has been profitable for religious conservative organizations. For example, the American Family Association sold more than 500,000 buttons and 125,000 magnets that were targeted to stop a "war on Christmas." See Simon, S. (2006, December 23). "Save Christmas: Send money: Christian groups raise funds as they sell items to counter a perceived war on the holiday." *Los Angeles Times*. Retrieved January 24, 2007, from Nexis database.

35. "The reason for the season" is language often used by those concerned with the secularization and/or commercialization of Christmas. See, for example, www.reasonfor theseason.com; Weaver, S. (2002, December 24). "The reason for the season." Retrieved October 20, 2006, from www.renewamerica.us. Concerns about commercialization notwithstanding, this language has also made its way onto T-shirts, bumper stickers, and yard signs. See, for example, www.christianshirts.net. On these issues more broadly, see Menendez, A. J. (1993). *The December wars: Religious symbols and ceremonies in the public square*. Buffalo, NY: Prometheus; Moore, R. L. (2003). *Touchdown Jesus: The mixing of the sacred and secular in American history*. Louisville, KY: Westminster John Knox; Schmidt, L. E. (1997). *Consumer rites: The buying and selling of American holidays*. Princeton, NJ: Princeton University Press. The language of "put Christ back into Christmas" has become familiar in recent years. A 1999 book by Vanessa Snyder and Deron Snyder, for example, offered *50 ways to put Christ back in Christmas: And keep the spirit all year*. Silver Spring, MD: Beckham. And, like "the reason for the season," this language has made its way onto T-shirts, bumper stickers, and yard signs. See, for example, www.victorystore.com.

36. Since Roosevelt took office in 1933, there have been only three instances in which the president did not speak on the occasion of the annual tree lighting. In 1961, Vice President Lyndon Johnson spoke instead of John Kennedy, because Kennedy was spending time with his ill father. See the National Park Service's history of the tree lighting at www.nps.gov/whho/historyculture/people.htm for this information. In 1971, Vice President Spiro Agnew spoke instead of Richard Nixon, because Nixon was meeting with heads of state overseas until the day prior to the tree lighting. This information about Nixon's absence was provided by Sahr Conway-Lanz, archivist for the Richard Nixon Presidential Materials, located at the National Archives in College Park, Maryland. In 1972, Agnew again gave the address. Two people independently identified all references to Christ in the 71 addresses that presidents since 1933 have given on the occasion of the lighting of the national Christmas tree (45 of these addresses were given prior to 1981 and 26 were given between 1981 and 2006). For this analysis, we also counted references to Him and He when they clearly referred to Christ. Agreement between the readers was .93, which was .86 after accounting for agreement by chance. See Scott, W. A. (1955). "Reliability of content analysis: The case of nominal scale coding." *Public Opinion Quarterly, 19*, 321–325.

37. In total, this analysis included 34 formal Christmas messages (8 that occurred prior to 1981 and 26 that occurred between 1981 and 2006). Although tree-lighting addresses and formal Christmas messages are the primary ways in which presidents mark the occasion of Christmas, they are not the only ways. Presidents have also regularly issued Christmas greetings to U.S. soldiers and Foreign Service personnel: Roosevelt, Johnson, Nixon, Bush, Clinton, and Bush all did so at least once. And, on occasion, presidents have made remarks at other Christmas celebrations. Because these messages were far less consistent across presidents, they were not included in this analysis. Notably, modern presidents have emphasized Christmas far more than Easter, another important Christian holy day. Reagan was the first to issue a formal Easter statement in 1981, in which he mentioned Christ six times. Reagan also sometimes used his weekly national radio address to mention Easter, a pattern that George H. W. Bush followed. Clinton was the first to fully engage in this signal, issuing a formal Easter statement each of his final seven years in office. Bush Jr. continued this pattern, making a formal Easter statement every year of his term (through 2007) with the exception of 2003, when the timing of his weekly radio address allowed him to speak about Easter without issuing a formal statement. Interestingly, Bush emphasized Christ much more in his Easter statements than did Clinton. Clinton averaged 2.3 references to Christ in his statements, whereas Bush averaged 8.2 references in his statements. In other words, Bush made more than three times as many references to Christ as did Clinton.

38. Roosevelt's address and all of the other quoted material in this section were retrieved from *Public Papers of the Presidents* at www.americanpresidency.org. Notably, Roosevelt's 1943 remarks on the tree lighting were combined with a formal fireside chat, which he delivered Christmas Eve. The address was therefore considerably longer and broader in scope than typical tree-lighting remarks.

39. The words "authentic engagement" are those of Mara Vanderslice, president of Common Good Strategies, a political consulting firm that worked with Democratic candidates during the 2006 campaign. See Martin, R. (2006, October 21). "Issues of faith and the fall campaign." National Public Radio's *Weekend Edition.* Retrieved October 29, 2006, from www.npr.org. Vanderslice was named by Religion News Service as one of the 12 most important voices in helping Democrats to connect with religious voters. See Burke, D. (2006, November 14). "Influential dozen seek to help Democrats bridge 'God gap.'" *Christian Century*, 15–16. This article also quoted Richard Cizik, vice president for governmental affairs for the National Association of Evangelicals, who said: "Simply using 'faith language' won't redound to the benefit of any candidate, Republican or Democrat, without some authenticity there."

## CHAPTER 5

1. Bush delivered this address on June 30, 1989. A transcript can be accessed at www .americanpresidency.org. The Supreme Court decision was *Texas v. Johnson*, decided in a 5–4 vote. At the time of the ruling, 48 states had laws prohibiting flag desecration, all of

which were enacted between 1897 and 1932. The best available data on acts of flag desecration are maintained by the Citizens Flag Alliance and can be accessed at www .cfa-inc.org. As an example of the rarity of flag burning, consider that in 1995, the first year for which the group has complete records, there were only nine reported acts of flag desecration in the United States. Of those nine acts, seven included burning the flag. From 1996 to 2006, the average number of acts of desecration per year was just over 11, not all of which included burning.

2. Fully 74% of born-again U.S. adults reported that they had discussed the issue with family, friends, or coworkers, and 54% said they had followed news about the issue "very closely" (Protestants in general reported this same level of news interest). Numbers are from the Times Mirror News Interest Index for July 1989, available upon request from the Pew Research Center for the People and the Press at http://people-press.org. On public opinion regarding flag burning in general, see Black, C. (1989, June 29). "Bush backed on flag-burning." *Boston Globe*. Retrieved September 8, 2006, from Nexis database. Poll also retrieved September 9, 2006, from the Roper poll center at the University of Connecticut, available in Nexis database. See Times Mirror (1989, October 8, Roper accession number 0281840). On the lukewarm sentiment toward Bush among religious conservatives, see Oreskes, M. (1989, July 26). "Old guard's gone, but Right finds new strength." *New York Times*. Retrieved September 8, 2006, from Nexis database.

3. Bush expressed his "personal, emotional response" to the flag-burning decision on June 22, 1989, at a luncheon hosted by the New York Partnership and the Association for a Better New York. A transcript can be accessed at www.americanpresidency.org. For news reports containing Bush's words, see, for example, Battle, M. (1989, June 23). "Poll: 69% want flag protected." *USA Today*. Retrieved September 21, 2006, from Nexis database; Mashek, J. W. (1989, June 23). "Bush blasts flag burning, but upholds law." *Boston Globe*. Retrieved September 21, 2006, from Nexis database; Phillips, D., & Dewar, H. (1989, June 23). "Flag ruling angers Congress: Bush denounces desecration." *Washington Post*. Retrieved September 21, 2006, from Nexis database; "Wrapped up in the flag." (1989, June 27). *New York Times*. Retrieved September 21, 2006, from Nexis database. A transcript of the press conference in which Bush announced his desire for a constitutional amendment can be accessed at www.americanpresidency.org. For insight into the president's thinking about the amendment, see Mashek, J. W. (1989, July 1). "Bush pushes amendment to outlaw flag desecration." *Boston Globe*. Retrieved September 8, 2006, from Nexis database. On all of these issues more broadly, see Goldstein, R. J. (1996). *Burning the flag: The great 1989–1990 American flag desecration controversy*. Kent, OH: Kent State University Press.

4. Rather than an amendment, Congress passed and Bush signed the Flag Protection Act of 1989, which the Supreme Court ruled unconstitutional on June 11, 1990, in *United States v. Eichman*. On signing the act, Bush again repeated his belief that an amendment was necessary. The former Boston University professor quoted in the *Globe* was Whitney Smith, director of the Flag Research Center and one of the world's foremost experts on flags. The center's Web site can be accessed at www.flagresearchcenter.com. Quote in

Alters, D. (1989, July 2). "Historical dilemma colors the debate over Old Glory." *Boston Globe*. Retrieved March 7, 2007, from Nexis database.

5. On support for a flag-burning amendment by the Knights of Columbus, see Knights of Columbus (2005, August 4). "Resolution on respect for the flag." Retrieved March 12, 2007, from www.kofc.org/news/releases/detail.cfm?id=20372. In 2006, 64% of white evangelicals said the flag-burning issue was "very important." The second highest group was white Catholics, at 58%. See Pew Research Center (2006, June 27). "Democrats more eager to vote, but unhappy with party." Retrieved September 9, 2006, from http://people-press.org/reports. For the Christian Coalition's "action alert" in support of the amendment, see www.cc.org/content.cfm?id=342. For the *National Liberty Journal*'s support, see "Washington confidential." (2006, June 6). *National Liberty Journal*. Retrieved March 6, 2007, from www.nljonline.com. For Perkins's support, see Perkins, T. (2006, April 28). "Washington update." Retrieved September 9, 2006, from www.frc.org.

6. "Seismic shock" quote from Neuhaus, R. J. (1987). "What the fundamentalists want." In R. J. Neuhaus & M. Cromartie (Eds.), *Piety and politics: Evangelicals and fundamentalists confront the world* (5–18). Washington, DC: Ethics and Public Policy Center. Over the years, concern about school prayer has become intertwined with a desire to protect the Pledge of Allegiance, particularly the phrase "one nation under God." In 2000, James Dobson wrote:

> When I was a kid, the Pledge of Allegiance was recited by each student, after which the class joined in saying the Lord's Prayer in unison. That was the way many public schools in America began each day, which was followed by a healthy dose of reading, writing and arithmetic. But as we have seen, the Pledge is under attack, and reciting the Lord's Prayer would send the ACLU into spasms of apoplexy. These two fundamental creeds—God and country—were central to school curricula in the not-so-distant past. Unfortunately, those beliefs and values have fallen into disfavor.

Dobson, J. (2000, September). "One nation under God?" *Focus on the Family Newsletter*. Retrieved August 23, 2006, from www.family.org/docstudy/newsletters/a0012735.cfm.

7. Falwell quote in "Hart-Mondale race, school prayer, Assad's power at home." (1984, March 5). Public Broadcasting Service's *MacNeil/Lehrer NewsHour*. Retrieved September 6, 2006, from Nexis database. The words "moral revolution" are borrowed from Ed McAteer, founder of the organization Religious Roundtable. In "Religious Right goes for bigger game." (1980, November 17). *U.S. News & World Report*. Retrieved September 7, 2006, from Nexis database. Weyrich quote in Conaway, J. (1983, March 22). "Righting Reagan's revolution: Paul Weyrich, moral tactician, at war with incompetence, moderates about the GOP." *Washington Post*. Retrieved September 7, 2006, from Nexis database. Bill Bright, founder of the theologically conservative Campus Crusade for Christ, told a U.S. House of Representatives committee in 1980: "The Supreme Court decision [in 1963] puts us in a straitjacket. . . . What is happening is not far removed from what is happening in the Soviet Union, preparing our students for no God." See Sinclair, W. (1980, July 31). "School prayer advocates blame '63 ruling for

social evils." *Washington Post*. Retrieved September 5, 2006, from Nexis database. And in 1995 religious conservatives distributed resource kits with suggestions for how teachers and students could observe the National Day of Prayer in public classrooms. Shirley Dobson told the *Washington Post*:

> Many of our religious freedoms are being stripped by our government since prayer was taken out of schools in 1962 . . . [and] we're in what many people call a moral free fall. Our country stands at a great crossroads, not unlike the crisis that threatened the stability during the Civil War. . . . and just as our forefathers sought God in times of trouble, so must we seek His face.

In Goodstein, L. (1995, May 4). "U.S. prayer day takes on more political tone: Organizers turn up the heat as constitutional debate nears." *Washington Post*. Retrieved September 5, 2006, from Nexis database. A few months later, Pat Robertson's chief legal counsel, Jay Sekulow, said, "Our public schools began as ministries of the church; now it is time to return them to the Lord." In Anderson, T. (1995, September 7). "The religious Right perils our freedoms." *Buffalo News*. Retrieved September 5, 2006, from Nexis database.

8. On morality politics, see Billings, D. B., & Scott, S. L. (1994). "Religion and political legitimation." *Annual Review of Sociology, 20*, 173–201; Gusfield, J. R. (1963). *Symbolic crusade: Status politics and the American temperance movement.* Urbana: University of Illinois Press; Lakoff, G. (1996). *Moral politics: What conservatives know that liberals don't.* Chicago: University of Chicago Press; Luker, K. (1984). *Abortion and the politics of motherhood.* Berkeley: University of California Press; Meier, K. J. (1994). *The politics of sin: Drugs, alcohol and public policy.* Armonk, NY: Sharpe; Miceli, M. (2005). "Morality politics vs. identity politics: Framing processes and competition among Christian Right and gay social movement organizations." *Sociological Forum, 20*, 589–612. On the importance of morality and values more generally, see Abramson, P., & Inglehart, R. (1995). *Value change in global perspective.* Ann Arbor: University of Michigan Press; Brooke, S. L. (1993). "The morality of homosexuality." *Journal of Homosexuality, 25*, 77–99; Brown, R. D., & Carmines, E. G. (1995). "Materialists, postmaterialists, and the criteria for political choice in U.S. presidential elections." *Journal of Politics, 57*, 483–494; Domke, D., Shah, D. V., & Wackman, D. (1998). " 'Moral referendums': Values, news media, and the process of candidate choice." *Political Communication, 15*, 301–321; Moen, M. (1984). "School prayer and the politics of life-style concern." *Social Science Quarterly, 65*, 1065–1071; Monroe, K. R. (1995). "Psychology and rational actor theory." *Political Psychology, 16*, 1–21; Rokeach, M. (1973). *The nature of human values.* New York: Free Press.

9. The key Supreme Court decisions on school prayer were *Engel v. Vitale* in 1962 and *Abington School District v. Schempp* in 1963. In the former, the Court said public schools could not mandate that students say a prayer. In the latter, the Court said that required Bible reading in public schools was unconstitutional. The key Supreme Court decisions on abortion were *Roe v. Wade* in 1973, which held that the right to obtain an abortion in the early months of pregnancy was legally protected, and *Planned Parenthood of Southeastern Pennsylvania v. Casey* in 1992, which affirmed this precedent. The key Supreme Court

decision on same-sex relationships was *Lawrence v. Texas* in June 2003, in which the Court ruled that states may not prohibit same-sex sexual activity (what had been legally known as sodomy) between two consenting adults. In addition, in November 2003, the Massachusetts Supreme Court upheld same-sex marriage as legal under the state constitution, a ruling that religious conservatives worried would encourage other states to do the same.

10. Falwell, J. (1980). *Listen, America.* Garden City, NY: Doubleday, 221. On the judicial blueprint, see Broder, D. (1980, November 22). "New Right sounds attack on courts." *Washington Post.* Retrieved September 7, 2006, from Nexis database; Sniffen, M. J. (1980, November 8). "Conservatives seek curbs on federal judges." *Associated Press.* Retrieved September 7, 2006, from Nexis database. The book project on judicial reform was directed by the Free Congress Research and Education Foundation, headed by Paul Weyrich. See Rader, R. R., & McGuigan, P. B. (1981). *A blueprint for judicial reform.* Washington, DC: University Press of America. Interestingly, this publication was mentioned in the confirmation hearings of Supreme Court chief justice John Roberts in 2005. See McGuigan, P. B. (2005, September 8). "Reading the whole book: Forgiving, not forgetting." Retrieved from September 7, 2006, from www.freecongress.org/commentaries/2005/050908.asp.

11. Perkins, T. (2005, April). "Justice Sunday: Stop the filibuster against people of faith." Family Research Council special publication. Retrieved September 7, 2006, from www.frc.org/get.cfm?i=LH05D02. See also Wallsten, P. (2005, April 25). "Battle over benches spills across pews." *Los Angeles Times.* Retrieved August 4, 2005, from Nexis database.

12. Quote from Haider-Markel, D. P., & Meier, K. J. (1996). "The politics of gay and lesbian rights: Expanding the scope of the conflict." *Journal of Politics, 58,* 332–349. By using such language, politicians were seeking to justify their actions. On the nature of justifications in political speech, see Campbell, K. K., & Jamieson, K. H. (1990). *Deeds done in words: Presidential rhetoric and the genres of governance.* Chicago: University of Chicago Press; Cherwitz, R. A., & Zagacki, K. S. (1986). "Consummatory versus justificatory crisis rhetoric." *Western Journal of Speech Communication, 50,* 307–324; Kuypers, J. (1997). *Presidential crisis rhetoric and the press in the post–Cold War world.* Westport, CT: Praeger; Scott, M. B., & Lyman, S. M. (1968). "Accounts." *American Sociological Review, 33,* 46–62; Ware, B. L., & Linkugel, W. A. (1973). "They spoke in defense of themselves: On the generic criticism of apologia." *Quarterly Journal of Speech, 59,* 273–283.

13. Rarely in the past few decades have religious conservatives' policy goals been realized at the national level. Perhaps the most notable exceptions are the Defense of Marriage Act in 1996 and the Partial-Birth Abortion Ban Act in 2003. On the political value of taking stands on "moral" issues, see Domke, D., Shah, D. V., & Wackman, D. (2000). "Rights and morals, issues, and candidate integrity: Insights into the role of the news media." *Political Psychology, 21,* 641–665; Glendon, M. A. (1991). *Rights talk: The impoverishment of political discourse.* New York: Free Press; Just, M. R., Crigler, A. N., Alger, D. E., Cook, T. E., Kern, M., & West, D. M. (1996). *Crosstalk: Citizens, candidates, and the media in a presidential campaign.* Chicago: University of Chicago Press; Luker, *Abortion and the politics of motherhood.* For U.S. public opinion as of 2006 on abortion, stem

cell research, and same-sex relationships, see Pew Research Center (2006, August 3). "Pragmatic Americans: Liberal and conservative on social issues." Retrieved September 5, 2006, from http://people-press.org/reports. For longer trends regarding public attitudes on these issues as well as school prayer and the Equal Rights Amendment, see Brewer, P. R., & Wilcox, C. (2005). "The polls: Same-sex marriage and civil unions." *Public Opinion Quarterly, 69,* 599–616; Nisbet, M. C. (2004). "The polls: Public opinion about stem cell research and human cloning." *Public Opinion Quarterly, 68,* 131–154; Servin-Gonzales, M., & Torres-Reyna, O. (1999). "The polls: Religion and politics." *Public Opinion Quarterly, 63,* 592–612; Shaw, G. M. (2003). "The polls: Abortion." *Public Opinion Quarterly, 67,* 407–429; Simon, R. J., & Landis, J. M. (1989). "The polls: Women's and men's attitudes about a woman's place and role." *Public Opinion Quarterly, 53,* 265–276; Turner, C. F., Villarroel, M. A., Chromy, J. R., Eggleston, E., & Rogers, S. M. (2005). "The polls: Same-gender sex among U.S. adults: Trends across the twentieth century and during the 1990s." *Public Opinion Quarterly, 69,* 439–462.

14. Specifically, the average length of Republican and Democratic platforms 1932–2004 was 16,536 words: 18,102 for the GOP and 14,970 for the Democrats. For more on the nature of party platforms, see David, P. T. (1971, May–June). "Party platforms as national plans." *Public Administration Review, 31,* 303–315; Gomberg, A. M., Marhuenda, F., & Ortuno-Ortin, I. (2004). "A model of endogenous political party platforms." *Economic Theory, 24,* 373–394. On party platforms' importance for government action and public opinion, see Budge, I., & Hofferbert, R. I. (1990). "Mandates and policy outputs: U.S. party platforms and federal expenditures." *American Political Science Review, 84,* 11–131; Monroe, A. D. (1983). "American party platforms and public opinion." *American Journal of Political Science, 27,* 27–42. For a general review of the literature on political parties, see Stokes, S. C. (1999). "Political parties and democracy." *Annual Review of Political Science, 2,* 243–267. On platforms as a tool to signal support for specific constituencies, see Fine, T. S. (1994). "Interest groups and the framing of the 1988 Democratic and Republican party platforms." *Polity, 26,* 517–530; Glaeser, E. L., Ponzetto, G. A. M., & Shapiro, J. M. (2005). "Strategic extremism: Why Republicans and Democrats divide on religious values." *Quarterly Journal of Economics, 120,* 1283–1330.

15. Two people read all of the platforms, noting discussion of each of the five issues: school prayer, abortion, research on stem cells, the Equal Rights Amendment, and same-sex relationships. We identified content that directly discussed these topics, through explicit usage of the issue's terminology. General platitudes about the values that underlie these issues (such as equality for the ERA) were included in our analysis only if they were explicitly connected to the issue itself. The full texts of Republican and Democratic party platforms are available at www.americanpresidency.org.

16. In the 1994 elections, close to 60% of victorious GOP congressional candidates received backing from the Christian Coalition. See Gallagher, J., & Bull, C. (1996). *Perfect enemies: The religious Right, the gay movement, and the politics of the 1990s.* New York: Crown, 229. Further, exit polls showed that, among white evangelicals, Republican candidates for the House outpolled Democratic candidates at a rate of more than 2–1. See Soper, J. C. (1996). "The politics of pragmatism: The Christian Right and the 1994

elections." In P. A. Klinkner (Ed.), *Midterm: The elections of 1994 in context* (115–124). Boulder, CO: Westview, 118. See also Edwards, L. (1999). *The conservative revolution: The movement that remade America*. New York: Free Press.

17. The considerable increase over time in words devoted to morality politics is not simply the result of an increase in total words included in the platforms. The average word count of a party platform from 1932–1976 was 10,358; from 1980–2004 the average was 27,127. This is an increase of 162%, which falls far short of the 2,335% increase in words devoted to morality politics over the same period (17 words per platform from 1932–1976; 414 words per platform from 1980–2004).

18. The quote from Beverly LaHaye and the information on Concerned Women for America were retrieved September 7, 2006, from the organization's Web site, at www .cwfa.org/history.asp. The Eagle Forum can be located at its Web site at www.eagleforum .org. For insight into the role of Phyllis Schlafly in the demise of the Equal Rights Amendment, see Bumiller, E. (1982, July 1). "Schlafly's gala goodbye to ERA." *Washington Post*. Retrieved September 7, 2006, from Nexis database. More generally, see Balmer, R. (2006). *Thy kingdom come: How the religious Right distorts the faith and threatens America*. New York: Basic, 1–34; Boles, J. K. (1979). *The politics of the Equal Rights Amendment: Conflict and the decision process*. New York: Longman; Falwell, J. (1987). "An agenda for the 1980s." In R. J. Neuhaus & M. Cromartie (Eds.), *Piety and politics: Evangelicals and fundamentalists confront the world* (109–123). Washington, DC: Ethics and Public Policy Center; Miller, A., & Greenberg, H. (1976). *The Equal Rights Amendment: A bibliographic study*. Westport, CT: Greenwood; Soule, S. A., & Olzak, S. (2004). "When do movements matter? The politics of contingency and the Equal Rights Amendment." *American Sociological Review, 69*, 473–497; Steiner, G. Y. (1985). *Constitutional inequality: The political fortunes of the Equal Rights Amendment*. Washington, DC: Brookings Institution.

19. Sidney Blumenthal, who would later serve as an adviser in the Clinton administration, in the 1980s said that Republicans intentionally did not deliver on the policies sought by religious conservatives, because this approach worked to the party's advantage. See Blumenthal, S. (1987). "The religious Right and Republicans." In R. J. Neuhaus & M. Cromartie (Eds.), *Piety and politics: Evangelicals and fundamentalists confront the world* (269–286). Washington, DC: Ethics and Public Policy Center.

20. For this analysis, we identified all instances of Constitution, constitutional, constitutionally, or unconstitutional in each party's platforms for our analysis of Constitution invocations (the term "unconstitutionally" did not appear in the platforms), and we identified all instances of judges, justices, courts, judiciary, or Supreme Court for our analysis of judiciary references.

21. As a reminder of where this chapter began, the GOP also sought a constitutional amendment to ban flag burning, another issue of concern to religious conservatives. The Republican Party platforms also regularly called for a constitutional amendment to balance the federal budget.

22. Scholar Duane Murray Oldfield says of family, "No institution is more important to the Christian Right's agenda." See Oldfield, D. M. (1996). *The Right and the righteous: The Christian Right confronts the Republican party*. Lanham, MD: Rowman & Littlefield, 66.

Indeed, the combination of "faith and family" is a familiar one among religious conservatives. For example, Richard Land, president of the Southern Baptist Convention's Ethics and Religious Liberty Commission, hosts a nationally syndicated radio program called *For Faith and Family*, which reaches some 1.5 million listeners. Land has parlayed the success of that program into a broader religious organization of the same name. And the Family Research Council, a prominent religious conservative organization, describes its mission as "defending family, faith, and freedom." The pairing of faith and family is also common in other religious circles, particularly among Catholics. There is a Catholic magazine called *Faith & Family*, and Women for Faith and Family is a Catholic organization that was founded in 1984. On the agenda of "family values," see Bendroth, M. L. (2002). "Fundamentalism and the family: Gender, culture, and the American pro-family movement." In B. Reed (Ed.), *Nothing sacred: Women respond to religious fundamentalism and terror* (259–280). New York: Thunder's Mouth Press/Nation Books; Gallagher, S. K. (2003). *Evangelical identity and gendered family life*. New Brunswick, NJ: Rutgers University Press.

23. In this analysis of faith language, we included the terms "Almighty," "God," "Christ," "Creator," "Divine," "Jesus," "Lord," "Providence," and all faith invocations used in chapter 2. We call all of this "faith language" here for the sake of simplicity. For family language, we identified all instances of family, families, marriage, wife, husband, and all forms of the terms parent, father, and mother. We did not include any form of the term child, because child and its variants were often used as general references to young people and were therefore not distinctly about family.

24. For the Traditional Values Coalition's statement, see Traditional Values Coalition (2004, August 25). "TVC praises GOP platform on marriage." Retrieved March 7, 2007, from www.traditionalvalues.org/modules.php?sid=1840. For Crouse's quote, see White, G. (2004, September 4). "Religious Right out of GOP spotlight: Skipped on TV but heeded on platform." *Atlanta Journal-Constitution*. Retrieved March 5, 2007, from Nexis database. For the Christian Coalition's statement, see Christian Coalition (2004, August 26). "Christian Coalition applauds Republican Party National Convention platform for supporting tough prolife position and the federal marriage amendment." Retrieved March 7, 2007, from www.cc.org/content.cfm?id=149&srch=platform.

25. U.S. religion historian Randall Balmer declares that there is a widespread "abortion myth" that suggests the religious conservative movement began in direct response to the *Roe v. Wade* decision. According to Balmer, who cites several leading figures of conservative politics, this is not what happened. Rather, Balmer contends, the religious conservative movement coalesced when the Carter administration sought to revoke the tax-exempt status of Bob Jones University in 1975 because the school's regulations forbade interracial dating. Balmer quotes, among others, Ed Dobson, a close associate of Jerry Falwell: "The Religious New Right did not start because of a concern about abortion. I sat in the non–smoke-filled back room with the Moral Majority, and I frankly do not remember abortion ever being mentioned as a reason why we ought to do something." See Balmer, *Thy kingdom come*, 1–34. On the importance of abortion and same-sex relationships as political issues for religious conservatives, see Kuo, D. (2006). *Tempting faith: An inside story of political seduction*. New York: Free Press, 24–35.

26. Harding, S. F. (2000). *The book of Jerry Falwell: Fundamentalist language and politics.* Princeton, NJ: Princeton University Press, 194. For Warren quote, see Warren, R. (2004, October 27). "Why every U.S. Christian must vote in this election." *Ministry Toolbox,* 178. Retrieved September 5, 2006, from www.pastors.com/RWMT/?ID=178. On the organization Catholic Answers, see Cooperman, A. (2006, September 29). "Religious-Right voter guides facing challenge from Left." *Washington Post.* Retrieved September 29, 2006, from www.washingtonpost.com.

27. Interest groups and key constituencies often contribute to the language in party platforms. For example, in August 1992, the Republican Party held its national convention in Houston. A month later, Martin Mawyer, the founder and president of the Christian Action Network, said this during an interview with CNN: "You must be reading a different Republican Party platform than the one I read when I was in Houston and the one I helped to construct." See "Politics and God—a dangerous mix?" (1992, September 14). Cable News Network's *Larry King Live.* Retrieved September 29, 2006, from Nexis database. For a review of scholarship on how interest groups influence the formulation of policy and the behavior of political leaders, see Baumgartner, F. R., & Leech, B. L. (1998). *Basic interests: The importance of groups in politics and political science.* Princeton, NJ: Princeton University Press.

28. Balmer, *Thy kingdom come,* 5. See also Frank, T. (2004). *What's the matter with Kansas? How conservatives won the heart of America.* New York: Metropolitan, 181–189. Republicans in their 2000 platform added that the practice of late-term abortion "shocks the conscience of the nation." In 2004, after Congress had passed a ban on this practice, the GOP's platform language focused on praising the legislation and warning that the judiciary might overturn it: "And while the vast majority of Americans support a ban on partial birth abortion, this brutal and violent practice will likely continue by judicial fiat."

29. See Gilgoff, D. (2005, July 25). "Democrats kick off a multifront campaign to connect with religious voters." *U.S. News & World Report.* Retrieved September 14, 2006, from Nexis database.

30. Bauer quote in Shorto, R. (2005). "What's their real problem with gay marriage? (It's the gay part)." *New York Times Magazine.* Retrieved June 21, 2005, from www.nytimes.com. Opposition to same-sex marriage was "non-negotiable" in 2004, according to Rick Warren and the organization Catholic Answers. See Warren, "Why every U.S. Christian must vote in this election"; Cooperman, "Religious-Right voter guides facing challenge from Left." Both Warren and Catholic Answers listed a total of five nonnegotiable issues for Christians: opposition to abortion, stem cell research, same-sex marriage, cloning, and euthanasia. Cooperman notes that Catholic Answers declared, "No one endorsing the wrong side of these issues can be said to act in accord with the Church's moral norms." See also Gallagher & Bull, *Perfect enemies.* Weyrich quote in Bennetts, L. (1980, July 30). "Conservatives join on social concerns." *New York Times.* Retrieved September 7, 2006, from Nexis database. Dobson, J. (2003, September). "Marriage on the ropes." *Focus on the Family Newsletter.* Retrieved September 7, 2006, from www.family.org/docstudy/newsletters/a0027590.cfm.

31. See Balmer, *Thy kingdom come,* 22, 24.

32. The GOP's opposition to same-sex relationships focused primarily on marriage, but it also was manifest in platform language that argued homosexuals should not be allowed to serve in the military and that sexual orientation should not be included among other protected minority characteristics.

33. The emphasis on the term families in this quote was added by the authors for the sake of clarity.

34. See Freligh, R. (1996, May 28). "Sending an earful to Bill Clinton." *Cleveland Plain Dealer*. Retrieved September 14, 2006, from Nexis database; Purdum, T. S. (1996, May 23). "President would sign legislation striking at homosexual marriages." *New York Times*. Retrieved September 14, 2006, from Nexis database; Rosenbaum, D. (1996, May 27). "Politics: The issues: Many disillusioned liberals see no alternatives to president." *New York Times*. Retrieved September 14, 2006, from Nexis database; Serrano, B. (1996, May 28). "Gay marriage rises as issue for candidates in fall election: Podlodowski leaves Clinton campaign." *Seattle Times*. Retrieved September 14, 2006, from Nexis database; Vobejda, B. (1996, May 24). "Clinton defends record on gay rights, opposition to same-sex marriage." *Washington Post*. Retrieved September 14, 2006, from Nexis database.

35. Following the 2004 campaign, a number of books by Democratic Party activists and insiders argued that the party's soul and vision were inadequately defined. See, for example, Armstrong, J., & Zuniga, M. M. (2006). *Crashing the gate: Netroots, grassroots, and the rise of people-powered politics*. White River Junction, VT: Chelsea Green; Carville, J., & Begala, P. (2006). *Take it back: Our party, our country, our future*. New York: Simon & Schuster; Hart, G. (2006). *The courage of our convictions: A manifesto for Democrats*. New York: Holt. Carville and Begala write:

> You can blame John Kerry if it makes you feel better. But the problem is much bigger than one candidate in one campaign. The problem, in part, is that on some important issues, people think Democrats are out of step with the mainstream. But the bigger problem is that people don't know what it is the party stands for. That's a problem we must solve. . . . Democrats must say loud and clear what it is they believe in. (*Take it back*, 3–4)

36. Dobson quote in Kirkpatrick, D. D. (2005, January 1). "Evangelical leader threatens to use his muscle against some Democrats." *New York Times*. Retrieved September 22, 2006, from Nexis database. Over the years, conservatives have even adopted a mantra: "No more Souters." Robert Bork's nomination was defeated in the Senate, 58–42. The oppositional rhetoric to Bork was so strong among the Democratic Party that new verbs "to bork," "borking," and "borked" emerged to signify a political appointee whose character was vilified in public. In 1996, Bork published *Slouching towards Gomorrah: Modern liberalism and American decline*. New York: Regan. The book was endorsed by Ralph Reed, Jr., and William Bennett, and Pat Robertson declared the book to be "brilliant." See Rich, F. (1996, October 9). "The war in the wings." *New York Times*. Retrieved September 23, 2006, from Nexis database. On the treatment of Bork, see Battiata, M. (1987, September 26). "Beverly LaHaye and the hymn of the Right: Leading her women in support of Reagan, Bork and SDI." *Washington Post*. Retrieved September

23, 2006, from Nexis database; Bronner, E. (1989). *Battle for justice: How the Bork nomination shook America*. New York: Norton; Dionne, E. J., Jr. (2001, May 11). "No more 'borking.'" *Washington Post*. Retrieved September 23, 2006, from Nexis database.

37. This quote comes from voiceover material in the introduction to Justice Sunday I. Video of the event was retrieved from www.dailykos.com/story/2005/4/24/20035/5837. Transcription was done by the authors. Transcripts and video of Justice Sunday II and III were retrieved from the Web site of the Family Research Council at www.frc.org. On the political machinations in the Senate over judicial nominees during this period, see Babington, C. (2005, January 16). "GOP moderates wary of filibuster curb: A few holdouts could block move to cut off debate on judicial nominees." *Washington Post*. Retrieved September 22, 2006, from Nexis database; Pisano, M. (2005, January 23). "Politics, judicial appointments to decide fate of Roe vs. Wade: Democrats will likely filibuster to block anti-abortion justices." *San Antonio Express-News*. Retrieved September 22, 2006, from Nexis database. On public opinion about these Senate maneuvers, see Pew Research Center (2005, May 16). "Disengaged public leans against changing filibuster rules." Retrieved September 22, 2006, from http://people-press.org/reports. See also polls retrieved September 23, 2006, from the Roper poll center at the University of Connecticut, available in Nexis database: *Newsweek* (2005, March 17–18, Roper accession number 1619522); Gallup (2005, April 29–May 1, Roper accession number 1623556); and Gallup (2005, May 20–22, Roper accession number 1625120).

38. Strictly speaking, the events were often sponsored by Focus on the Family Action and FRC Action. These are the legislative lobbying arms of Focus on the Family and the Family Research Council, respectively, and are legally separate from their parent organizations. Perkins quote in Cooperman, A. (2005, July 4). "Evangelical groups plan aggressive drive for nominee: Campaign seeks solid conservative." *Washington Post*. Retrieved September 23, 2006, from Nexis database. Well-known evangelist Pat Robertson went further than Perkins, praying for more Supreme Court seats: "Take control, Lord! We ask for additional vacancies on the court." In Kirkpatrick, D. D. (2005, August 3). "DeLay to be on Christian telecast on courts." *New York Times*. Retrieved September 18, 2006, from Nexis database. Prior to nominating Alito, George W. Bush nominated Harriet Miers for the open seat. Miers, a long-time Bush friend who was serving as White House counsel, ultimately asked Bush to withdraw her nomination. Notably, after nominating Miers, Bush focused considerable energy on promoting her religiosity, particularly among conservative religious leaders. See Associated Press (2005, October 13). "Finding her religion: Bush says aides discussed Miers' religion with conservatives." *Chicago Tribune*. Retrieved April 17, 2006, from ProQuest database.

39. The broadcast audience numbers are according to the organizers of the event. By Justice Sunday III, organizers claimed that the event was reaching 80 million households. Notably, there was a small number of other party-affiliated politicians who spoke as part of these events as well. All of them were Republicans.

40. In the days leading up to the rally, Frist was criticized by some in the Senate as well as by some in the moderate religious community, including the head of the Presbyterian church, Frist's own denomination. See Shepard, S. (2005, April 24). "From 'Justice

Sunday' to the White House? Christian event may mark Frist's plans for '08 bid." *Atlanta Journal-Constitution*. Retrieved September 17, 2006, from Nexis database. See also Kirkpatrick, D. D. (2005, April 25). "In telecast, Frist defends his effort to stop filibusters." *New York Times*. Retrieved September 18, 2006, from Nexis database. In regard to Frist's need to appeal to religious conservatives, former Republican strategist John Pitney noted at the time, "[A] Republican will have a hard road to the convention unless he or she is acceptable to evangelical voters." See Shepard, "From 'Justice Sunday' to the White House?" Ultimately, Frist's concerns about broader public perceptions were so substantial that he put out a message before the event explaining that his participation was "not about faith, but fairness . . . [and] giving these nominees . . . a fair up-or-down vote." This is according to Frist's spokesperson, Bob Stevenson. See Shepard, "From 'Justice Sunday' to the White House?"

41. Abraham Lincoln was referenced by several speakers in the Justice Sunday events, including Charles Colson, who said:

> And remember when you hear that talk about . . . don't impose your will on us. You know where that started? That didn't start with Jerry Falwell and Pat Robertson in the 1980s. It started with Abraham Lincoln in the 1860 campaign when he was setting out to abolish slavery, and people said he will impose his moral will on us. Well, thank God he did. He brought the moral will of the people and hit the conscience of the people as the church must always do.

42. It was not only Perkins among the event's leaders who testified to DeLay's religious credentials. DeLay was followed in the speaking order by Charles Colson, who began his remarks with these words:

> I just have to say a word about my friend, Tom DeLay. I've worked with him over the years and have watched him up on Capitol Hill [at] a Majority Leader's lecture series where he and I together have worked to teach Biblical worldview to members of Congress. He does that year in, year out. . . . That's a man who lives his faith and proves the ground is level at the foot of the cross. Thank you, Tom DeLay.

## CHAPTER 6

1. Weyrich quote in Hook, J. (2006, November 8). "Democrats take control of House." *Los Angeles Times*. Retrieved November 8, 2006, from www.latimes.com. For the goals and views of Karl Rove, see Rove's speech to the Republican National Committee on January 20, 2006. Retrieved November 16, 2006, from www.real clearpolitics.com/Commentary/com-1_21_06_Rove.html. See also his speech to the New York Conservative Party on June 22, 2005. Retrieved November 8, 2006, from www.freerepublic.com/focus/f-news/1429250/posts. More broadly, see Fineman, H. (2004, December 6). "Rove unleashed." *Newsweek*. Retrieved November 8, 2006, from

Nexis database; Moore, J., & Slater, W. (2006). *The architect: Karl Rove and the master plan for absolute power.* New York: Crown. In a 2005 interview, *Dallas Morning News* reporter Wayne Slater, who had covered Bush and Rove since their Texas days, said:

> Karl Rove's model is beyond electing and re-electing George Bush. It is building a Republican Party not simply for years but for decades. It is the [William] McKinley model. It is the [Franklin] Roosevelt model. It is decades and decades of fundamental realignment of our government. To do that, in part, you have to build a base of supporters, and no one is more important in this base than conservative evangelicals for a Christian, a conservative like George Bush, and [the] Republican Party, who can use this group very successfully as part of its political base.

Slater, W. (2005, March 2). Interview for *Karl Rove: The architect* (Television broadcast). Boston: Public Broadcasting Service.

2. From quote in Swarns, R. L., & Caldwell, D. (2003, December 6). "Democrats try to regain ground on moral issues." *New York Times*, A-11. Religious leaders running for the presidency have not done so only as Republicans, of course. Most notably, the Reverend Jesse Jackson was a candidate for the Democratic Party's presidential nomination in 1984 and 1988. Unlike Pat Robertson and Gary Bauer, however, Jackson was also a racial minority—a status that defined his presidency to a much greater degree than did his religious groundings. For example, a full-text search of *New York Times* coverage in Nexis database from January 1, 1984, through November 15, 1984, found 359 items when using the search terms of "Jesse Jackson and God or faith or relig*" and 788 items when using the search terms of "Jesse Jackson and black or African or African-American." For parallel dates in 1988, the numbers were 276 items for the former, 656 for the latter.

3. The results for the presidential elections are drawn from National Election Studies data, which formed the basis for the figures in chapter 1. Results from the 2006 House of Representatives election are drawn from exit polls, which were conducted by Edison Media Research and Mitofsky International, and were retrieved November 9, 2006, from www.cnn.com.

4. According to a Gallup poll, 89% of Americans approved of the way George H. W. Bush was handling his job in early March 1991, as the Gulf War drew to a close. See "Poll: Bush's approval at historic high." (1991, March 2). *United Press International.* Retrieved November 17, 2006, from Nexis database. A Pew survey found 84% public approval for Bush a few days later. See Pew Research Center (1991, March 22). "GOP collects big war dividend." Retrieved November 17, 2006, from http://people-press.org/reports.

5. On Quayle's speech to the Christian Coalition's rally, see Lacitis, E. (1992, August 18). "Among his people in Houston, the press has Quayle all wrong." *Seattle Times.* Retrieved November 11, 2006, from Nexis database; Sarasohn, D. (1992, August 19). "The hymn battle of the Republicans." *Oregonian.* Retrieved November 11, 2006, from Nexis database. On Falwell's seating arrangements, see Urban, J. (1992, August 20). "Convention '92: Evangelicals lining up for Bush: New coalition to campaign on his

behalf." *Houston Chronicle.* Retrieved November 11, 2006, from Nexis database. Regarding the noted party platform decisions, each was driven by religious conservatives. See Hall, M. (1992, August 14). "Platform battles mirror the party's struggles." *USA Today.* Retrieved November 13, 2006, from Nexis database; Von Drehle, D. (1992, August 18). "Convention journal: A celebration by religious Right as platform panel sees the light." *Washington Post.* Retrieved November 11, 2006, from Nexis database. Regarding the convention speeches of Buchanan and Robertson, both struck deals with GOP strategists that allowed them to deliver speeches not subjected to the usual editing process for convention addresses, provided that they endorsed Bush. They were the only two speakers who were given this privilege. See Jones, A. T. (2006). "George Bush and the religious Right." In M. J. Medhurst (Ed.), *The rhetorical presidency of George H. W. Bush* (149–170). College Station: Texas A&M University Press. Buchanan delivered his address on August 17, 1992. A transcript can be accessed at www.americanrhetoric.com. In this address, Buchanan also called the Democratic National Convention a "giant masquerade ball at Madison Square Garden—where 20,000 radicals and liberals came dressed up as moderates and centrists—in the greatest single exhibition of cross-dressing in American political history." Notably, Buchanan delayed his speech 15 minutes so that all television networks could carry it live; as a result, the following speaker—Ronald Reagan—was bumped from a prime-time slot. It was the final time Reagan would address a Republican Party convention. See Jones, "George Bush and the religious Right." On Pat Robertson's address, see Turner, D., & Roberts, T. (1992, August 22). "Republicans give stage to the religious Right." *St. Petersburg Times.* Retrieved November 11, 2006, from Nexis database.

6. For the Schlafly quote, see Hall, "Platform battles mirror the party's struggles." For the Reed quote, see Von Drehle, "Convention journal: A celebration by religious Right as platform panel sees the light." Reed was referring directly to a group of prochoice Republicans who had been trying to modify platform language that opposed abortion. Another notable indicator of religious conservative strength at the convention was that some 300 of the roughly 2,000 party delegates were members of the Christian Coalition. Again, see Von Drehle, "Convention journal." The quote from an unnamed convention volunteer was drawn from Hall, M. (1992, August 20). "Moderates feeling shut out." *USA Today.* Retrieved November 11, 2006, from Nexis database. On some moderates leaving the convention before its close, see Urban, "Convention '92: Evangelicals lining up for Bush." For the quotes from McInturff and the Reagan cabinet member, see Wilkie, C. (1992, August 18). "GOP compass direction: The far Right." *Boston Globe.* Retrieved November 11, 2006, from Nexis database. For the Rosenbaum quote, see Hall, "Moderates feeling shut out."

7. Bush spoke on August 22, 1992, before the National Affairs Briefing. The last time this group had convened prior to 1992 was in 1980, when the featured speaker was presidential hopeful Ronald Reagan. A transcript of Bush's address can be accessed at www.americanpresidency.org. For the *Times*'s response, see Suro, R. (1992, August 23). "The 1992 campaign: The religious Right: Bush gets full support at religious gathering." *New York Times.* Retrieved November 11, 2006, from Nexis database; "Mr. Bush,

crossing the line." (1992, August 26). *New York Times*. Retrieved November 11, 2006, from Nexis database.

8. Robertson wrote this in a letter aimed at stopping an Iowa equal rights measure. The letter was funded by the Christian Coalition and then given free to the Iowa Committee to Stop ERA. The letter was ultimately distributed to families nationwide that had made contributions to the Christian Coalition. For media coverage, see "Pat Robertson says feminists want to kill kids, be witches." (1992, August 26). *Atlanta Journal-Constitution*. Retrieved November 11, 2006, from Nexis database. See also Associated Press (1992, August 26). "Robertson letter attacks feminists." *New York Times*. Retrieved November 11, 2006, from Nexis database; Schwartz, M., & Cooper, K. J. (2006, August 23). "Equal rights initiative in Iowa attacked." *Washington Post*. Retrieved November 11, 2006, from Nexis database. Some media couldn't resist poking fun at Robertson's rhetorical excess. For example, the *St. Louis Post-Dispatch* editorialized tongue-in-cheek that "Iowans are to be on the alert for covens of women armed with broomsticks and hiding out in cornfields." See "Broomsticks over Iowa." (1992, August 27). *St. Louis Post-Dispatch*. Retrieved November 11, 2006, from Nexis database.

9. This televised question-and-answer session took place on October 22, 1992. A transcript can be accessed at www.americanpresidency.org. The public opinion data about moderates came from a poll retrieved November 13, 2006, from the Roper poll center at the University of Connecticut, available in Nexis database. See Times Mirror (1992, August 25–27, Roper accession number 0183535). See also Pew Research Center (1992, September 17). "The people, the press, & politics: Campaign '92: Survey XI." Retrieved November 17, 2006, from http://people-press.org/reports. In this report, Pew concluded:

> The Bush campaign's emphasis on family values appears thus far to have back-fired. The theme is antagonizing as many voters as it attracts. . . . Unlike four years ago when Bush's early September campaign efforts unified all of his core groups, his current strategy is having the opposite effect. While the family values emphasis appears to have increased the President's core support among social agenda "Moralist" Republicans, it has done little to attract socially moderate, yet economically conservative "Enterpriser" Republicans and independent "Upbeats" who until recently leaned heavily to the Republican party.

10. Will, G. (1992, August 26). "Republican campaign in need of some values." *Toronto Star*. Retrieved November 11, 2006, from Nexis database. Information on National Council of Churches letter in Lehigh, S. (1992, August 31). "Values campaign divides clergy: Republicans' use of religion draws praise and criticism." *Boston Globe*. Retrieved November 11, 2006, from Nexis database. The Clinton campaign did everything it could to highlight how Bush had embraced religious conservatives. For example, during and after the Republican convention, Clinton took to calling the GOP the party of "Pat Buchanan, Pat Robertson, Phyllis Schlafly and Jerry Falwell." The Clinton campaign seemed to recognize immediately that Bush's shift to the right was hurting him. Campaign strategist James Carville reportedly smiled after reading the headline "Tougher

GOP stance on social issues reflects surge of the religious Right," saying: "We've gotta like that one." See Maraniss, D. (1992, August 20). "Clinton takes to the stump in Michigan: Bush called captive of Republican Right." *Washington Post*. Retrieved November 11, 2006, from Nexis database.

11. On the symbolic significance of Schiavo for some religious conservatives, see Easton, N. J. (2005, March 22). "Social conservatives see advance of right-to-life effort." *Boston Globe*. Retrieved November 13, 2006, from Nexis database. The Schiavo case dominated the attention of several religious conservative organizations for much of March 2005. The Family Research Council and Focus on the Family, for instance, both sent their members regular e-mail updates about the situation. See Allen, M. (2005, March 24). "Conservative groups' steady support." *Washington Post*. Retrieved November 13, 2006, from Nexis database. Further, religious conservatives encouraged GOP leaders to act on their behalf. Keith Appell, a political strategist involved with the Schiavo case, said of religious conservatives: "They've played a major role. There's been an enormous amount of pressure brought to bear on conservative members of Congress to get involved." See Thomma, S. (2005, March 21). "How GOP base flexed its political muscle." *Seattle Times*. Retrieved November 13, 2006, from Nexis database. On the Republican Party's memo about the issue's political value, see Allen, M., & Roig-Franzia, M. (2005, March 20). "Congress steps in on Schiavo case: Lawmakers to pass bill to resume feeding, allow court review." *Washington Post*. Retrieved November 13, 2006, from Nexis database. On Bush's return to Washington to sign the legislation, see Babington, C., & Allen, M. (2005, March 21). "Congress passes Schiavo measure: Bush signs bill giving U.S. courts jurisdiction in case of Fla. woman." *Washington Post*. Retrieved November 13, 2006, from Nexis database. The president's trek to Washington, DC—the first time Bush had interrupted a vacation to return to Washington—to sign the Schiavo bill was noted by religious conservatives. For example, Richard Cizik, vice president for governmental affairs for the National Association of Evangelicals, praised Bush for "his willingness to interrupt his vacation to make a statement. And not just to make a statement, because we're not playing games here, but to make a difference, too." See Bumiller, E. (2005, March 21). "Supporters praise Bush's swift return to Washington." *New York Times*. Retrieved November 13, 2006, from Nexis database.

12. Dobson quote in Hulse, C., & Kirkpatrick, D. D. (2005, April 1). "Even death does not quiet harsh political fight." *New York Times*. Retrieved November 13, 2006, from Nexis database. In the same article, Family Research Council president Tony Perkins said, "It is a tragic, unfortunate but avoidable event that should awaken Americans to the problem of the courts. It is no longer theoretical. It is life or death." On Christian conservatives and Schiavo's fate, see Gilgoff, D. (2007). *The Jesus machine: How James Dobson, Focus on the Family, and evangelical America are winning the culture war*. New York: St. Martin's Press, 124–132. Delay quote in Hulse & Kirkpatrick, "Even death does not quiet harsh political fight." DeLay was criticized for this remark and later apologized, calling his words "inartful." See Allen, M. (2005, April 14). "DeLay apologizes for comments: Leader wouldn't say whether he wants Schiavo judges impeached." *Washington Post*. Retrieved November 20, 2006, from Nexis database. Danforth quote from

Danforth, J. C. (2005, March 30). "In the name of politics." *New York Times.* Retrieved November 16, 2006, from Nexis database. Two months later, Danforth published another op-ed in the *Times*, with the headline "Onward, moderate Christian soldiers." This piece included these words:

> In the decade since I left the Senate, American politics has been characterized by two phenomena: the increased activism of the Christian Right, especially in the Republican Party, and the collapse of bipartisan collegiality. I do not think it is a stretch to suggest a relationship between the two. To assert that I am on God's side and you are not, that I know God's will and you do not, and that I will use the power of government to advance my understanding of God's kingdom is certain to produce hostility.

See Danforth, J. C. (2005, June 17). "Onward, moderate Christian soldiers." *New York Times.* Retrieved November 16, 2006, from Nexis database. Danforth further developed these critiques in his 2006 book *Faith and politics: How the "moral values" debate divides America and how to move forward together.* New York: Viking.

13. See Smerconish, M. (2006, November 10). MSNBC's *Scarborough Country.* Transcript retrieved November 13, 2006, from www.msnbc.msn.com. The 2005 polls were retrieved November 13, 2006, from the Roper poll center at the University of Connecticut, available in Nexis database. See Gallup (2005, April 1–2, Roper accession number 1622166) and CBS News (2005, March 21–22, Roper accession number 1621399). For the 2006 poll data, see Pew Research Center (2006, January 5). "Strong public support for right to die." Retrieved November 17, 2006, from Nexis database; ABC News Poll (2006, March 27). "Looking back, more than six in 10 still support decision in Schiavo case." Retrieved November 17, 2006, from http://abcnews.go.com/Health/PollVault/story?id=1771492.

14. Poll retrieved November 13, 2006, from the Roper poll center at the University of Connecticut, available in Nexis database. See Hart and McInturff (2006, July 21–24, Roper accession number 1662131). When Frist first announced in July 2005 that he would support the stem cell bill, Reverend Patrick Mahoney, director of the Christian Defense Coalition, said: "He cannot be pro-life and pro-embryonic stem cell funding. Nor can he turn around and expect widespread endorsement from the pro-life community if he should decide to run for president in 2008." See Bixler, M., & Dart, B. (2005, July 30). "Frist breaks away: Stage set for stem cell battle: Senate leader defies Bush's rigid policy." *Atlanta Journal-Constitution.* Retrieved November 13, 2006, from Nexis database.

15. See "A move away from extremism." (2006, November 17). *National Catholic Reporter.* Retrieved November 27, 2006, from http://ncronline.org; Gergen, D. (2006, November 9). CNN's *Anderson Cooper 360 Degrees.* Transcript retrieved November 20, 2006, from Nexis database. A picture of George W. Bush during the veto ceremony surrounded by "snowflake" children—those born from embryos previously frozen—was the lead item on the National Right to Life Committee's Web site for months afterward. Its Web site (accessed October 20, 2006) is available at www.nrlc.org. Focus on the Family founder James Dobson had this to say in praise of Bush's veto: "[Bush] campaigned

for the White House on the promise that he would work to build a culture that values life, and he did just that with his veto." See Mulkern, A. C., & Soraghan, M. (2006, July 20). "Bush fulfills pledge to veto boost in stem-cell funding: House falls shy of two-thirds needed to override president." *Denver Post*. Retrieved November 13, 2006, from Nexis database. For public opinion about stem cell research after the veto, see Pew Research Center (2006, August 3). "Pragmatic Americans: Liberal and conservative on social issues." Retrieved September 5, 2006, from http://people-press.org/reports. On the electoral calculus of Karl Rove, see Balz, D., & Allen, M. (2004, November 7). "Four more years attributed to Rove's strategy: Despite moments of doubt, adviser's planning paid off." *Washington Post*. Retrieved November 14, 2006, from www.washingtonpost .com; Roth, B. (2002, November 9). "From behind scenes, Rove has GOP in front." *Houston Chronicle*. Retrieved November 14, 2006, from Nexis database. In regard to the 2006 election, one senior Bush adviser explained that in midterm elections "there's less energy" so the key is to get "your base as inspired as possible." Quote in Barnes, F. (2006, May 1). "Turnout is destiny: Karl Rove's new assignment is to get the faithful to the polls." *Weekly Standard*. Retrieved November 14, 2006, from Nexis database.

16. Dean was elected chair of the Democratic National Committee on February 12, 2005. The day before, Pinellas-Pasco Circuit Court judge George Greer in Florida refused the request of Terri Schiavo's parents to prevent Schiavo's husband from removing her feeding tube. The response to this decision by Schiavo's parents and religious and political activists propelled Schiavo's condition into the national consciousness. The 50-state strategy is featured on the Democratic National Committee's Web site (accessed on November 15, 2006) at www.democrats.org/a/party/a_50_state_strategy. In some of his southern campaign stops in 2004, Dean added another element to his list of issues that should be left out of electoral politics: school prayer. See VandeHei, J. (2003, December 8). "Dean crafts own 'southern strategy.'" *Washington Post*. Retrieved November 15, 2006, from Nexis database; Wallis, J. (2003, December 28). "Putting God back in politics." *New York Times*. Retrieved November 15, 2006, from Nexis database. On criticism of Dean after he switched course and began to speak of the importance of faith, see "Is Dean pandering to religious voters?" (2003, December 29). Fox News Channel's *Hannity & Colmes*. Transcript retrieved November 15, 2006, from Nexis database; King, C. I. (2004, January 10). "Dean's faith-based folly." *Washington Post*. Retrieved November 15, 2006, from Nexis database; Roberts, C., & Roberts, S. (2004, January 16). "Dean unconvincing with religious contradictions." *Chicago Sun-Times*. Retrieved November 15, 2006, from Nexis database.

17. On the Kaine campaign, see Dionne, E. J., Jr. (2005, November 10). "A party finds the right words." *Washington Post*. Retrieved November 15, 2006, from Nexis database; Fineman, H. (2005, November 21). "A faith-based initiative: What the Democrats can learn from Kaine's Virginia victory." *Newsweek*. Retrieved November 15, 2006, from Nexis database; Homan, T. (2005, April 26). "Raising Kaine." *American Spectator*. Retrieved November 15, 2006, from Nexis database. On Santorum's importance among religious conservatives, see Biema, D., Booth-Thomas, C., Calabresi, M., Dickerson, J. F., Cloud, J., Winters, R., & Steptoe, S. (2005, February 7). "The 25 most

influential evangelicals in America." *Time*. Retrieved November 25, 2006, from Nexis database. Regarding Casey's campaign strategy, Casey hired a consulting firm, Common Good Strategies, to assist him in his religious outreach. Common Good Strategies was founded and headed by Mara Vanderslice. In 2004, Vanderslice worked on religious outreach for John Kerry; afterward, she began to work with Democratic Party candidates in several states to help them connect with religiously inclined voters. Personal interview with Mara Vanderslice, November 15, 2006. Casey's address at Catholic University was delivered as the 38th Annual Pope John XXIII Lecture, on September 14, 2006. A transcript can be accessed at http://inquirer.philly.com/rss/news/091406caseyremarks .pdf. In the election returns, Casey received 62% of mainline Protestant and 59% of Catholic votes. These percentages are from exit poll data, which were retrieved November 9, 2006, from www.cnn.com.

18. Casey Sr. was the defendant in the 1992 Supreme Court decision of *Planned Parenthood of Southeastern Pennsylvania v. Casey*, which reaffirmed a woman's right to have an abortion. There is some disagreement over the reason for Casey's being denied a speaking opportunity at the 1992 Democratic Party convention. An overview of news coverage about the convention and Casey was accessed on March 7, 2007, at www .washingtonmonthly.com/archives/individual/2005_03/005787.php. Whatever the full story, Democrats' refusal to provide a speaking opportunity for Casey was seized upon by those seeking to build an alliance between religious and political conservatives. For example, Pat Buchanan in his speech at the 1992 Republican Party convention said that when Casey "asked to say a few words on behalf of the 25 million unborn children destroyed since *Roe v Wade*, he was told there was no place for him at the podium of Bill Clinton's convention, no room at the inn." In subsequent years, Casey was a rare Democratic speaker at Christian Coalition events, addressing family and his opposition to abortion. See Griffith, P. (1995, September 9). " 'Our issues will not be ignored': Cream of GOP woo 4,100 Christian Coalition conference faithful." *Pittsburgh Post-Gazette*; Reed, R., Jr. (1993, September 25). "Shared faith, divergent politics." *Washington Post*. Retrieved November 16, 2006, from Nexis database. On Casey Jr. being recruited, see Finkel, D. (2006, October 15). "Low-key Democrat leads high-stakes Senate race: Social conservative Bob Casey is an unlikely party hero." *Washington Post*. Retrieved November 17, 2006, from Nexis database. Casey was elected as Pennsylvania state treasurer in 2004. Finkel writes that "within days of [Casey's] election as state treasurer, the Democrats were contacting him about running against [Rick] Santorum."

19. On Strickland's campaign Web site, the "About Ted" page began with these words:

> After Ted Strickland was first reelected to Congress, he placed a plaque in his office with the following quote from Scripture: "And what does the Lord require of you but to do justice, and to love kindness, and to walk humbly with your God?"—Micah 6:8. Throughout his service as a minister, a psychologist, a professor and a Member of Congress, Ted has worked to exemplify those simple, powerful words.

Strickland's Web site at www.tedstrickland.com was accessed on November 17, 2006. See also Haddock, V. (2006, November 5). "Democrats get religion." *San Francisco Chronicle*. Retrieved November 17, 2006, from Nexis database; Hallett, J., & Niquette, M. (2006, November 6). "Governor candidates put faith in voters." *Columbus Dispatch*. Retrieved November 17, 2006, from Nexis database. Information about the campaign activities of Strickland and Granholm also was provided by Mara Vanderslice in a personal interview, November 15, 2006. According to Vanderslice, the invitation for Granholm to speak at Hope College came after her campaign "spent months developing relationships at seminaries and religious colleges, with pastors and professors. These were 'listening meetings' where we sought to better understand the role of religion in public life." Vanderslice added that Granholm received a standing ovation at Hope, a reaction that "stunned" her staff. Regarding election returns, in Ohio, Strickland received 60% of the popular vote, including 57% of votes among Protestants and 58% among Catholics. The exit polls in the state did not include a question that allowed the differentiation of evangelical versus mainline Protestants. In Michigan, Granholm received 56% of the popular vote, including 62% of votes among mainline Protestants and 56% among Catholics. The vote totals are from actual counts; the religious breakdowns are from exit polls. Notably, in Ohio and Michigan, the Republican Party fielded candidates known for staunchly religiously conservative views: Kenneth Blackwell in Ohio and Dick DeVos in Michigan.

20.  Ford quote in Haddock, "Democrats get religion." In his campaign commercial, Ford said, "I started church the old-fashioned way. I was forced to. And I'm better for it. I'm Harold Ford, Jr. Here, I learned the difference between right and wrong, and now [Republican] Mr. [Bob] Corker is doing wrong." In the background throughout the commercial is a cross. This advertisement was accessed on Ford's campaign Web site at www.fordfortennessee.com on October 13, 2006. The final debate between Ford and Corker was October 28, 2006, and was broadcast live nationally on C-SPAN. Democratic campaigns in other states also emphasized religious views. In North Carolina, Heath Shuler spoke often about his faith. See Weeks, L. (2006, November 4). "Back on home turf: Former Redskin Heath Shuler is hoping to return to Washington, this time as a congressman." *Washington Post*. Retrieved November 17, 2006, from Nexis database. The *Post* said in a story on Shuler: "Religion is important to Shuler. He doesn't campaign on Sundays. He says, 'If it weren't for my belief in Jesus Christ, I wouldn't be what I am today.'" In Missouri, Claire McCaskill did not wither in her campaign against openly religious incumbent Jim Talent. At a speech in Springfield, Missouri—a city known as the "buckle of the Bible belt" because it includes 200 churches and five Christian colleges— McCaskill said: "It's time that we start reading the Bible instead of knocking people over the head with it." See Murray, S. (2006, October 9). "A balancing act in the upper South: Hopeful Democrats tread warily on social issues." *Washington Post*. Retrieved November 17, 2006, from Nexis database.

21.  Much of the scholarship in the "civil religion" tradition takes this perspective. See, for example, Bellah, R. (1967). "Civil religion in America." *Daedalus, 96*, 1–21; Bellah, R. (1975). *The broken covenant: American civil religion in time of trial*. New York: Seabury;

Marty, M. E. (Ed.). (1992). *Modern American Protestantism and its world: Civil religion, church and state.* New York: KG Saur; Parsons, G. (2002). *Perspectives on civil religion.* Burlington, VT: Ashgate; Pierard, R., & Linder, R. (1988). *Civil religion and the presidency.* Grand Rapids, MI: Academie. For examples of popular commentary taking or critiquing this perspective, see Cooperman, A. (2004, September 16). "Openly religious, to a point: Bush leaves the specifics of his faith to speculation." *Washington Post*, A-1; Klinghoffer, D. (2004, November 16). "Moral values aren't just Christian." *Christian Science Monitor.* Retrieved November 25, 2004, from Nexis database; Olson, L. R. (2004, November 22). "Most believers back GOP." *Newsday.* Retrieved November 25, 2004, from Nexis database; Zelizer, G. L. (2004, October 25). "When religion and politics mix." *USA Today.* Retrieved November 25, 2004, from Nexis database.

22. Gerson's quote came in a December 2004 speech in Key West, Florida. Transcript retrieved November 21, 2006, from www.beliefnet.com/story/159/story_ 15943.html. In regard to U.S. public opinion about the nation's Christian roots, see Pew Research Center (2006, August 24). "Many Americans uneasy with mix of religion and politics." Retrieved November 20, 2006, from http://people-press.org/reports. In 1996, 60% of randomly sampled U.S. adults said yes when asked "Is the U.S. a Christian nation?" This percentage rose to 67% in 2002, to 71% in 2005, and was at 67% in 2006.

23. We use "founding fathers" to refer to both those responsible for the Declaration of Independence and those responsible for the U.S. Constitution. Strictly speaking, these two groups were fairly distinct. Only 8 of the 56 signers of the Declaration of Independence attended the Constitutional Convention of 1787: George Read of Delaware; George Clymer, Benjamin Franklin, Robert Morris, and James Wilson of Pennsylvania; George Wythe of Virginia; Roger Sherman of Connecticut; and Elbridge Gerry of Massachusetts. (Notably, Wythe and Gerry attended the convention but did not sign the Constitution.) Of course, both groups of founders were central to the nation's successful development and have come to be referred to interchangeably.

24. Kennedy delivered his address on September 12, 1960. A transcript can be accessed at www.americanrhetoric.com. Jefferson's metaphor comes from a letter he wrote to the Danbury Baptist Association in 1802. In the letter he said:

> Believing with you that religion is a matter which lies solely between Man & his God, that he owes account to none other for his faith or his worship, that the legitimate powers of government reach actions only, & not opinions, I contemplate with sovereign reverence that act of the whole American people which declared that their legislature should "make no law respecting an establishment of religion, or prohibiting the free exercise thereof," thus building a wall of separation between Church & State.

A transcript can be accessed through the Library of Congress at www.loc.gov. The words by Bush came when he was speaking to reporters on January 29, 2001, following an Oval Office meeting with congressional leaders. A transcript can be accessed at www.americanpresidency.org.

25. Medhurst, M. (2005). "Forging a civil-religious construct for the twenty-first century." In R. P. Hart & J. L. Pauley II (Eds.), *The political pulpit revisited* (151–160). West Lafayette, IN: Purdue University Press. Others have identified this transformation as well. For instance, former president Jimmy Carter discussed the "entwining of church and state" in his 2005 book, *Our endangered values: America's moral crisis.* New York: Simon & Schuster.

26. See Concerned Women for America (1998, April 10). "Debunking the myth of separation of church & state." Retrieved December 2, 2006, from www.cwfa.org. See also the Alliance Defense Fund's pamphlet entitled *The truth about separation of church and state.* Retrieved December 2, 2006, from www.alliancedefensefund.org. The Texas Republican Party platform can be accessed at www.texasgop.org/site/PageServer? pagename=library_platform.

27. This is particularly notable because the views of this group are often at odds with the will of the majority. Consider that in 2006, a Pew Research Center poll asked U.S. adults which should be the more important influence on U.S. laws: "the Bible" or "the people's will, even when it conflicts with the Bible." The public in general chose the people's will at a rate of nearly 2:1. However, one group notably deviated from this outlook: fully 60% of white evangelical Protestants selected the Bible. See Pew Research Center, "Many Americans uneasy with mix of religion and politics." Appleby quote in "Divine intervention." (2003, July/August). *Foreign Policy, 136*, 14. For more on the principles of manifest destiny in modern foreign policy communications, see Coles, R. L. (2002). "Manifest destiny adapted for 1990s' war discourse: Mission and destiny intertwined." *Sociology of Religion, 63*, 403–426; Pfaff, W. (2007, February 15). "Manifest destiny: A new direction for America." *New York Review of Books.* Retrieved February 13, 2007, from www.nybooks.com.

28. See Johnson, P. (1999). *A history of the American people.* New York: Harper Perennial. (Original work published in 1997); Noll, M. A. (Ed.). (1990). *Religion and American politics: From the colonial period to the 1980s.* New York: Oxford University Press.

29. *Newsweek* editor Jon Meacham put it this way: "The great good news about America—the American gospel, if you will—is that religion shapes the life of the nation without strangling it. Belief in God is central to the country's experience, yet for the broad center, faith is a matter of choice, not coercion, and the legacy of the Founding is that the sensible center holds. It does so because the Founders believed themselves at work in the service of both God and man, not just one or the other. Driven by a sense of providence and an acute appreciation of the fallability of humankind, they created a nation in which religion should not be singled out for special help or particular harm. The balance between the promise of the Declaration of Independence, with its evocation of divine origins and destiny, and the practicalities of the Constitution, with its checks on extremism, remains perhaps the most brilliant American success." See Meacham, J. (2006). *American gospel: God, the founding fathers, and the making of a nation.* New York: Random House, 5.

30. This is not to deny that religion has been used for ill at various points in U.S. history. Some of the nation's most heinous deeds—including slavery, segregation, and the

decimation of Native Americans—were justified at least partially in religious terms. In many of these instances, however, religion was not so much the cause of the violence as a way for those engaging in it to rationalize their actions.

31. Lattin, D. (2000, March 4). "Christian Right ready for push to the polls: Impetus is McCain, marriage measure." *San Francisco Chronicle*. Retrieved November 22, 2006, from Nexis database.

32. Kerry delivered his address on September 18, 2006. A transcript was retrieved November 21, 2006, from www.washingtonpost.com. Notably, there is the chance that informal religious tests for office make formal tests easier to support. Indeed, despite the constitutional directive to the contrary, formal religious tests are not unheard of. The Texas state constitution, for example, has this clause: "No religious test shall ever be required as a qualification to any office, or public trust, in this State; nor shall any one be excluded from holding office on account of his religious sentiments, *provided he acknowledge the existence of a Supreme Being*" (Article I, section 4, emphasis added). See http://tlo2.tlc .state.tx.us/txconst/articles/cn000100.html. Although this test is almost certainly not applied today, it highlights the tensions that exist between the ideal of church-and-state separation and the historical realities.

33. On the nature, value, and lack of religious literacy in America, see Prothero, S. (2007). *Religious literacy: What every American needs to know—and doesn't*. San Francisco, CA: HarperSanFrancisco.

34. The book was part of Jefferson's private collection, which was used to replace the congressional library after it was destroyed in the War of 1812. See "True faith and allegiance." (2007, January 5). *Boston Herald*. Retrieved February 12, 2007, from Nexis database. Ellison is not the first politician to use a book other than the Bible for the oath of office. In 1825, John Quincy Adams took the presidential oath by placing his hand on a book of laws rather than on the Bible. Since then, some politicians have used Hebrew versions of the Bible and others have opted to "affirm" the oath rather than "swear" it, the former being viewed as a more secular option. See Sacirbey, O. (2006, December 9). "Conservatives attack use of Koran for oath: Sacred and secular books have subbed for Bible." *Washington Post*. Retrieved February 12, 2007, from Nexis database. For Prager's quote and Goode's comments, see "Taking an oath on Koran should be OK." (2006, December 31). *Denver Post*. Retrieved February 12, 2007, from Nexis database. On the religious makeup of the new members of Congress, see "Newsmakers." (2007, March 14). *Houston Chronicle*. Retrieved March 16, 2007, from Nexis database; Stone, A. (2006, December 1). "Newly elected Muslim lawmaker under fire." *USA Today*. Retrieved February 12, 2007, from Nexis database; "Two Buddhists in Congress." (2007, January 7). *St. Petersburg Times*. Retrieved February 12, 2007, from Nexis database.

35. Scholars have long noted that it is through various social institutions that cultural norms and understandings are established and passed from generation to generation. This is the process of socialization. On socialization generally, see Goslin, D. A. (Ed.). (1969). *Handbook of socialization theory and research*. Chicago: Rand McNally; Grusec, J. E., & Hastings, P. D. (Eds.). (2007). *Handbook of socialization: Theory and research*. New York:

Guilford. On socialization and the media, see Preiss, R. W., et al. (Eds.). (2007). *Mass media effects research: Advances through meta-analysis*. Mahwah, NJ: Erlbaum. On socialization and the educational system, see Brint, S. (2006). *Schools and societies* (2nd ed.). Stanford, CA: Stanford University Press. On socialization and religion, see Heft, J. L. (2006). *Passing on the faith: Transforming traditions for the next generation of Jews, Christians, and Muslims*. New York: Fordham University Press.

36. For these data, see Weaver, D. H., Beam, R. A., Brownlee, B., Voakes, P. S., & Wilhoit, G. C. (2007). *The American journalist in the 21st century*. Mahwah, NJ: Erlbaum, 14–16. Since the early 1970s, this research has tracked characteristics among journalists working full time at daily and weekly newspapers, general interest news magazines published more than once a month, radio and television stations with news departments, and wire service bureaus. See also Lichter, S. R., Rothman, S., & Lichter, L. S. (1986). *The media elite: America's new powerbrokers*. Bethesda, MD: Adler & Adler; Pew Research Center (2004, May 23). "Bottom-line pressures now hurting coverage, say journalists." Retrieved August 30, 2005, from http://people-press.org/reports; Silk, M. (1995). *Unsecular media: Making news of religion in America*. Urbana: University of Illinois Press; Underwood, D. (2002). *From Yahweh to Yahoo! The religious roots of the secular press*. Urbana: University of Illinois Press. The Pew data show that mainstream journalists hold different views about the relationship between religious faith and morality from many in the U.S. public. According to Pew, 58% of the U.S. public in 2002 said that a belief in God "is necessary to be moral." In contrast, 6% of journalists at national media outlets and 18% of journalists at local media outlets said the same in 2004.

37. DeYoung quote in Kurtz, H. (2004, August 12). "The Post on WMDs: An inside story: Prewar articles questioning threat often didn't make front page." *Washington Post*, A-1. On mainstream journalists' reliance on government officials, see also Bennett, W. L., Lawrence, R. G., & Livingston, S. (2007). *When the press fails: Political power and the news media from Iraq to Katrina*. Chicago: University of Chicago Press; Domke, D. (2004). *God willing? Political fundamentalism in the White House, the "war on terror," and the echoing press*. London: Pluto; Entman, R. M. (2004). *Projections of power: Framing the news, public opinion, and U.S. foreign policy*. Chicago: University of Chicago Press; Zaller, J. (1994). "Elite leadership of mass opinion: New evidence from the Gulf War." In W. L. Bennett & D. L. Paletz (Eds.), *Taken by storm: The media, public opinion and U.S. foreign policy in the Gulf War* (186–209). Chicago: University of Chicago Press.

38. Murrow delivered this address to the Radio-Television News Directors Association Convention on October 15, 1958. Transcript retrieved November 28, 2006, from www.rtnda.org/resources/speeches/murrow.shtml.

39. Quote by *New York Times* leadership in Siegal, A. M., et al. (2005, May 2). "Preserving our readers' trust: The Credibility Group." Retrieved August 5, 2005, from www.nytimes.com. See also Keller, B. (2005, June 23). "Assuring our credibility." Retrieved August 5, 2005, from www.nytimes.com. The *Post* and *Newsweek* collaboration, *On Faith*, can be found at http://newsweek.washingtonpost.com/onfaith. The quotes were drawn from this site on November 27, 2006. Information about beliefnet's awards was accessed November 27, 2006, from www.beliefnet.com/about/index.asp.

40. In August 1995, the Department of Education under Bill Clinton first issued formal guidelines regarding the acceptable practice of religion in the public schools. This was done partly to avoid a showdown with conservatives who were pushing for a constitutional amendment to facilitate greater school-time religious activity. See Holmes, S. A. (1995, August 26). "Clinton defines religion's role in U.S. schools." *New York Times*. Retrieved February 5, 2006, from Nexis database; "Refresher course: As school resumes, Clinton has some pointers on prayer." (1995, August 30). *Pittsburgh Post-Gazette*. Retrieved February 5, 2006, from Nexis database. In February 2003, as part of the No Child Left Behind Act, the Department of Education under George W. Bush issued the "Guidance on Constitutionally Protected Prayer in Public Elementary and Secondary Schools" (available online at www.ed.gov/policy/gen/guid/religionandschools/prayer_guidance.html). To some, these guidelines went too far in allowing religious activity in schools. See Toppo, G. (2003, February 11). "School prayer gets a boost." *USA Today*. Retrieved February 5, 2006, from Nexis database. See also Americans United for the Separation of Church and State's critique of these guidelines, available online at www.au.org/site/DocServer/public_school_guidance.pdf?docID=186.

41. This document is available online at www.au.org/site/PageServer?pagename=issues_publicschools_joint. The authors of the document describe its purpose this way: "The organizations whose names appear below span the ideological, religious and political spectrum. They nevertheless share a commitment both to the freedom of religious practice and to the separation of church and state such freedom requires. In that spirit, we offer this statement of consensus on current law as an aid to parents, educators and students." Other signers of the statement included the American Humanist Association, the Baptist Joint Committee, B'nai B'rith, the Christian Legal Society, the Christian Science church, the Lutheran Office for Governmental Affairs, the General Conference of Seventh-day Adventists, the Interfaith Alliance, and the Reorganized Church of Jesus Christ of Latter-Day Saints.

42. Along these lines, Albright suggested that the secretary of state be provided "more religious advisers." See Maher, H. (2006, October 13). "U.S.: Albright speaks out on religion, politics, and Bush." *Radio Free Europe*. Retrieved December 1, 2006, from www.rferl.org.

43. In Canada, Prime Minister Stephen Harper is the most vocally religious leader the nation has had in years. An evangelical Christian, Harper regularly closes his speeches with "God bless Canada." See Campbell, C. (2006, February 20). "The church of Stephen Harper." *Maclean's*. Retrieved November 29, 2006, from Nexis database. In Great Britain, former Prime Minister Tony Blair's religious beliefs received uncommon attention. For example, Blair was accused of giving religious groups unfair sway in government decisions, and his tendency to draw stark contrasts between good and evil led some to compare his particular Christian vision to that of George W. Bush. In July 2006, Danish prime minister Anders Fogh Rasmussen criticized Blair and Bush for their use of religious language, calling God and politics "a dangerous cocktail." See "Danish PM advises Blair and Bush 'Keep God out of speeches.'" (2006, July 6). *BBC Monitoring International Reports*. Retrieved November 29, 2006, from Nexis database; Fitchett, J.

(2003, January 24). "Tony Blair builds his stature on the shifting sands of Iraq." *International Herald Tribune*. Retrieved November 29, 2006, from Nexis database; Walker, J. (2005, October 21). "Blair's faith under scrutiny." *Birmingham Post*. Retrieved November 29, 2006, from Nexis database. On the history and current status of the Southeast Asia conflicts, see Dossani, R., & Rowen, H. S. (Eds.). (2005). *Prospects for peace in South Asia*. Stanford, CA: Stanford University Press; Kaur, R. (2005). *Religion, violence, and political mobilisation in South Asia*. Thousand Oaks, CA: Sage. In Africa, tensions between Christians and Muslims have a long history, and they continue to play a role in the affairs of many African nations. See Ellis, S., & Ter Haar, G. (2004). *Worlds of power: Religious thought and political practice in Africa*. New York: Oxford University Press; Fletcher, R. (2004). *The cross and the crescent: Christianity and Islam from Muhammad to the Reformation*. New York: Viking; Mazrui, A. A. (1996). *Christianity and Islam in Africa's political experience: Piety, passion and power*. Washington, DC: Center for Muslim-Christian Understanding. Similarly, in Ireland, the historic conflict between Protestants and Catholics continues to be a central factor in many of the nation's political and cultural developments. See "A promise of peace." (2005, July 25). *Chicago Tribune*. Retrieved November 29, 2006, from Nexis database; Tanner, M. (2001). *Ireland's holy wars: The struggle for a nation's soul, 1500–2000*. New Haven, CT: Yale University Press. On some of the conflicts centered around Muslim immigration to Europe, see Cowell, A. (2006, February 8). "West coming to grasp wide Islamic protests as sign of deep gulf." *New York Times*. Retrieved November 30, 2006, from Nexis database; Nickerson, C. (2006, May 22). "Europe raises bar for immigrants." *Boston Globe*. Retrieved November 30, 2006, from Nexis database. One recent example of this clash of cultures in Europe is the decision of the French school system to prohibit students from wearing "conspicuous" religious symbols, including the head scarves commonly worn by Muslim females. See "Headscarf defeat riles French Muslims." (2005, November 1). *BBC News*. Retrieved November 29, 2006, from http://news.bbc.co.uk; Sciolino, E. (2004, October 22). "France turns to tough policy on students' religious garb." *New York Times*. Retrieved November 29, 2006, from Nexis database. On the religious issues that have arisen in the debate about Turkey's entrance into the European Union, see Moore, M. (2006, November 30). "Turkey set back in bid for E.U. membership: Move follows pope's support of effort." *Washington Post*. Retrieved December 1, 2006, from Nexis database; Tavernise, S. (2006, November 28). "Allure of Islam signals a shift within Turkey." *New York Times*. Retrieved December 1, 2006, from Nexis database.

44. Thomas, C., & Dobson, E. (2000). "Blinded by might." In E. J. Dionne, Jr., & J. I. DiUlio, Jr. (Eds.), *What's God got to do with the American experiment?* (51–55). Washington, DC: Brookings Institution Press. See also Thomas, C., & Dobson, E. (1999). *Blinded by might: Can the religious Right save America?* Grand Rapids, MI: Zondervan. Scholar Patrick Glynn, associate director of the George Washington University Institute for Communitarian Policy Studies, put it this way: "A too direct coupling of religion and politics in the public square is usually pernicious, not only for politics but also for religion itself. The result is typically not the sanctification of politics but the politicization of religion." In

Glynn, P. (2000). "Conscience and the public square." In Dionne & DiUlio, *What's God got to do with the American experiment?* (81–89). Graham quote in Michaels, M. (1981, February 1). "Billy Graham: America is not God's only kingdom." *Parade*, 6–7.

45. The Confessing church's founding faith statement, the Barmen Declaration, was written primarily by Karl Barth and opened with these words: "In view of the errors of the 'German Christians' and of the present Reich Church Administration, which are ravaging the Church and at the same time also shattering the unity of the German Evangelical Church, we confess the following evangelical truths," the first of which concluded with this statement: "We reject the false doctrine that the Church could and should recognize as a source of its proclamation, beyond and besides this one Word of God, yet other events, powers, historic figures and truths as God's revelation." A copy of the Barmen Declaration is available online at www.ucc.org/faith/barmen.htm. Barth lost his professorship in Bonn in 1935 and moved to Switzerland after refusing to take a loyalty oath. Niemöller was a prominent Confessing church pastor in Germany, and beginning in 1936 he spent seven years in Nazi prisons and concentration camps. Bonhoeffer was the head of the Confessing church's seminary in Finkenwalde, Germany, from 1935 to 1937, when it was closed by the Nazis. Thereafter he was a speaker, author, and activist in the German resistance as a symbol of the Confessing church. Bonhoeffer's efforts in helping a group of Jews escape to Switzerland contributed to his imprisonment in 1943, and he was hanged in 1945 in a concentration camp. See "The Nazi challenge to the German Protestant Church," written by Victoria G. Barnett, director of church relations for the U.S. Holocaust Museum in conjunction with the documentary *Bonhoeffer*, which aired in a condensed format on the Public Broadcasting Service on February 2, 2006. The essay and information about the documentary were accessed November 30, 2006, at www.pbs.org/bonhoeffer and at www.bonhoeffer.com. See also the U.S. Holocaust Memorial Museum's online exhibition on Bonhoeffer at www.ushmm.org/bonhoeffer; and the International Dietrich Bonhoeffer Society, accessed on November 30, 2006, at www.dbonhoeffer.org/node/3. See also Floyd, W. W. (2000). *The wisdom and witness of Dietrich Bonhoeffer*. Minneapolis, MN: Fortress; Kelly, G. B., & Weborg, C. J. (Eds.). (1999). *Reflections on Bonhoeffer: Essays in honor of F. Burton Nelson*. Chicago: Covenant.

46. King, M. L., Jr. (1963). *Strength to love*. New York: Harper & Row, 47; "A move away from extremism." (2006). *National Catholic Reporter*. Retrieved March 7, 2007, from http://ncronline.org/NCR_Online/archives2/2006d/111706/111706r.htm; Kuo, D. (2006). *Tempting faith: An inside story of political seduction*. New York: Free Press.

47. This victory came in North Africa at El Alamein, where Allied forces led by Generals Harold Alexander and Bernard Montgomery and the British Eighth Army routed Axis forces led by Germany's Erwin Rommel. This was a turning point in what Churchill called the Battle of Egypt. Churchill made these particular comments as part of the Lord Mayor's Dinner at the Mansion House in London on November 10, 1942. His speech was reported in the *New York Times* on the following day. See Associated Press (1942, November 11). "Prime Minister Churchill's speech." *New York Times*. Retrieved November 27, 2006, from ProQuest database.

## EPILOGUE

1. Lusk and Warren quotes in Nussbaum, P. (2006, January 8). "The purpose-driven pastor." *Philadelphia Inquirer*. Retrieved December 5, 2006, from www.philly.com/mld/ inquirer/living/religion/13573441.htm. In 2004, Warren sent an e-mail newsletter to more than 130,000 ministers about voting priorities; see Warren, R. (2004, October 27). "Why every U.S. Christian must vote in this election." *Ministry Toolbox*, 178. Retrieved September 5, 2006, from www.pastors.com/RWMT/?ID=178. As 2007 dawned, he told the *Orange County Register*:

> I don't know if I would ever do a letter again. I think people know where I stand on issues, and I still stand firmly on those . . . issues. I'm just trying to broaden the agenda to say there's more issues than that. I don't think in today's world you can ever be just a single-issue person. I think when it comes to [politicians], you have to look at the person's character, you have to look at their policy beliefs, you have to look at their leadership ability, you have to look at the stability of their family, you have to look at their track record. There are numerous things, and people who only choose one of those things, and that's all they look at. . . . I don't think that's using your vote in the wisest way.

In Driscoll, G. (2006, December 31.) "Rick Warren in his own words." *Orange County Register*, A-14. Regarding the status of *The Purpose Driven Life*, it had sold 25 million copies as of late 2006, making it the highest-selling nonfiction hardcover title in U.S. publishing history. See Mead, W. R. (2006, September). "God's country?" *Foreign Affairs*. Retrieved March 9, 2007, from Nexis database; Rose, C. (2006, August 17). "Why 'Purpose Driven Life' author turns eye on the global AIDS pandemic: Evangelical author explains why mixing politics and religion is 'destroying the church.'" Interview for *The Charlie Rose show* (Television broadcast). Retrieved March 9, 2007, from Nexis database.

2. A transcript of Brownback's remarks was retrieved February 27, 2007, from Congressional Quarterly, Inc., in Nexis database. Notably, Brownback bridges the two Christian perspectives in the religious Right: he was an evangelical Protestant before converting to Catholicism in 2002. On Brownback's faith, his involvement in issues related to Africa, and the support for Brownback among religious conservatives, see Milbank, D. (2007, January 23). "Despite 1% poll standing, Brownback is a winner among antiabortion Right." *Washington Post*. Retrieved March 8, 2007, from Nexis database; Neuman, J. (2006, December 5). "Conservative Sen. Brownback explores presidential run: The Kansan could fill 'a vacancy on the right' in the Republican field: Social issues are a focus." *Los Angeles Times*. Retrieved March 9, 2007, from Nexis database; Sharlet, J. (2006, January 25). "God's senator: Who would Jesus vote for? Meet Sam Brownback." *Rolling Stone*. Retrieved March 8, 2007, from www.rollingstone.com/politics/story/ 9178374/gods_senator; Swarns, R. (2007, January 21). "Kansas senator announces bid for presidency." *New York Times*. Retrieved March 8, 2007, from Nexis database.

3. Obama spoke at the Democratic Party convention on July 27, 2004, at the Fleet Center in Boston. A transcript can be accessed at www.americanrhetoric.com. The phrase "audacity of hope" comes from a sermon given by Obama's pastor, the Reverend Jeremiah A. Wright, Jr. See Obama, B. (2006). *The audacity of hope: Thoughts on reclaiming the American dream.* New York: Crown, 356. For the reaction of news media and pundits to Obama's speech, see, for example, Basu, M. (2004, July 29). "Election 2004: Speech buzz lifts star for Obama." *Atlanta Journal-Constitution.* Retrieved December 4, 2006, from Nexis database; Benedetto, R. (2004, July 29). "Address throws Illinois' Obama into whirlwind of political hope." *USA Today.* Retrieved December 4, 2006, from Nexis database; Hooper, E. (2004, July 29). "Speaker's words felt by every American." *St. Petersburg Times.* Retrieved December 4, 2006, from Nexis database; Jurkowitz, M. (2004, July 29). "With one speech, neophyte's political stock soars." *Boston Globe.* Retrieved December 4, 2006, from Nexis database; "Our turn: Every few years, speech transcends: Lovers of oratory were rewarded this week when Barack Obama electrified the Democratic convention." (2004, July 29). *San Antonio Express-News.* Retrieved December 4, 2006, from Nexis database. In June 2006, Obama delivered the keynote address at the Call to Renewal conference, hosted by the progressive religious organization Sojourners, which is headed by Jim Wallis. Obama was on the cover of *Time*'s October 23, 2006 issue. The cover story, by Joe Klein, was titled "Why Barack Obama could be the next president." Obama appeared on Comedy Central's *The Daily Show with Jon Stewart* via satellite on November 7, 2005. He appeared with his wife on *The Oprah Winfrey Show* on October 18, 2006.

4. There were more than 2,000 in the audience, many of them ministers, gathered from some 39 states and 18 nations. See Finnegan, M. (2006, December 2). "AIDS fight needs churches, Obama says: Senator disagrees on condom issue, but tells evangelicals that moral guidance is needed." *Los Angeles Times.* Retrieved December 5, 2006, from Nexis database. On the relationship of Obama and Warren, see Mehta, S. (2006, November 30). "Obama an unlikely guest at O.C. church: Evangelical minister angers peers as he reaches across the aisle for his AIDS conference." *Los Angeles Times.* Retrieved December 4, 2006, from Nexis database.

5. Warren quote in Finnegan, "AIDS fight needs churches, Obama says." In his public statement about Obama's abortion position, Warren said: "Let it be made very clear that Pastor Warren and Saddleback Church completely disagree with Obama's views on abortion and other positions he has taken, and have told him so in a public meeting on Capitol Hill." See Mehta, "Obama an unlikely guest at O.C. church." Obama also released a statement about the matter, saying: "While we will never see eye-to-eye on all issues, surely we can come together with one voice to honor the entirety of Christ's teachings by working to eradicate the scourge of AIDS, poverty and other challenges we all can agree must be met." On these statements and the quoted opposition to Obama's visit, see Cooperman, A. (2006, November 30). "Church is urged to disinvite Obama." *Washington Post.* Retrieved December 6, 2006, from Nexis database; "Church leaders distressed over Obama visit." (2006, November 28). *Christian Newswire.* Retrieved December 6, 2006, from www.christiannewswire.com.

6. A transcript of Obama's remarks was retrieved March 8, 2007, from Congressional Quarterly, Inc., in Nexis database. On the audience reaction to Obama's speech, see Dionne, E. J., Jr. (2006, December 5). "Message from a megachurch." *Washington Post.* Retrieved December 6, 2006, from Nexis database; Finnegan, "AIDS fight needs churches, Obama says"; Harnden, T. (2006, December 4). "Democrat preaches to the unconverted." *Daily Telegraph.* Retrieved December 6, 2006, from Nexis database.

7. Obama appeared on the show on December 1, 2006. Transcription was done by the authors.

8. Jakes quote in Zahn, P. (2005, February 8). Cable News Network's *Paula Zahn Now* (Television program). Retrieved December 7, 2006, from Nexis database. Jakes delivered the sermon at the National Day of Prayer service at the National Cathedral in Washington, DC, on September 16, 2005. George W. and Laura Bush, Dick and Lynne Cheney were all in attendance. See also Biema, D., Booth-Thomas, C., Calabresi, M., Dickerson, J. F., Cloud, J., Winters, R., & Steptoe, S. (2005, February 7). "The 25 most influential evangelicals in America." *Time.* Retrieved November 25, 2006, from Nexis database. The One Campaign's Web site can be accessed at www.one.org. In a widely circulated open letter to President George W. Bush in 2005, Warren was joined by Billy Graham in declaring that global poverty "is an issue that rises far above mere politics. It is a moral issue . . . a compassion issue. . . . America, as the most blessed nation on our planet, has the greatest obligation to help those who are stuck in poverty around the world." A copy of this letter was accessed on December 5, 2006, at www.beliefnet.com/story/168/story_16821_1.html. The letter was sent to more than 150,000 evangelicals across America. See Rossi, H. L. (2005). "Evangelicals embrace new priorities." Retrieved December 5, 2006, from www.beliefnet.com/story/168/story_16822_1.html.

9. Cizik quote in Sullivan, A. (2006, April). "When would Jesus bolt?" *Washington Monthly.* Retrieved December 5, 2006, from www.washingtonmonthly.com/features/2006/0604.sullivan.html. A copy of the Evangelical Climate Initiative was accessed December 5, 2006, at www.christiansandclimate.org/statement. A list of signatories was accessed on the same day at www.christiansandclimate.org/signatories.

10. Hunter quotes upon accepting the position in Pinsky, M. (2006, October 7). "Orlando pastor to lead coalition." *Orlando Sentinel.* Retrieved December 5, 2006, from www.theledger.com/apps/pbcs.dll/article?AID=/20061007/NEWS/610070419/1326. Hunter also told the *Los Angeles Times* in October 2006, "We're not abandoning our previous positions: We're still pro-life, pro-traditional marriage, pro-morality. But one or two issues can't adequately express the Gospel." See Simon, S. (2006, October 19). "Evangelicals ally with Democrats on environment: Religious leaders hope the global-warming campaign sends a message to the GOP." *Los Angeles Times.* Retrieved December 5, 2006, from Nexis database. Hunter quotes upon resignation in Mariano, W. (2006, November 24). "Christian group leader resigns: Incoming president-pastor had dispute with group about conservative philosophy." *Orlando Sentinel.* Retrieved December 5, 2006, from Nexis database. See also Cooperman, A. (2006, November 29). "Second new leader resigns from the Christian Coalition." *Washington Post.* Retrieved December 5, 2006, from Nexis database. See also Hunter, J. (2006). *Right wing, wrong bird: Why the*

*tactics of the religious Right won't fly with most conservative Christians.* Longwood, FL: Distributed Church Press.

11. This opposition was headed by the Interfaith Stewardship Alliance, which wrote a public letter that was accessed December 5, 2006, at www.interfaithstewardship.org. See also Goodstein, L. (2006, February 8). "Evangelical leaders join global warming initiative." *New York Times.* Retrieved December 5, 2006, from Nexis database. On the National Association of Evangelicals' commitment to "creation care," see "For the health of the nation: An evangelical call to civic responsibility," located at www.nae.net/images/civic_responsibility2.pdf. See also Goldstein, P. (2006, October 10). "The big picture: Believers preach gospel of green." *Los Angeles Times.* Retrieved December 5, 2006, from Nexis database.

12. Dobson et al. wrote a public letter, dated March 1, 2007, to L. Roy Taylor, chair of the board of the National Association of Evangelicals, in which they requested that Cizik stop talking about global warming or be asked to resign his NAE position. This letter was accessed March 9, 2007, at www.citizenlink.org/pdfs/NAELetterFinal.pdf. On the NAE's affirmation of Cizik and commitment to combating global warming, see Cooperman, A. (2007, March 11). "Evangelical body stays course on warming; conservatives oppose stance." *Washington Post.* Retrieved July 10, 2007, from Nexis database; Goodstein, L. (2007, March 14). Evangelical group rebuffs critics on right. *New York Times.* Retrieved July 10, 2007, from Nexis database.

13. See Abramson, P. R., & Inglehart, R. (1986). "Generational replacement and value change in six West European societies." *American Journal of Political Science, 30,* 1–25; Braungart, R. G. (1974). "The sociology of generations and student politics." *Journal of Social Issues, 30*(2), 31–54; Jennings, M. K., & Niemi, R. (1980). *Generations and politics.* Princeton, NJ: Princeton University Press; Mannheim, K. (1952). "The problem of generations." In P. Kecskemeti (Ed.), *Essays on the sociology of knowledge* (276–332). London: Routledge; Schneider, B. (1988). "Political generations in the contemporary women's movement." *Sociological Inquiry, 58,* 4–21; Sears, D. O., & Valentino, N. A. (1997). "Politics matters: Political events as catalysts for pre-adult socialization." *American Political Science Review, 91,* 45–65. On the civil rights movement specifically, see Carmines, E. G., & Stimson, J. A. (1989). *Issue evolution: Race and the transformation of American politics.* Princeton, NJ: Princeton University Press; Fiorina, M. (1974). *Representatives, roll calls, and constituencies.* Lexington, MA: Lexington; Whitby, K. J., & Gilliam, F. D., Jr. (1991). "A longitudinal analysis of competing explanations for the transformation of southern congressional politics." *Journal of Politics, 53,* 504–518.

14. See Shaheen, J., et al. (2006, April 11). "Redefining political attitudes and activism: A poll by Harvard's Institute of Politics." Retrieved December 5, 2006, from www.iop.harvard.edu/pdfs/survey/spring_poll_2006_execsumm.pdf.

# INDEX

✻